The Taming of the Troops

CONTRIBUTIONS IN SOCIOLOGY

Series Editor: Don Martindale

Black Belonging: A Study of the Social Correlates of Work Relations Among Negroes
Jack C. Ross and Raymond H. Wheeler

The School Managers: Power and Conflict in American Public Education
Donald J. McCarty and Charles E. Ramsey

The Social Dimensions of Mental Illness, Alcoholism, and Drug Dependence
Don Martindale and Edith Martindale

Those People: The Subculture of a Housing Project
Colette Pétonnet. Rita Smidt, Translator

Sociology in Israel
Leonard Weller

The Revolutionary Party: Essays in the Sociology of Politics
Feliks Gross

Group Interaction as Therapy: The Use of the Small Group in Corrections
Richard M. Stephenson and Frank R. Scarpitti

Sociology of the Black Experience
Daniel C. Thompson

The Incomplete Adult: Social Class Constraints on Personality Development
Margaret J. Lundberg

Handbook of Contemporary Developments in World Sociology
Raj Mohan and Don Martindale, Editors

The New Social Sciences
Baidya Nath Varma, Editor

The Population Challenge: A Handbook for Nonspecialists
Johannes Overbeek

THE TAMING OF THE TROOPS
Social Control in the United States Army

LAWRENCE B. RADINE

Contributions in Sociology, Number 22

GREENWOOD PRESS
WESTPORT, CONNECTICUT • LONDON, ENGLAND

Library of Congress Cataloging in Publication Data

Radine, Lawrence B
The taming of the troops.

(Contributions in sociology; no. 22).
Includes bibliographical references.
1. Sociology, Military. 2. Social control.
3. United States. Army—Personnel management.
I. Title.
U21.5.R32 301.5'93 76-5262
ISBN 0-8371-8911-X

Library of Congress Catalog Card Number: 76-5262
ISBN: 0-8371-8911-X

First published in 1977

Greenwood Press, Inc.
51 Riverside Avenue, Westport, Connecticut 06880
Printed in the United States of America

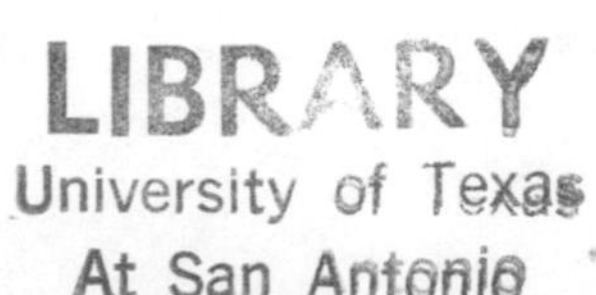

To Glenda

Contents

Preface

This study emerged out of conversations with anti-war Army soldiers during the Vietnam War. These men were asking themselves why they were so ineffective as resistance organizers at a time when there seemed to be such strong anti-war and anti-Army feelings among both soldiers and civilians. There are many ways to answer this question, but one answer that kept cropping up in our discussions was in the nature of the Army itself, particularly its techniques of social control. But in looking at how the Army prevented leftist political expression among its troops, I was drawn to some wider issues. I found the Army used techniques of control on dissidents that it had been developing for use on a much wider array of deviant soldiers and personnel problems. It seemed that anti-military political dissent was only one (and probably a minor) form of deviance for which the Army has developed its modern social controls. As a result, this project became a general study of social control in the United States Army.

I wrote this book with a concern for what I see as the progressive erosion of freedom in bureaucratic contexts. In my view, the widening span of control of bureaucracies results in a declining spontaneity, a delimiting of the human variety, and a diminution of the power of lower participants within organizations. This can occur through manipulative controls as well as coercive ones. The difficulty with manipulative controls is that they extend the sphere of control into wider areas of thought and feeling. Herbert Marcuse, in *One Dimensional Man*, argues that the most gratifying, rational, inclusive controls can also be the most de-politicizing. I think the capabilities of suppressing resistance through these co-optive techniques are frequently underestimated, even by those with some political organizing experience. Manipulative controls are difficult to recognize because they are subtle and rational and seem liberal in contrast to coercive controls.

But could this view of co-optation be overextended? If I were to characterize the mentality surrounding co-optation as a cynical and manipulative one (as I frequently do), how would I deal with a situation where an officer perceives an enlisted man's grievance as legitimate and tries to right it? The difficulty may perhaps be resolved by distinguishing among different types of explanations. I am less concerned with the motives or intentions of Army officials in their use of modern controls than on the effects of these controls on resistance. In other words I look for the functions these controls play for the Army. Co-optive, paternal, and coercive techniques can be used by concerned as well as cynical men. The intent of this book is *not* to castigate or to reform the Army but to illuminate the nature of bureaucratic control, in all its diversity and subtlety. This book does not advocate one policy or another; rather, it assesses policies in terms of the effects on personal and political freedom.

The Taming of the Troops develops two key themes: (1) the overall shift in Army controls from coercion to manipulation and (2) the change in military controls to more closely resemble civilian controls. These developments occur with some strains, and much of the change comes through psychologists, sociologists, psychiatrists, correctional therapists, and lawyers. Of course, soldiers who refuse to be submissive provide the pressure for change. The result is an organization that, in my opinion, is all the more capable of controlling deviant and politically outspoken soldiers.

To some extent these pressures for modernization exist in all the U.S. armed forces. There are many parallels in changes—for example, in leadership style and the increasing reliance on behavioral science—in both the Air Force and the Navy. In addition, there are some structural similarities among the services: they all share the military legal code and the maximum-security prison at Fort Leavenworth. So although I focused both in interviews and in documentation on the Army, much of what I say here applies to the U.S. armed forces in general.

Furthermore, some of the techniques developed in the Army have been borrowed by civilian sectors; for example, milieu therapy, crisis intervention, and similar techniques used in psychiatry today originated in the armed forces. Intelligence testing and the use of dossiers underwent great development in the Army. Some leadership and organizational principles discussed in this book have been taken up by industrial organizations. However, the extent of influence the Army has had on civilian life is outside the scope of this work. The point is that the Army can be viewed as a vanguard bureaucracy in the development of new techniques of control, as well as a recipient of civilian controls.

The Taming of the Troops is about a class relationship within a bureaucracy. It analyzes that relationship in terms of controls used by those in authority and the nature of resistance expressed by those without it. The reader may find my use of the term *resistance* to be broader than the customary usage. While I certainly would not say that every instance of AWOL or disrespect to an officer is an act of political dissent, some of this sort of activity can be considered primitive or prepolitical forms of rebellion. In this book, I argue for a broadened definition of what is political.

In using interviews to describe an organization as complex as the Army, a writer has to discriminate between typical patterns and the peculiarities of one post, one brigade, or one point in time. Soldiers can go through the Army and report markedly different experiences. As much as possible, I tried to "triangulate" my interviews and use here personal accounts with more generalizing studies, such as survey research reports and modernization project evaluations.

The first chapter describes a "career" or a series of stages that a typical dissident soldier would be likely to go through if he were actively trying to organize other soldiers into an anti-war movement. This chapter counterposes this experience with the reports of how post commanders use their resources for dealing with potential dissidence. Most of the techniques of control that are introduced in this chapter are discussed more fully in later chapters.

In Chapters 2, 3, and 4, we see more of the variety in styles of troop control and leadership, arranged along a continuum from the most despotic to the most modern. As controls modernize, they are based less on personal, direct confrontation, so these three chapters can also be viewed in terms of a range from the most personal to the most "situational." Chapter 2 analyzes the most despotic and direct controls. Chapter 3 shows how ideological elements and control through group morale can be added to the personal control of a more protective officer. Chapter 4 discusses co-optive and rational controls and describes what I believe to be the future basis of Army social control. It also sets down principles that receive some further analysis in Chapters 5 and 7 on psychiatry and corrections.

Soldiers who try to escape the military have used a variety of routes, but one of the most common has been via the psychiatric casualty or mental unfitness route. In Chapter 5 the ways the military has influenced the practice of psychiatry to preclude this form of exit—and even deviance—will be taken up.

After the deviant soldier has exhausted the legal ways of noncooperation, he typically runs afoul of the military justice system. Chapter 6 explores the operation of the courts and the uniqueness of military law. The military justice system has many aspects that are remarkably fair, yet it is able to prosecute almost any of the usual forms of resistance or noncooperation, whether it be political dissent or apolitical troublemaking. Finally, we follow the deviant soldier into the military prison system, with its odd array of modern enlightened—and manipulative—forms of rehabilitation as well as old-fashioned "county jail" brutality.

Acknowledgments

I am happy to acknowledge my indebtedness to Tom Fellows and Sam Andes for the many discussions that helped to formulate the questions for this research and for their determined efforts to introduce me to as great a variety of military people for interviewing as they could find at Fort Leonard Wood. I also want to express my appreciation to Carl Rogers and other GI anti-war movement organizers, NCOs, officers, GIs, Vietnam veterans, lawyers, and psychiatrists who were so generous with their time and patient with uncomfortable questions.

I wish to thank the following for generously granting me permission to republish parts of their publications: Physicians Postgraduate Press, *Harper's* magazine, Association of Military Surgeons of the U.S., American Psychiatric Association, U.S. Army Research Institute for the Behavioral and Social Sciences, General Research Corporation (formerly Research Analysis Corporation), and the American Political Science Association. I also thank Empire State College for giving me permission to draw from the module "The Sociology of the Military: A Study of the Operations of Complex Organizations" by Lawrence B. Radine.

I want to thank Alvin W. Gouldner and Ken Neubeck for valuable suggestions at the outset of this study, and George Rawick for his continued encouragement. Peter Amann, Stan Peabody, Freddie Greene, Ethel Kertz, and Patsy West criticized parts of the manuscript, and I very much appreciate their help. Marian Wilson's and Chris Vroom's conscientious typing is much appreciated. I particularly want to thank my wife, Glenda, who, as the work progressed, successively became my research assistant, sounding board, and editor.

The Taming of the Troops

1

The Detection and Suppression of Dissidence

Techniques of domination exist in two kinds of configurations: in relation to each other and in relation to techniques of resistance. In one pattern, techniques of domination interact over a period of time with techniques of resistance to such a degree that each comes to be strongly influenced and shaped by the other. The second configuration, the relation of each technique of domination to a set of techniques of domination, shows that these techniques are generally far more effective when they are applied in a coherent pattern, particularly a pattern of increasing severity.

A sequence of gradually increasing oppressiveness, or "repression on the installment plan," was one of the explanations that Raul Hilberg used to account for the effectiveness of Nazi techniques of domination of Jews.[1] Hilberg traced Nazi techniques of domination beginning with the original seemingly harmless, but crucial, definition of the Jew. This was followed, shortly thereafter, by proscriptions against Jews in civilian bureaucracy. These still were not viewed as directly threatening for most Jews, however. Somewhat later, the Nazi bureaucracy forced Jewish businessmen, financiers, and industrialists to sell their corporations—again, of little immediate concern to most Jews. Still later, the bureaucracy prohibited the ownership of houses by Jews. Thus, the previously assimilated German Jews had to move to ghettos. One of the last stages in this process was to transfer Jews to what were described to them as work camps. Each of these stages was separated from the others long enough so that the Jews and Germans might have a chance to accommodate themselves to it.[2]

This pattern of increasing oppressiveness is effective because repression is difficult to respond to when it is applied in small increments; no one step is sufficient cause to rally opposition around. The gradual adaptation of the demoralized and subjugated subordinate population to each new, more intense state of repression makes any resistance difficult. Thus, repression on the installment plan can institute a form of domination that would almost inevitably be resisted if one of the later steps were applied too early. The German bureaucracy encountered relatively little resistance, according to Hilberg, and it rarely made mistakes (such as placing one step out of order). Thus, there is an internal logic to techniques of domination: they are most effective when applied in a sequential pattern.

In most situations of domination, the subjugated are not likely to be as demoralized and overpowered by the domination as were the Jews, and they may have their own techniques of resistance that interact with techniques of domination. There are many examples of the interactive nature of resistance and authority, ranging from Hegel's abstract view of the master-slave relationship[3] to perhaps the escalating series of resistance and domination that occurs in Ken Kesey's graphic novel *One Flew over the Cuckoo's Nest*.[4] The history of the relationship of the American working class to the managerial class can be seen as a kind of dialectical interaction between resistance and authority. In this light, Taylorism can be considered a managerial response to the American worker's attempt to insert elements of play (such as loafing and horseplay) into an otherwise miserable work setting.[5] Workers responded to the rationalization of the work process partly by forming small groups at the work place by which they could regulate the pace of production themselves through the various small-group processes of social control over group members. One managerial response to the discovery of small-group social controls, according to Loren Baritz,[6] was the implementation of a counseling program designed to undermine resistive small-group solidarity and anti-company attitudes. Other responses to anti-management, working-class cohesion included training supervisors in psychological and social sciences, surveying attitudes, and perhaps using various forms of propaganda. The American workers' response to these and many other manipulative forms of control has been to withdraw cynically from interaction with the company, and to some degree from other workers, and to become increasingly involved in escapist, egotistic pleasures both at work (such as drugs or fantasies)[7] and off work.[8] Management's countermoves have included the recent emphasis on team functioning,[9] work modules,[10] and "job enrichment"[11] to re-create involvement at work. The point is that these techniques of resistance and authority exist in interaction; the response of one side conditions the activity of the other.

I have suggested that bureaucratic techniques of domination can exist in a sequence along with other techniques of domination and that they can be influenced by the nature of resistance. In later chapters I will show that knowledge of how to use the techniques can be retained in an institution to lie fallow or to unfold as needs arise.

The interaction of a GI anti-war organizer and military authority displays some of these characteristics of techniques of domination. The majority of people who enter the Army intending to organize within fail to anticipate the Army's response to them and are rendered ineffective, becoming greatly demoralized in the process; however, the pattern of responses that the Army makes is neither capricious nor unpredictable. The Army's tactics can be anticipated, as evidenced by the uniformity of its sequence of responses at a variety of bases. Furthermore, the Army's response to the resisters is determined in some part by the activity of the resisters themselves. This latter influence is more likely to occur when the Army is just learning to deal with a new kind of resister.

Through interviews with GI resisters (some of whom found their resistive careers ended fairly early in the process, while others were more successful) and through published accounts of relatively successful organizers,[12] a composite picture can be formed of the pattern of the Army's techniques of domination over individual GI organizers. I will also use the testimony to a congressional committee of military intelligence agents to verify some aspects of the organizers' accounts.[13] This composite picture demonstrates the Army's techniques of domination over those resisters who attempt to organize. In any single case, however, one or more of the steps may be missing or the Army may decide not to follow through with its own pattern. I will contrast this experience of Army repression with some other activities that post commanders carry out to prevent resistance from spreading. This information will be drawn from post commanders' detailed responses to survey research questionnaires. The following, then, is an account of the career of a hypothetical GI organizer who is both strongly committed to his values and competent at organizing.[14]

The first in this series of techniques of domination is the Army's identification of the potential resister. There are many ways it can use to obtain this information. Every recruit is asked to fill out a standard form that asks if he belongs to any of a list of organizations designed subversive by an attorney general. If he checks that he does belong to one of these, the Army would already have a notion that he might cause trouble. Alternatively, the Army may find out about a potential activist's intent to organize because, in a surprising large number of instances, he announces prior to his entry in the service his plans to organize within the Army.[15] The Army has other means of identifying some potential activists in addition to the latter's self-disclosure.

In the rare case that the resister enters the Army as an officer, the routine FBI background check conducted on each candidate would alert the Army if he had an activist past. It would not be surprising if the Army were to extend this background research to apply to all potential recruits in a future smaller and more technologically advanced military setting. As we shall see in another chapter, the Army and the Selective Service system attempted during World War II to institute a similar technique of background checks by using social workers to preclude letting in those disposed toward psychiatric problems. The fact that the plan failed does not necessarily mean that the Army lost interest in it or that the Army could not use a background check to predict other kinds of difficulties that a recruit might have in a military environment.

Another possible technique for identifying potential troublemakers, which can also be traced back to World War II, is the use of a personality test to predict those who might have difficulty adjusting to the Army. The personality test used during World War II was inadequate, but the Army continues to research this area. Recently one of the Army's psychological researchers announced that his group was developing a method of spotting potential AWOLs from personality tests from which a numerical score for each recruit could be generated and recorded in his personnel file.[16]

These latter techniques were, of course, not designed specifically to identify political organizers but to locate potential disciplinary offenders in general. Political organizers have not been a sufficiently serious problem for the Army to research predictive behavioral science methods in great detail. Nevertheless some Army contract researchers have developed a profile to identify potential dissidents in the Army. This research was carried out partly through the use of personnel files (201 files were examined) of earlier GIs who had made dissident expressions while they were in the Army.[17] Thus, if the problem of organized dissidence ever did become serious, the Army could rely on this profile (or a newer version) to help it handle these kinds of organizers.[18]

If an individual resister is considered to be a security risk, evidenced by his having belonged to a subversive organization or committing certain politically motivated acts, his personnel file is flagged.[19] His file is thus spotted as belonging to someone whom the Army will not assign to certain positions, such as missile duty, Army intelligence, and so forth. The early identification of a "potential troublemaker" can give the Army a considerable edge over the resister. It can use special leadership techniques and careful assignments to certain areas, it can discharge the soldier, or it can even preclude his entry. The Army can keep a watchful eye on the organizer's activity, which in the early stages would otherwise be rather difficult to detect. In many cases the resister does not know he has been identified; thus he makes no response to the Army's treatment of him as an organizer at this stage in his organizing career.

The competent resister will do no real organizing during basic (combat) training for several reasons. As we shall see in the next chapter, basic trainees are usually too psychologically disorganized and overwhelmed to think of formulating a coherent resistive response. At least in the past, trainees have often been terrified of the Army, particularly in the early weeks. They are also physically tired during basic training and only want to relax or perhaps explore their new environment during their off-duty time. Recruits do not know each other well enough at this period to develop the relations of trust and affection that are necessary for organizing a resistance movement. The Army appears to watch the trainees most closely during basic training, and it seems to give noncommissioned officers (NCOs) and officers more license to use their power and authority than at nearly any other time during a soldier's experience in the Army.

Another reason the organizer should not attempt any organization at this time is to protect his own ego. Many people maintain a fiction of their omnipotence: they feel that if they were really committed to something, they would not back down to any power. But GIs I have interviewed have asserted that the Army, at least during basic training, seems to be interested in destroying that self-confident state of mind that is so important for resistance. The way to destroy this attitude is to draw out the resistance of a recruit and then deal with it with all the power the organization has at its disposal. It is a shock to many young men to have the awareness so overwhelmingly thrust upon them that in fact they can be made to back down, and with surprising ease. This kind of threat to the self-image of a young man makes it difficult for him to maintain his own personal equilibrium, much less to even think of organizing other GIs.

Although the competent organizer does no active organizing

at this stage, he does begin to get to know fellow recruits and their backgrounds. The contacts he develops may prove useful later on, should he be stationed with the same people with whom he went through basic training.

Once out of basic training (and advanced individual training) and into a more "permanent party" or garrison duty kind of situation, the typical organizer will begin to talk informally with soldiers in his barracks or in his work section. He does not ask them to do anything but merely talks with them, in a relaxed way, about concerns that he feels they might share. This is what organizing always begins with: getting people to understand some aspects of the social structure by relating to their problems but without asking them to do very much. A competent organizer will begin with issues such as the manner in which GIs are treated in the Army, and somewhat later he will attempt to link this discussion with some more political and ideological issues, such as U.S. foreign policy, the conduct of war, and perhaps some issues of socialism versus capitalism.[20]

Before the organizer entered the Army, he might have been more likely to restrict himself to talking with potential constituents about ideological issues exclusively. If he persisted in this in the Army, he would alienate most GIs. However, once in the Army and through basic training, this organizer can better understand and sympathize with the GIs' overwhelming concern with harassment and the way the individual is treated in the Army.[21] Some civilian anti-war, anti-military organizers' unceasing emphasis on the correct "analysis" and attendant ideological issues and the relative neglect of a concern of the day-to-day treatment of the GI led the GI to think of this kind of radical as just one more in a series of people who are trying to manipulate him, rather than one who respects him as an individual in his own right.[22] This alienation from politics is partly a class phenomenon. The sense of "being a fall guy for everyone else" has recently become a central concern of working-class youth.[23] This may be contrasted with the greater concern with ideology and perhaps a relatively more theoretical orientation that characterizes the middle class, or at least the more highly educated radicals. Thus one might say that the Army's repression of the radical organizer when he becomes a GI helps to make him a better organizer because he is forced to understand his fellow soldiers more deeply and he will find it much more difficult to ignore problems of the treatment of the individual.

The Army's usual response to the discussions this organizer has been initiating is to assign him quietly to a different work section, probably one in which he has minimal contact with other soldiers.[24] The Army is able to make this move partly because it is already aware of the presence of a potential troublemaker and has been watching him for precisely this reason. Some of these organizers have verbal skills and end up as clerk-typists or similar kinds of duties, and there are many such jobs they could be assigned to that would keep them isolated from other soldiers during work hours.[25]

If a GI becomes politically outspoken only after entering the Army, his personnel file may be flagged at this later point.[26] Rather than being carefully assigned, a flagged soldier may temporarily be unassigned to any permanent work detail or base but held in what is called a holdover company. Thus while everyone he knows is sent off to various bases, he exists in a kind of limbo, unable to develop his organization or maintain contacts.[27]

Except for the case of holdovers, most organizers do not recognize that they have been deliberately isolated on a given work section until further along in their career in the Army when they have a chance to reflect on what has happened to them.[28] Soldiers are assigned to different jobs as a matter of course, and a reassigned soldier would not ordinarily suspect that he is being watched and manipulated.

The Army, using techniques on the installment plan, is not likely to use its most repressive technique at the outset. To court-martial someone for this kind of casual, though political, discussion tends to make a cause célèbre of him and generally to lower troops' morale as other GIs are forced to face more directly the oppressive aspects of the Army.[29]

The Army, an organization with a history, has the capacity to learn from its mistakes. When GI organizers first appeared in the Army (in 1967 and 1968), the Army commonly erred and overreacted by severely punishing the people who took these early steps.[30] But as Theodore Mataxis advises, the Army can better handle the problem of organizers by avoiding early overreaction.[31] It is, incidentally, much cheaper and takes less effort and time to use milder, less obvious techniques and hope the resister ceases his organizing.

Some GIs learn to expect an overreaction from a commander, which could consist of charging the resister with some violation of the Uniform Code of Military Justice (UCMJ), and, as a consequence, they study military law themselves.[32] This phenomenon in which an enlisted man learns some military law is contemptuously called (by officers, that is) a "barracks lawyer." The barracks lawyer puts officers, who are also subject to the UCMJ, on the defensive and makes them hesitant to use the judicial machinery. They are thus more likely to use bureaucratic techniques rather than the military justice system to control the dissident. The barracks lawyer is taking a chance in hoping he can bluff his commanding officers into leaving him alone. Even his attempt to read the copy of the UCMJ, which is kept in the orderly room, communicates his intentions to his officers, who will duly take note.

Transferring a GI from one work section to another may fail to prevent him from continuing to politicize others through discussions in the barracks (work sections are often run independently of barracks assignments)[33] or in other off-work activities and settings. The technique of transferring may be used again; the Army may transfer this resister to another barracks. Sometimes the two kinds of transfer may occur simultaneously.

The transfer may be carried out entirely within one base or, perhaps less likely, from one post to another, particularly one in a different state.[34] Of course, the effectiveness of the transfer is maximized when the organizer is moved to an entirely different base. On the other hand, it is more difficult and time-consuming for the Army to transfer a single GI to another base, and there may be organizational limitations on carrying this out because the Department of the Army (the Pentagon), rather than the base commander, has to make this assignment. (I would suppose that few organizers are viewed as threatening enough to influence the Army to carry out this transfer technique.)[35] During the Vietnam War, occasionally a GI organizer was sent to Vietnam as a result of his political efforts.[36]

If it could be shown in court that this transfer to a war zone was a result of the soldier's unsanctioned political activity and therefore not routine, it would be designated a "punitive transfer," which is illegal. The charge of punitively transferring an organizer can cause the Army some embarrassment, and it may be reluctant to use this technique in less than the most serious cases.[37]

The transfer is a widely used technique of handling dissidence and other problems in many bureaucratic structures.[38] Military leadership textbooks mention it as a useful technique of control.[39] The transfer is likely to be considered fairly early in a series of techniques of domination because it is not likely to elicit much of a resistive response. It is not as harsh as discharging or arresting someone, so supporters have little justification to complain. It seems so neutral and ordinary that the organizer may not even know it has been carried out intentionally. The transfer is a particularly effective technique because it tends to remove the individual from people he knows and trusts, which might demoralize him, and it forces him to build new relationships, which takes valuable time and effort. It may severely damage a nascent movement because it is often sufficient to stop a potential organizer in the Army. This is especially true if the organizer has only a few months left in the Army and feels that it would not be worth the effort to attempt to build anew. The transfer is also easy on the commanding officer because it allows him to export the problem rather than deal with it.

Several organizers have recounted how another technique was used on them, either in conjunction with the first time they were transferred or in conjunction with a second transfer.[40] The Army labeled the incoming organizer as a troublemaker by telling company members that a communist was being transferred into their unit. When this labeling occurred, the announcement was made one or two weeks in advance of the transfer. This technique, called *red-baiting*, identifies the organizer in a deviant and unfavorable way. When he does appear, he is taken aback by the fact that people are not responding to him in their usual ways; they seem to be actually shunning him.

The enlisted men's attitude toward communism is rather different from that of the officers. Young working-class GIs are considerably less ideological and are likely to view a communist as someone who is somewhat idealistic and maybe a little bit foolish but, usually, not someone who is dangerous. They may even be vaguely curious about him.[41] While red-baiting may have worked for a previous generation of working-class youth, it probably is less meaningful today.[42] It is also not likely to be effective for very long with competent organizers. Once an organizer realizes that a red-baiting process has preceded him in his new barracks situation, he can deal with it. Probably the best way to handle the labeling, if he were indeed a communist or a socialist, would be not to hide his beliefs but be willing to talk about them. He should explain his views, being careful not to push them very strongly. It is important for him to be honest and straightforward about his political persuasion; lying about his true feelings would tend to confirm the deviant status that the Army has tried to confer on him. "Owning up" to his values probably will not hurt him very much. Toward the end of the Vietnam War the Army ceased to use this kind of labeling, according to some of my interviewees.

If the organizer is able to surmount the effects of isolation, transferring, and labeling and begins organizing in earnest, the Army's next response is likely to be to directly confront the resister and attempt to intimidate him. It may use inspections for this purpose. An unusual inspection is considered a form of harassment and may turn up evidence that could provide excuses for more severe punishment. Inspections can also provide the Army with a sense of the magnitude of the problem.[43] It might find, for example, that many soldiers have radical literature in their lockers.

Inspections are only one form of harassment that a commander could use. He could directly threaten a soldier in a "counseling" session, or he could have the soldier arrested for reasons that have no connection with his link to an organization.[44] This kind of arrest has the advantage of effectively inhibiting a soldier without appearing to violate his civil rights. This demonstrates the usefulness of a military justice system in which substantive law[45] is based on protecting the organization from the individual rather than the reverse. The commander could also use the "treatment," a pattern of nonlegal harassment with participation by other soldiers, which involves isolation, unpleasant assignments, excessively close supervision, and ridicule.

The experiences of several anti-war organizers during the 1960s show that the command structure will shift to a different agency from the personnel and administrative (command) sectors that have been handling him thus far.[46] Military intelligence or military police investigators may interrogate the organizer and his supporters. Such an interrogation is a highly threatening event. For example, the interrogator could explain to a supporter who wanted to go back to college or to a professional school that any kind of court-martial would effectively close his future career. One of my interviewees wanted to be a high school teacher and was warned during an interrogation that a court-martial or even a bad discharge from the Army would destroy that career. So the Army, by finding out what kinds of career aspirations the individual has, can better organize its ability to terrorize him. The training military intelligence men receive for handling enemy prisoners of war can easily be put to use in intimidating anti-war GIs.[47]

The good organizer should expect that he will be interrogated and threatened at some point, but it is important that he warn his supporters that they may also be questioned or transferred. Once they have been recognized and threatened, some soldiers may feel that there is little more to lose in continuing their activities, and consequently they become more outspoken. The next step on the part of the GI organization will probably be to move off base and start thinking about publishing a GI anti-Army, anti-war paper. The move off base may not initially require as great a readjustment as might be supposed because many soldiers ordinarily live off post in nearby towns.

This is the stage at which the movement is likely to enlist civilian support. The organization off base may include project houses, coffeehouses, and military counseling centers, all of which require a supporting staff of civilians because the GIs are so likely to be transferred from the base.

By far the most common organizing strategy is to put out a paper. The Army reported a total of 245 GI anti-war papers produced during the Vietnam conflict.[48] Some of these lasted for only a couple of issues; others lasted for several years. Probably the greatest number of papers published at any one time would have been around ninety. Although a GI anti-war newspaper is generally produced subsequent to the interrogation and threats, it can precede the interrogations and be partly an inciting cause of them. The difference depends upon how closely the Army is watching the group and how threatening it considers its activities.

At one time, the military viewed GI anti-war papers and their distribution off post as serious and highly threatening events.[49] In order to handle this problem, military intelligence or military police infiltrated organizations and tried to find out as much as they could about them, including their civilian support.[50] The military spy would attempt to assess the threat and size of possible upcoming demonstrations and perhaps would make himself aware of issues that, if exploited, could cause splits among organization members. Some organizers whom I have interviewed were aware of the possibility that a military spy could act as an agent provocateur, pushing the group to an even more militant stance and especially to put itself into a situation in which legal charges could be brought against members of an organization. A particularly useful technique of the agent provocateur would be to introduce drugs, which political activists (at least those among my interviewees) would normally shun.

Hearings before the House Committee on Internal Security in 1972 have disclosed that Army spying on GI anti-war groups did occur and that the tpying had been considerably curtailed as a result of the civilian criticism of Army spying on civilians.[51] In other words, the directives outlawing Army spying on civilian groups have had some spillover into spying on GI anti-war groups. This does not mean that spying on GIs has ended. In order to place a spy in a GI anti-war group, special permission now has to be granted from the Defense Investigative Review

Council. This agency's director has testified that every request to carry out "covert surveillance" on a GI anti-war group has been granted.[52] Spying remains a technique of domination that the Army is likely to use when it perceives a serious threat.

The next step in the social control of the GI anti-war group is taken by yet a different agency, this one not even military. Local police have taken the initiative in threatening and investigating GI anti-war groups and project houses.[53] In fact, since the curtailing of Army spying, the Army does not seem to need to give much overt support to these local police because they, rather gratuitously, seem to take on the burden and expense of suppressing these groups.[54] They may suppress them by staging marijuana "busts" or by working with the courts and city councils to deny parade permits to radicals who want to "work within the system."[55] The small towns that so many Army bases are near—and provide considerable income for—support the Army, almost without being asked. Generally local police have with military police and military intelligence "an excellent relationship" and "full cooperation," especially in the areas of anti-war GIs and demonstrations.[56] Many coffeehouses have been closed by local civilian authorities. Even local citizens assist in the task, occasionally shooting at GI project houses and coffeehouses as they pass by in cars.[57]

If the organizers are not intimidated by the hostile and sometimes vicious responses from the civilian community, the dialectic of repression takes one more step: the organizers may be charged for some offense of the UCMJ. Given the vagueness of military law, even the most competent organizer can be arrested eventually by a military authority.[58] In the case of a court-martial, the competent organizer makes certain that soldiers on post and many civilians are aware of the proceedings so that the court-martial takes place in a publicized context with a courtroom packed with civilian and GI supporters, and even some news reporters. The organizer almost certainly would be represented by a civilian lawyer with some experience in military law. Even a court-martial can be turned to the partial advantage of the resister if he knows how to handle it. But the military can anticipate this by shifting the scene of the trial.[59]

The alternative to the court-martial is an undesirable or dishonorable discharge, which are quiet and convenient ways of getting rid of a resister; in addition, they can have some effect on ruining the resister's future so others will not be inclined to follow his example. A competent organizer, however, can fight such a "punitive discharge" through a military appeal system.

In 1969 the Army produced a directive, "Guidance on Dissent," to assist commanding officers in handling dissent.[60] By specifying what activities he could prosecute and what activities he must tolerate, the directive tells the commander when the Army will back him up (thus he can "cover his ass") and when he is "taking the right action." This may make it more likely that a commanding officer will take action; the guidelines remove some elements of uncertainty and give the officer some clues as to what would be considered an overreaction that resisters could, as Mataxis argued, "blow up out of proportion" and "make the regulations look ridiculous and the officers look brutal."[61] While the guidelines were a clear recognition of the presence of an organized anti-war movement within the Army, the letter probably did more to give the commander the confidence to take action against resisters and to protect himself from their techniques than it did to protect the resisters' rights. The commander otherwise might not have known what severe penalties the law places at his disposal for certain specified acts of resistance. "Guidance on Dissent" was an indication of both the Army's sensitivity to public relations and its capacity to learn from its experiences with resisters and to regularize social control.

The Army thus has a definite sequential repertoire of techniques of dealing with an organizer: identification, isolation and transferring, labeling, intimidation, espionage, reliance on outside agencies, and incarceration or expulsion. However, there were many situations, especially toward the end of the Vietnam War, in which leftist papers continued to be published and no one was court-martialed or punitively discharged. The Army had become less enthusiastic about prosecuting political resisters, for several reasons: the bad publicity it seemed to bring; the negative effect on a commanding officer's record to have an outbreak of open resistance or a poorly run repression strategy; the difficulty of legally carrying out surveillance on organizations; and so on. But the most important reason could be that officers in the Army came to recognize that the anti-war organizations were not the *cause* of serious problems for the military but perhaps a *consequence* of such problems. The problems of soldiers' refusals to fight in Vietnam and other outbreaks of rebellion, such as fragging, seemed to be independent of the ineffective, organized GI anti-war movement.[62]

The Army's dialectic of repression today may not unfold to its full extent. But this set of techniques will remain available to it, and it could bring them up if in the future it faces more seriously debilitating resistance. In 1967, when the Army probably did not know what to do with political resistance, its vacillating and capricious responses were said to be intended to keep organizers off balance. But by the end of the Vietnam War, the military had learned how to handle these resisters and, for the most part, decided not to bother.

The resister's career that I have outlined is constructed from the experiences and from the point of view of the anti-war organizer. The Army was simultaneously making other kinds of adaptations and responses that were not necessarily apparent to the organizer. Some of these tactics have been reported in a survey research study carried out by Research Analysis Corporation, a frequent contractor to the Army on personnel matters.[63] This organization surveyed the commanding officers of the following seventeen major Army posts within the United States: Fort Benning, Fort Bliss, Fort Bragg, Fort Campbell, Fort Carson, Fort Dix, Fort Gordon, Fort Hood, Fort Jackson, Fort Knox, Fort Leonard Wood, Fort Lewis, Fort Ord, Fort Polk, Fort Riley, Fort Sam Houston, and Fort Sill (the following post numbers are not related to the order of the above posts).

The following quotations from the research reports are summaries of post commanders' statements of their "methods used to deal with dissent":

> *Conventional Military Discipline and Courts-Martial Procedures*
>
> The consensus was that disciplinary measures appear to have been effective as a deterrent to the outright violation

of the legal restrictions on dissent. However, it was emphasized that these do little toward reducing dissent because the typical dissident is generally careful to be a good soldier while on duty, specifically to avoid punishment. The threat of court-martial does not exist insofar as the off-post activities of the dissident are concerned, provided he is not in uniform.

Changes in Regulations and Practices

Changes in regulations and practices that have been introduced for handling dissent or as preventive measures were listed as follows:

Post 1.

(1) Introduction of changes in military leadership techniques and disciplinary practices permitting a more flexible response to dissent.

(2) Maintenance of a close relationship with news media to assist in early identification of possible problems.

Post 3. [*sic*]

Conduct of a series of seminars which have oriented toward the race problem have been useful in reducing this area of possible dissent.

Post 4.

Modification of regulations pertaining to haircuts.

Post 5.

Change in duties and environment of known or suspected dissidents.

Post 6.

(1) Amplification of regulations concerning gatherings and distribution of literature to define better the responsibilities of the individual and actions to be taken within the command.

(2) Continuing command emphasis on duty, honor, and country through the chain of command down to and including the platoon sergeant.

Post 7.

(1) Team consisting of Commanding General, Chief of Staff, G-2, Provost Marshal, Information Officer and Staff Judge Advocate, formed to coordinate collection of information about dissidents, predict probable courses of dissident actions, and to formulate policies and procedures for dealing with dissent.

(2) Education program undertaken to make soldiers more aware of their responsibilities.

(3) Regulation revised concerning dissemination of publications on post.

(4) Directive issued establishing procedures to regulate civilian dissidents coming on post.

(5) Regulations pertaining to applying for CO status changed to curb its use as a means of dissent, while protecting the rights of the legitimate conscientious objector.

(6) Platoon-size reaction force created to augment military police element if needed.

(7) Emphasis placed on the welfare of the soldiers by commanders.

Post 8. Regulations prohibiting the distribution on post of certain types of publications changed to define more precisely the items within the purview of this restriction.

Post 9. Use of smooth and easy to use grievance channels, such as commander's open door policies, IG [Inspector General] and open discussions in command information sessions.

Post 10.

(1) Instituting SOP [standard operating procedure] for collecting underground newspapers distributed illegally on post.

(2) Emphasis on adequacy of information program and personnel services.

(3) Refusal to acknowledge or react to unwarranted attacks in underground newspapers.

Post 11. Broadening of regulations to make them more defensible legally.

Post 12. Keeping troops informed through character guidance classes, post newspaper, daily bulletin and commander's hour.

Post 13. Close coordination with on-post and off-post law enforcement and intelligence agencies to monitor dissident activities better.

Post 15. [*sic*]

(1) The revision of appropriate regulations has been beneficial in controlling demonstrations and the dissemination of dissident literature.

(2) Command information program expanded to counteract dissident activities.

(3) Command information class begun to explain US involvement in Vietnam.

Post 16.

(1) Increased emphasis on intelligence reporting of all incidents.

(2) Efforts concentrated on disciplining, eliminating, or transferring hard-core activists.

(3) Appointment of Field Officer of the Day (FOD) (in addition to normal Duty Officer) to operate daily from last light until one hour after closing time of clubs. The FOD visits service clubs, bus depots, theaters, etc., and maintains radio contact with military police.

(4) Establishment of two-man courtesy patrols by major unit commanders to patrol areas of responsibility from last light until one hour after closing of clubs. Patrols can alert the military police who will respond as required.

(5) Senior NCO required to remain in barracks at night.

(6) Platoon size ready force established in each major command, prepared to react on 30-minutes notice, to reinforce and assist the Provost Marshal as required.

(7) Armed guards established to guard weapons and ammunition, especially during training in the field.

(8) Emphasis on Command Information program. Two publications have been issued; one covers a discussion on dissidence, and the other deals with personal appearance.

(10) An acting IG has been appointed at battalion level to handle complaints and grievances promptly.

(11) Enlisted and officer advisory councils have been formed.

(12) Distribution of substandard personnel under constant review.

(13) PX's [post exchange] and commissaries stocked with specialized items, such as reading material, "soul" music, specific cosmetics, and "soul" food.

(14) Dissident Advisory Council established under Chief of Staff to evaluate dissident activities and recommend countermeasures.

(15) Narcotic Advisory Council established under G-1 [personnel].

Counseling with Dissidents

Most posts reported a passive attitude toward counseling with dissidents, namely, that individual soldiers are permitted access to commanders through established counseling periods and through the IG. It was stressed that counseling can be effective with followers or marginal dissidents, but that the hard-core dissident is dedicated to a radical policy and cannot be reached by logic or rational argument.

Surveillance of Dissidents

The questionnaire requested comments on a policy of observing dissident action closely, but taking no action until required. Eleven of the seventeen returns indicated that they considered this worthwhile and were using it in varying degrees. One return mentioned that, in addition to unobtrusive surveillance of known or suspected dissidents, obvious surveillance of troubled areas is maintained with a

> view to preventing violations rather than arresting after the fact.
>
> Those who appeared to prefer more direct action put forward the following points:
>
> (1) Immediate counseling is preferable to preclude the dissident from influencing others.
>
> (2) Delay often results in more harmful effects on the good order and discipline of the entire command.
>
> (3) Unfavorable publicity results if any action is taken against dissidents for activities other than outright violations of regulations. It is difficult to maintain surveillance and avoid charges of harassment.[64]

Commanders volunteered some additional comments that were also summarized in the report. Some felt that

> . . . with additional time in initial screening prior to induction, and by eliminating those individuals from induction that are troublemakers or have a background of dissent, the existing dissension problems would be eased. Continued leniency toward interpretation of the Bill of Rights and Army regulations, as well as clearly defined guidelines as to actions authorized, would greatly assist in dealing with dissension.
>
> Over the past few months, numerous AWOL and racial tension seminars determined that the major contributing factor to these problem areas is a lack of communication in the established chain of command. Policies or practices that strengthen or open up the existing chain of command offer the most fruitful relief to the problems of dissent. Control of dissidence must begin at the lowest command level. Activities of potential dissidents must be monitored by first-line supervisors who must initiate prompt legal corrective action and make necessary reports through the chain of command. . . . The extent of dissent should be gauged not only in terms of organized dissident meetings, coffee houses, and underground newspapers, but also in terms of increased disciplinary incidents, AWOL's and

other signs of disaffection or lowered discipline. The employment of professional opinion-sampling organizations, to ascertain scientifically the extent and causes of dissent and disaffection, is suggested. Such sampling would provide a firm basis for attacking the problem.

A major part of the response to the present situation would seem to lie in enlightened leadership which seeks to understand the young men of today and the environment from which they come, and employs such tools as unit newspapers and junior officer, NCO, EM [enlisted men], and race relations councils to this end. Further, military leaders must review traditional practices and procedures—some of which are "self-inflicted wounds" and are prime sources of irritation—to determine whether they are still militarily essential. Finally, major efforts should be made to stabilize military assignments—for both the leaders and the soldiers—since personnel turbulence is destructive of efforts to employ soldiers productively and to build morale and esprit within units.[65]

In another survey, most commanding officers reported no real changes in the procedures or actions taken by their military police.[66] Some reported that units (such as companies) are becoming reluctant to handle incidents such as the refusal of orders and disrespect toward superiors internally and prefer to report them to the military police. Others reported that military police monitor group actions but take little action themselves.[67]

In this report, which surveyed the same seventeen bases, the commanding officer of one of these bases made the following list:

Actions that have been taken to minimize the effects of dissident or racial incidents are:

(1) A close alignment of Military Police patrols, interior guards, courtesy patrols and staff duty personnel has been achieved which affords early detection, notification, prevention, and apprehension of offenders.

(2) Frequent analysis of all incidents involving violence

is made to determine trends in racial tensions, racially oriented offenses, dissident implications, and association with outside supporting sources.

(3) At post level, courses of instruction are presented in race relations and human relations which give opportunity to air opinions, complaints, or grievances in an atmosphere relatively free from the need to display violence. This safety valve aids in keeping racial problems at an absolute minimum.

(4) Thorough investigation of all offenses to identify offenders but also to detect racial or dissident implications.

(5) Complete coordination between commanders and staff on the identification, referral and counselling of possible dissident inclined individuals or those who stress racial violence.

(6) Close liaison is maintained with civilian police agencies in the surrounding area to insure early awareness of any protest type gatherings or the initiation of dissident activities.

(7) Regulations pertaining to petitions, distribution of literature, and meetings having protests as the basic purpose have been reviewed, clarified, and strengthened.

(8) Stress has been placed on reporting incidents to the Military Police that involve violence, indicate dissent, or reflect racial overtones.

(9) Command interest and review of all incidents where dissident or racial ramifications are indicated. This review is conducted with commanders and appropriate staff members and positive courses of action are decided for command supervision throughout the chain of command, Military Police prevention and enforcement efforts, and increased activities by other staff elements.

(10) The operation of a community advisory council and the close liaison/cooperation with the military affairs committees of surrounding communities leads the civilian com-

munity support to maintaining law, order, and discipline on and off post.[68]

And at another base, Actions "that have been taken to minimize the impact of dissident activities" included the following:

(1) Action was initiated within the command to identify persons as troublemakers, and subsequently to determine whether or not individuals so designated were suitable for retention. This effort resulted in an increase on the average of 30 soldiers a month being released by administrative actions.

(2) An enlisted men's council was organized in late 1969 to enable the Division Commander to have a feel for what really bugged the soldiers. This effort by no means was an attempt to circumvent the chain of command, but was truly designed to attain a sense of responsiveness to soldier problems. As a result of command support for the council down to the lowest level, the effort has materially assisted the overall control of dissidence and racial tensions.

(3) A Racial Harmony Committee was formed to better determine racial conditions at this post. Again there was no intent to circumvent the chain of command, but to give the Division Commander and his subordinate commanders a true evaluation of what factors are important in creating racial tensions and to identify the problems, either real or imagined, affecting minority groups. Significant improvement with regard to racial conditions has been realized from the efforts of this committee.

(4) Local criminal investigation, Military Police investigation, and Counterintelligence efforts have been used for the early identification of dissidence and violence. This effort is continuous around the clock. It has materially assisted, along with the Racial Harmony Committee and Enlisted Men's Council efforts, to control the environment.

(5) Project VOLAR [an acronym from Volunteer Army; this project was a field experiment in Army modernization

conducted at several bases]. while in its initial stages and implemented in January 1971, had an impact in decreased racial tensions and dissidence during the period late 1970 through publicity and the promise of a better lot for soldiers.

(6) The implementation of a drug center to assist the user of narcotics with regard to his individual problem has had a favorable impact. There are no statistics available to substantiate the above statement in light of racial tensions and dissidence. The impact of commencing the drug center program has brought the drug problem the attention it so sorely deserved. Commanders are acutely aware of the impact of drugs on order, discipline, and mission accomplishment. This acute awareness has led to early identification of drug users and pushers. The Military Police criminal investigation and civil police authority have effectively used available information to curtail drug traffic. During the period January 1971 to March 1971, the director assigned overall responsibility of the administration of the drug center. Activity reports a significant drop in the use of heroin. This may be attributed to the increasing command awareness, assistance to the user of narcotics, and excellent results attained by the local police community.

(7) Under the sponsorship of the local Chaplaincy, an on-post coffee house activity was initiated in 1969. This activity was favorably accepted by soldiers and has provided an additional outlet for gripes, grievances, and the opportunity to express such grievances. Command representatives, to include the Division Commander, have made themselves available on a periodic basis for "rap" discussions concerning everyday life at this installation. This activity has helped to reduce dissidence and racial tensions, and may have led to the reduction of soldier interest in the off-post coffee house.[69]

It is significant that the commanding officers who made these comments view some Army improvements and modernizations specifically as techniques to reduce dissent. In one questionnaire, from which I quoted, commanders were informed that the study was sponsored by the Office of the Provost Marshal General (head of the military police). Some of the above quotes were responses to a question that read, "please indicate what actions (MP actions, changes in procedures, etc.) have been taken at your post in response to each type of activity listed in Table 1, and how these activities affect the enforcement of discipline, law, and order."[70] The other questionnaire asked commanders to evaluate the various methods employed at their installation to manage dissent (with breakdowns of various methods in the questionnaire: use of conventional procedures, changes in regulations, counseling, and so on).[71]

These questionnaire responses illustrate an interesting aspect of social control: the way in which co-optive, "understanding" techniques can coexist with certain much more coercive techniques. For example, there seems to be no contradiction in the case of Post 7 (or Post 16), where the post commander emphasizes the welfare of the soldiers under his command but still creates a standby "reaction" force to quell any disturbances should his "concern" for his men be ineffective at preventing anti-war expressions. A more personal example of this continuity might be the experience of one black organizer, Private Leslie Williams, who was offered the choice between a seat on the enlisted men's council or a discharge with the promise that he leave the state of Texas. He was told that if he capitulated to either of these offers, court-martial charges (possession of marijuana) would be dropped.[72]

Some coercive techniques are too apparent and reduce the effectiveness of the co-optive ones, however. It is clear from these accounts that officers are relying on far more than mere coercion. For example, to contain dissent they are using propaganda (Post 15's and Post 16's command information program and Post 12's papers and commanding officers' hour), safety valves for the expression of tension (Post 9's use of the inspector general and the commanding officer's "open door" and Post 16's various councils), more communication (Post 5's various seminars), and the maintenance of soldier's identity and self-image (Post 12's character guidance and Post 7's education program). The shift to rely on and develop these modern tactics is the main concern of this book. While the dissident soldier may see Army social control in personal terms and with a certain amount of fear, the Army, as we shall see, is able to insulate itself from anti-war and anti-authority sentiments through a much broader range of techniques of control.

NOTES

1. Raul Hilberg, *The Destruction of the European Jews* (Chicago: Quadrangle Books, 1961).

2. Ibid., p. 31.

3. G. W. F. Hegel, *The Phenomenology of Mind*; trans. J. B. Baillie (New York: Harper & Row, 1967).

4. Ken Kesey, *One Flew over the Cuckoo's Nest* (New York: New American Library, 1962).

5. Samuel Haber, *Efficiency and Uplift* (Chicago: University of Chicago Press, 1964).

6. Loren Baritz, *The Servants of Power: A History of the Use of Social Science in American Industry* (New York: John Wiley & Sons, 1960).

7. Jason Ditton, "'Absent at Work' or How to Manage Monotony," *New Society* 21 (December 1972): 679-81.

8. Donald Clark Hodges, "Cynicism in the Labor Movement," in *American Society, Inc.: Studies of the Social Structure and Political Economy of the United States*, ed. Maurice Zeitlin (Chicago: Markham Publishing Co., 1970), pp. 439-48.

9. George E. Berkley, *The Administrative Revolution: Notes on the Passing of Organization Man* (Englewood Cliffs: Prentice-Hall, 1971).

10. Robert L. Kahn, "The Work Module—A Tonic for Lunchpail Lassitude," *Psychology Today* 6 (February 1973): 35ff.

11. *Work in America: Report of a Special Task Force to the Secretary of Health, Education and Welfare* (Cambridge: MIT Press, n.d.), pp. 93-120.

12. For especially complete accounts, see Dennis Davis, *G.I. Joe's a Red!* (Boston: New England Free Press, 1969); GI Alliance, *Strategy and Tactics for GI Organizing* (Tacoma: GI Alliance/Free Press, n.d.); Andy Stapp, *Up Against the Brass* (New York: Simon & Schuster, 1970); Fred Halstead, *GIs Speak Out Against the War: The Case of the Ft. Jackson 8* (New York: Pathfinder Press, 1970).

13. U.S. Congress, House, Committee on Internal Security, *Investigation of*

Attempts to Subvert the United States Armed Services, 92d Cong., 2d sess., pt. 2, November 9, 10, 16, 18, 1971, May 2, 3, 1972, pt. 3, May 9, 10, June 1, 20, 1972.

14. The lack of one or the other of these two characteristics (commitment and competence) is sometimes misleadingly interpreted as apathy. See, for example, the essay by David Riesman and Nathan Glazer, "Criteria for Political Apathy," in *Studies in Leadership: Leadership and Democratic Action*, ed. Alvin W. Gouldner (New York: Russell & Russell, 1950), pp. 531-47.

15. See the case of Edmund Jurenas in Committee on Internal Security, *Investigation of Attempts*, pt. 2, pp. 7204-15.

16. See Marion D. Wood, "Spotting Potential AWOLs from Personnel Data Cards," *ARMY* 20 (February 1970): 60-61.

17. See Howard C. Olson and R. William Rae, *Determination of the Potential for Dissidence in the US Army, Volume 1—Nature of Dissent*, RAC-TP-410 (McLean, Virginia: Research Analysis Corporation, 1971). Available from the National Technical Information Service, Department of Commerce, listed as AD884031. According to this study, "Factors of Army component [draftee or volunteer], geographic origin, religion, education level, Army Classification Battery (ACB) scores, and Military Occupational Specialty (MOS) proved to be significantly related to dissident activity." Ibid., p. 2.

18. The army has quietly discharged some recruits who appear likely to be dissidents. According to some of my interviewees, some black militants spend only two weeks in basic training before they are identified and discharged. See also the commanding officers' reports at the end of Chapter 1 for some evidence of the readiness to use administrative discharges to get rid of possible dissidents. Similarly, when former Secretary of the Army Howard Callaway was asked if he would agree to having "draft dodgers" and deserters "make up their time" by serving a year in the Army, he replied, "I don't want that kind of people in the Army." Quoted in "Army Seeks Idled Workers," *Ann Arbor News*, February 22, 1974.

19. The technique of "flagging" personnel files was first brought to my attention by some of my clerk-typist interviewees. The practice is also mentioned in Committee on Internal Security, *Investigation of Attempts*, pt. 2.

20. Ibid., pp. 7221-30.

21. "Harassment of the troops and the lack of personal freedom and dignity" were cited by soldiers as the key reason for dissidence. See R. William Rae, Stephen B. Forman, and Howard C. Olson, *Future Impact of Dissident Elements within the Army on the Enforcement of Discipline, Law and Order*, RAC-TP-441 (McLean, Virginia: Research Analysis Corporation, 1972), p. 73. Available from the National Technical Information Service, Department of Commerce, listed as AD 891558.

22. See "Case Study in Opportunism: The GI Movement," Fred Gardner, Exhibit 64, in Committee on Internal Security, *Investigation of Attempts*, pt. 3, pp. 7522-25.

23. Hodges, "Cynicism in the Labor Movement"; see also Chapter 4 below, which discusses attitude surveys, for other comments on this aspect of GIs' concerns.

24. Officers, when asked for their recommendations on how the Army could reduce dissidence, suggested (among many other things), "Spot insurgent leaders [and] try to isolate them and then give them other responsibilities." Rae, Forman, and Olson, *Future Impact of Dissident Elements*, p. 155.

25. In one case, the Army isolated an entire company suspected of having seven American Servicemen's Union (ASU) organizers. ASU was one of the larger dissident organizations during the Vietnam War. See *Camp News* 3 (February 15, 1972): 15.

26. According to the Army, this is a comparatively rare occurrence. In 1972 the Army claimed it had only fifteen soldiers flagged. Committee on Internal Security, *Investigation of Attempts*, p. 7089. Judging by the level of magnitude of the problem, one would suppose that there are many more flaggings that are not reported.

27. Another way to carry out the same function would be to detain him at a psychiatric facility. See *Camp News* 4 (April 15, 1972): 3.

28. Stapp, *Up Against the Brass*, pp. 27-28.

29. See the Harvey and Daniels case described in Sherrill, *Military Justice Is to Justice as Military Music Is to Music* (New York: Harper & Row, 1970), p. 41.

30. Mataxis feels that since the GI organizers benefited from the outcry and repression, they must therefore have wanted to elicit this excessive response. See Theodore C. Mataxis, "This Far, No Farther: How the Army Handles Dissenters in Uniform," *Military Review* 51 (March 1970): 74-82. His article, minus some right-wing vituperation against New Leftists, was reprinted in *Commander's Call*, thus ensuring it an even wider readership among officers than the more international-policy-oriented *Military Review* would ordinarily bring.

31. Ibid.

32. See, for example, Rivkin, *GI Rights and Army Justice* (New York: Grove Press, 1970).

33. On the problem dual authority engenders, see Moskos, *The American Enlisted Man, The Rank and File in Today's Military* (New York: Russell Sage Foundation, 1970), pp. 72-73.

34. See Halstead, *GIs Speak Out Against the War*, p. 7, and the Jurenas Case in Committee on Internal Security, *Investigation of Attempts*, pt. 2, pp. 7204-15.

35. Marine organizers of the *Semper Fi* paper were transferred out of Iwakuni on less than twenty-four hours' notice. See *Camp News* 3 (January 15, 1972).

36. See ibid., and ibid. (February 15, 1972).

37. The Army's acute concern over its public image has resulted in its establishing a "procedure for reporting all cases of suspected criminal conduct, wrong-doing, or mismanagement, which may result in damaging public confidence in the Army." The reports, code named "Blue Bell," include desertions, violent protests and sabotage, racial incidents, stockade disturbances, various dissident acts and protests, and fraggings (killing an officer with a fragmentation grenade). See Rae, Forman, and Olson, *Future Impact of Dissident Elements*, pp. 53-54.

38. On transfers within the federal prison system, see Howard Levy and David Miller, *Going to Jail: The Political Prisoner* (New York: Grove Press, n.d.).

39. See the "situational" studies in Samuel H. Hays and William N. Thomas, *Taking Command: The Art and Science of Military Leadership* (Harrisburg, Pennsylvania: Stackpole Books, 1967), pp. 265-92.

40. Stapp, *Up Against the Brass*, p. 28; and Davis, *G.I. Joe's a Red!* p. 50.

41. Davis, *G.I. Joe's a Red!* p. 50.

42. In a study of the attitudes of low-level (E1-E4) enlisted men, Army researchers asked nondissidents in the sample why they did not take part in dissident activities. Only 7 percent said protest was disloyal or unpatriotic. Other reasons for not participating in dissident acts included: the feeling that protest would do no good and they just want to get out of the Army (48 percent); no opportunity to participate (19 percent); fear of punishment (12 percent); and no reason to protest and/or complaints could be handled through the system (14 percent). Rae, Forman, and Olson, *Future Impact of Dissident Elements*, p. 44. Soldiers in general appear very tolerant toward dissident activities by other soldiers. Eighty-six percent of all E1-E4 respondents in the sample said the Army should take no action against soldiers' attendance at protest meetings off post, and 68 percent said the Army should take no action against on-post demonstrations. Ibid., p. 71.

43. See *Camp News* 3 (January 15, 1972).

44. See ibid. 2 (December 15, 1971): 2.

45. See Chapter 7 below for a discussion of this term.

46. See Stapp, *Up Against the Brass*, p. 37 and Davis, *G.I. Joe's a Red!* p. 49. See also *Camp News* 3 (December 15, 1972): 23, and (January 15, 1972): 3.

47. See Robert B. Rigg, "Made in USA," *ARMY* 18 (January 1968): 24-31.

48. See Committee on Internal Security, *Investigation of Attempts*, pt. 3, p. 7319.

49. "The Collapse of the Armed Forces," Robert D. Heinl, Jr., Exhibit 51, in ibid. pp. 7132-40.

50. Ibid., pt. 2, pp. 6924-25, 6955.

51. Ibid., pp. 6879-976.

52. Ibid.

53. This problem of local police repression was frequently commented upon in anti-war papers, such as *Camp News*, and it is noted in Committee on Internal Security, *Investigation of Attempts*, pt. 3, pp. 7305-07.

54. Committee on Internal Security, *Investigation of Attempts*, pp. 7259-93.

55. Ibid., pp. 7305, 7271.

56. Ibid., pp. 7259-93. See also the post commanders' comments in this chapter.

57. The People's House near Fort Campbell was teargassed and shot at by shotguns: some of the cars of those who frequented the house were firebombed, and others were run off the road. *Camp News* 2 (December 15, 1971). The Covered Wagon at Mount Home, Idaho, was burned down through arson. Ibid. The United Front in the Fort Sill area had a gas grenade tossed through the living

room window. Ibid. 4 (April 15, 1972): 6. A GI center in the Philippines was raided, probably illegally, by local police and the shore patrol. Ibid. Off the Runway, near Holyoke, Massachusetts, was closed for violation of city occupancy plumbing and other ordinances. Ibid., 2 (December 15, 1971). The examples of civilian harassment are so easily multiplied that it is an unusual project house or coffeehouse that had not experienced some form of terrorist attack (accompanied by local police indifference or illegal raids).

58. A few organizers have attempted to surmount the difficulty of distributing a paper (it is illegal to have more than one copy of an unauthorized paper in one's possession) by getting it approved by the post commander. The Army reports that nineteen papers have received such sanctioning. See Committee on Internal Security, *Investigation of Attempts to Subvert*, p. 7183.

59. See, for example, *St. Louis Post-Dispatch*, January 17, 1973.

60. There were two versions of this letter issued by the Department of the Army. Many officers thought the first letter, issued in May 1969, was much too permissive; in fall 1969 a second, stricter guideline was issued.

61. Mataxis, "This Far, No Farther," p. 81.

62. Committee on Internal Security, *Investigation of Attempts*, pt. 2, pp. 6979-7006.

63. Olson and Rae, *Determination of the Potential.*

64. Ibid., pp. 73-78.

65. Ibid., p. 81.

66. Rae, Forman, and Olson, *Future Impact of Dissident Elements*, pp. 163-75.

67. Ibid.

68. Ibid., p. 170.

69. Ibid., pp. 172-73.

70. Ibid., pp. 171, 180.

71. Olson and Rae, *Determination of the Potential*, pp. 88-89.

72. *Camp News* 3 (January 15, 1972): 10.

2

Coercive Control

A resister who has failed to organize a large group of soldiers may feel frustrated and wonder why he was so unsuccessful.[1] In the late 1960s radical anti-war soldiers' organizations typically consisted of only a few people, and demonstrations were usually quite small (perhaps thirty or forty soldiers plus as many civilian supporters). This contrasts markedly with demonstrations at middle-sized college campuses that could draw 3,000 students and with marches on Washington by 100,000 protesters.

One organizer disconsolately told me, "You can't organize in the Army. It's like a tar baby." He could have meant that striking the tar baby—the Army—would only cause one to be immobilized within its repressive machinery. But I think what this soldier meant was that the Army does not present many real, concrete issues around which to organize. It can be overpowering without being excessively vicious or saliently unfair. In addition, it is difficult for a resister to acquire a following because of the Army's system of coercive controls—and gratifications—that it employs on soldiers en masse.

This wide array of techniques for controlling soldiers collectively may be placed on a continuum, ranging from the most overt, coercive style to the most subtle, inclusive sort. It has often been pointed out that the Army's social controls have been changing for years from coercion to manipulation. In this and in the next two chapters, I will examine these controls in some detail, focusing on the effectiveness of each style. I will also examine some of the historical sources of modernization and suggest some of the forces leading to the transformation of techniques of control. For example, behavioral scientists' "imperialism," enlisted men's discontent, and the changes in the technology of warfare are forces for change in social control that I will discuss in these chapters. (There are other forces, such as civilian criticism of the military, that are outside the scope of this study.)

This chapter will look into the most coercive (and oldest) of Army styles of control, a style which is typically employed by the tough, brutal drill instructor or combat platoon sergeant of many Army stories and movies.[2] This chapter will characterize some of the assumptions underlying the coercive style of control, and it will focus on two patterns of despotic techniques—basic training and "the treatment." I will also look at some of the strains that result when Army support for despotic practices is withdrawn.

The coercive control style is based on a rather uncharitable view of human nature. It assumes that men are naturally lazy, uncooperative, and likely to avoid risks. Therefore a leader has to use coercive techniques—including physical punishments, mental harassment, docking pay, restriction of freedom of movement, and so on—to accomplish anything. The result of the reliance on coercive techniques, of course, is alienated and recalcitrant soldiers. There is a self-fulfilling prophecy at work here: coercion is assumed to be necessary given the pessimistic view of human nature, and the soldier responds with (suppressed) anger and resistance, which necessitates the continued use of coercive controls.

An NCO who was assigned to training recruits described this control style—and the results of relying only on coercion:

> One . . . example of ridiculous jobs is, on my committee they

have this training that takes 16 hours worth of training for each company that comes through there. OK, now, a certain number of hours, like 3 or 4, are set aside for "practical exercises." All that "practical exercises" pertains to is going out and filling sand bags. I mean how much training do you need on filling a sand bag before you're very proficient at it? One, two, three sandbags—not hours, sandbags. Then last week we had a company out there and it was my job to have a platoon and a half do nothing but unstack the sandbags around a bunker and then stack them up. Just for "practical exercises."So, I tell them, "look, this is what we have to do. This is what they told me to have you do. Just look busy so that if they come over here nobody gets hassled about it. So just to keep them off my back and off your back just look like you're doing something." And so everybody stands around and once in a while somebody throws a sand bag up. And that's all we got accomplished. Maybe in a total of 2 hours time, we actually moved a total of 12 or 15 sandbags. Everybody got along fine. I told them, "look, you're getting paid by the hour, not piece time. You get paid the same if this thing gets done today or a month from today. So why knock yourself out?" *You have to remember too that the Army is based on a set of negative reasoning whereas a man will not be commended or singled out for doing a good job, but he will be punished for doing a bad job.* And anybody subjected to this kind of reasoning is going to say fuck it, I'm going to do just enough to get by. Why should I knock myself out when I'll get no credit for it, no esteem whatsoever in anybody's eyes? But if I fuck it up I'll get an Article 15 [a fine or restriction], so obviously I'll do just enough to get by. They don't say like if you guys stay within the standards for haircuts we'll have a party at the end of the month. No, it's not like that. Do it or else. People are naturally going to rebel against something like that. If you walk up and slap me in the face I'm naturally going to be hostile to you. But if you walk up and shake my hand I'm going to be friendly towards you.

This soldier reflected some widespread complaints about Army life. A recent survey presented to the Army War College emphasized that enlisted men in the lower grade levels (lower ranks such as E1-E4) in the Army "are apparently far more sensitive to the use and misuse of their time than is commonly realized by leaders at all echelons."[3] This has been especially irritating during advanced individual training. The survey also identified NCOs' complaints that they did not have the authority they needed to reward good performance with time off.[4]

This soldier's commentary suggests that there are ways to resist the Army short of outright refusals, mutinies, assaults, or desertions. This recalcitrance is one of the consequences of relying on coercive measures for social control. In a separate interview, an officer spoke of similar problems from his perspective:

> The men [get] their frustrations out in [various ways such as] breaking the machinery. They were very good at breaking the trucks, or just getting their frustrations out by battering, breaking things, and by writing on toilet walls and by doing things half assed. You know, when they're told to do something they go through the motions but they don't really do it. There's just no professionalism, I would think. Or very, very little amongst a large body of the enlisted people. Any chance to screw an officer they will, by fouling up records and just by doing a generally sloppy job. Of course, why should they do a good job if they're getting abused? If you do a good job in the Army, it very rarely helps you. Usually you get in trouble for it. And also there's pure resentment. If this guy is doing a good job, well everybody looks at him and says well what the hell is wrong with you? So you're not going to get the peer approval if you're too effective. So that's why they have 20 guys out pushing one shovel. It takes that many.
>
> [The result in more general terms is a situation which] isn't felt out [that is, expressed openly] kind of resistance. . . . It's like trying to push a mule. The Army is like trying to pull a donkey or trying to push a mule and the mule is just

> going very slow because it doesn't want to get hassled. And the Army is used to, for the last 20 years or maybe for 100 years, accepting this kind of performance as being up to snuff. In other words, this is all right. Of course, we always have enough bodies to do the job. If 100 can't do it, we'll draft another 1,000, what's the difference?

The few rewards consistent with the coercive style of control usually involve getting away from the Army. These include weekend passes (during training), leaves, and "early outs" (discharge from the Army before one's tour is officially over). With one or two striking exceptions (noted in the account of basic combat training in this chapter) rewards are not connected with military objectives. Rewards characteristic of this style are sometimes viewed by soldiers as rights they already had (prior to entering the service). An enlisted man explained how soldiers have to earn these rewards:

> The first thing they do is take away everything you've got that you've taken for granted. They take away your right to go home, they take away your hair, your clothes. They take away your right . . . to sit there and drink a beer. They hit [you with] stuff that's all new to you, language wise. They take away your right that when you don't like something [you should be able to] tell them about it. Take away your privacy. Take away your bed, everything. They give you everything that's green. They give you all this crap. And then they make you [earn it] back. And, for instance, a pass is the ideal thing. They say, well a pass isn't a right, it's a privilege and you've got to earn it. Well, the first time someone doesn't do something you want, well he doesn't get a pass. They control your time and they limit you to this whole area, about 1/3 block in size. And tell you that if you leave the area you're in trouble and say that they're going to call you out any time they want to and if you're not there they're going to throw you in jail. All this kind of crap. They try to make you earn back these things.

Another soldier complained of endless, close supervision. "The

Army's system is kind of like the pecking order of birds. Nobody just rides around by himself. There's always somebody who's pressuring you."

These comments refer to coercive practices used in a garrison or noncombat situation. Because there is little intrinsic motivation in such a setting, coercive measures are likely to be turned to. In contrast, soldiers I have spoken to mention coercive practices less often in combat, perhaps because there is a clearer purpose behind officers' orders or because the officers themselves are more motivated to avoid these practices with the concomitant resistance.

Coercive leadership in combat was described by Norman Mailer in his novel *The Naked and the Dead*.[5] Mailer's platoon sergeant uses fear and continual power confrontations to ensure obedience. He has the power of military authority behind him, but he normally uses his own personal style of belligerence to cow any resistance in his platoon. He is willing to use any force at his disposal, such as his own rifle, and he attempts to cull out resistance, to dare it to appear, because he is confident he can beat it down. His power is enhanced by demonstrating the impotence of the men rather than by allowing them to lull themselves into thinking that they could resist if they chose to.

Correspondingly, the general in Mailer's book uses privilege as an adjunct to fear. Class hostility of enlisted men versus commissioned officers is exacerbated by the continual allocation of privileges and scarce resources to the officers. The theory is that the separation enhances discipline and the class hostility will be displaced onto the enemy. Soldiers, according to this view, fight because they hate, not because they love (other soldiers).

At first glance, coercion seems to be a simpleminded and counterproductive way to maintain control. But coercion affects the victim in peculiar ways, sometimes actually integrating him into the organization by altering his self-concept. This alteration of the self—becoming a soldier—occurs primarily through the process of basic training. One of my interviewees asserted that basic training is probably the most important reason that the Army was able to prevent the wholesale transfer of the civilian anti-war movement in the 1960s into its own ranks.

Writing in the 1960s, Peter Bourne, an Army psychiatrist, divided basic training into four stages.[6] First, there was a stripping away of civilian cues, which are ways of telling the world how one wants to be interacted with and identified. This was done to more easily inculcate new identities and appearances. Second, there was a process of insults and mortifications that were intended to break down the individual's pride in himself, which is essential to his capacity to resist. In the third stage the Army began to rebuild and reorganize the personality by providing a few, much desired rewards. Finally, there was some kind of final test of proficiency and often a graduation ceremony. Let us look at these tactics in more detail.

The first few days a recruit experienced in the military were a period of great stress and shock for him.[7] In this first stage, he actually did very little except respond to routine induction procedures such as filling out forms, being issued uniforms, and so forth. He was filled with all sorts of impressions and fears about the Army, and there was little that he could do to alleviate his tension. Depersonalization of the recruit began with the physical examination—most civilians are not accustomed to being forced to stand naked in front of others who are unfamiliar. The "skinhead" haircut and the uniform functioned to reduce the recruit's ability to cue others to treat him as an individual.[8]

The second stage, in which the recruit began to train, was accompanied by a marked decrease in his near-panic stress state.[9] During this stage, however, the self-image of the recruit was directly assaulted; he was forced to do unfamiliar tasks, which created confusion and uncertainty. For example, some trainees were forced to imitate animals (to bark like dogs, and the like). The personal disorganization of the individual was exacerbated and reflected by the tight training schedule in which he was kept uninformed of what was in store for him. The Army's power was enhanced by its appearance of precise planning while the recruit hardly knew what to anticipate. Recruits quickly learned the do's and don'ts that would please the drill instructor and would keep them from being picked out for embarrassing individual harassment in front of others. The closeness of traditional barracks life, in which perhaps thirty men slept in one large room, further encouraged the submergence of individuality in the military group. Bathrooms in these barracks had no walls around the toilets.

Recruits had been allowed early in basic training to see other recruits in later stages being beaten for such "transgressions" as not keeping up in a forced march.[10] Drill instructors attempted to communicate extraordinary prerogatives even within the military. As one trainee reported, his drill instructor's introductory comment was, "Yo' ass belongs to me and only incidentally to the U.S. Army, when I'm tru' wi' it."[11]

Physical exercise has been one of the hallmarks of basic training. Certainly there is no denying that effective soldiers must be in good physical condition, but constant, excessive exercise is not the most efficient way to accomplish this. There must regularly be some days allotted for the body to recuperate. Physical exercise in basic training had the more important function of providing drill instructors with legitimate ways of punishing those who did not respond to orders with the snap and zeal they would like. An order to drop for twenty push-ups at some trivial infraction is an effective tool of control. It is quick, and learning occurs best when the results are quickly transmitted back to the learner. Physical exercise as punishment also functioned to avoid clogging the Army's judicial machinery. Even minor legal punishment cannot be used to the extent that the coercive style would require in basic training. Exercises done in front of others served not only to show the others what to expect but to humiliate the offender.

In the third stage of basic training, some of the recruit's repressed desires were allowed to come to the fore—for example, a recruit's desire for individuality and recognition—and the Army made use of them.[12] One of the first rewards bestowed in basic training was a score resulting from rifle practice. Shooting is the point at which the killing function of the military is inescapable. But this was also the point where the recruit was given what he most craved—some personal recognition of success and competence.[13]

Recruits who excelled in basic training were given the informal rank of squad leader. This early reward divided the men and co-opted (included) some of the more capable, who might have otherwise later organized resistance. Recruits learned that the way to beat the system was to excel in it.

Uncooperative recruits were isolated and ostracized with ridicule and insults, which even the other recruits joined in. Uncooperative individual acts could be cast in a group context; the overall score of the unit would be lowered, and rewards such as passes would be lost to the unit. Recalcitrance would be defined as incapacity, or incompetence (which may, in fact, actually be the case), which would make a resister at this stage an unsympathetic character. Tauber reports that recruits in his training company began to swagger and affect southern drawls, identifying with their drill instructors.[14] A "blanket party," in which informally authorize the event. The recalcitrant recruit would know that his fellow trainees, not just the drill instructor, were beating him, and this demoralized and diffused his resistance.

The harassment (although mixed with rewards) that continued through this third stage functioned ostensibly to ensure that soldiers would follow direct orders immediately. If a drill instructor recognized that his harassment was driving a good man to quit, he would drop him a short compliment: "You can't quit. You'll make a good trooper."[15]

The last stage was a more accepting and rewarding stage that occurred near the end of basic training.[16] There was often a graduation ceremony, replete with rituals expressing the Army's desire to accept the recruits as members of the team. That the men had to endure harassment for so long would influence them to have a greater commitment to the organization; it was the only way they could justify putting up with their treatment. Consequently, GIs expected to feel different—like supermen—because they had endured the hardships of basic training. The soldiers Bourne studied were somewhat disappointed that they had not really changed, and some wished the Army had been tougher with them.[17] Interestingly, recent changes in Army basic training may cause this disappointment to grow. While Bourne's description may apply to several previous decades of basic training, the Army in the 1970s appears to be relying on some different principles of control in its newer, less mortifying basic training process. These new techniques are taken up in Chapter 4.

A man's integration with the Army and his self-image as a soldier are complex entities. He can feel like a soldier and yet bitterly resent the process that caused his transformation. He may continue to hate various aspects of the Army. Other soldiers may want to be part of the military but may be too personally disorganized to be able to conform within a bureaucratic context. For example, during the Vietnam war many of these soldiers were successful "in country" (rural Vietnam) but not in stateside duty. They could perform only in an atmosphere of informality, relaxed authority, and fairly identifiable objectives and goals (fighting the enemy and coming home). Once stateside, these goals were not replaced, and the harassment and capricious discipline (allegedly maintained to keep the men in a state of readiness) caused them to fly into a rage.

Certain soldiers—some decorated combat veterans, some middle-level NCOs with many years of experience but frustrated by Army liberalizations, and various others—are singled out by their company commander as troublemakers. Once a recalcitrant soldier is considered as a troublemaker he may experience an organized set of despotic techniques that James Jones called *the treatment* in his novel *From Here to Eternity.*[18]

The treatment in the novel requires various officers and NCOs to act in concert to pressure a soldier to conform. These pressures entail social isolation, extra duty, disallowing of passes, withholding expected promotions, and assignment to unpleasant details such as KP (kitchen patrol). The NCOs keep a close watch for possible chargeable offenses, and there are many extra, stiffer inspections and vague threats of violence. In marches, the resisting soldier is continually called for being out of step, even if he is marching perfectly. Physical exercise is also used as a punishment.

The soldier is endlessly ridiculed along whatever lines the NCOs think he would be sensitive, such as maligning his ethnicity or race, or insulting his masculinity, or insulting the women in his family, or labeling him a bolshevik. A man's pride is his weakest point, observes Jones.[19] Questioning one's manly honor provides one of the most easily manipulated and effective levers of control.

Thus the soldier, who, except for his expression of anti-Army sentiment, has been soldiering perfectly can be expected to explode in his frustration. Once he does, he is bound to do some outright, undeniably illegal act for which the military can severely punish him.

Jones was writing about a U.S. Army garrison (in Hawaii) just prior to World War II. How has the treatment evolved since then? In the recently more disorganized Army with an increased diversity of officers and enlisted men and a greater presence of legal officers, we might expect that the repression in concert would be difficult to achieve. But the changes seem rather minor, according to the experiences of some of my interviewees.

An Army legal officer who initiated a law suit against the Army to defend his own political activism commented on his experience with the Army's treatment. He said the Army usually appears to be disorganized as long as resistance is not organized.

> When they focus on a problem they go berserk, like the way they focused on me. The day I started the suit in federal court (the paper and the radio had it on the air at midnight) and by 4 A.M. they had everybody out—you know, the generals, the colonel, everybody. They were going around seeing what kinds of shit they could dig up on me by 8 o'clock in the morning. Once they get hot on a problem, it's just like fighting a war to them. The dissidents in the Army are the enemy. And they mobilize their full efforts to drive the guy nuts, to get rid of him, or disband a unit, or how can we court martial him, or put him in a stockade, or do something. In other words, as soon as a resistance builds up they get very strong.

Jones's account of the treatment suggests an interesting aspect of rules: they work best when they are ordinarily not rigidly enforced.[20] When there is some kind of resistance, the application of the rules can be tightened up against the resisters, thereby providing a much greater capacity to control without exceeding legal limits. This selective enforcement of certain rules (which may be unrelated to the real "offense") can be seen in the following comment by an enlisted man:

> Every enlisted man does a certain number of things that he can be punished for. But usually isn't punished for because they're not big enough to take notice of. Things like taking off early from work and having a Sgt. cover for you. Or getting to work late. Haircut. Little things like this. But if you're ever in a position where you give a lifer like our 1st Sgt. trouble. . . . Here's an example: this guy is living off post with his wife. He beats his wife, I guess. . . . She called his company commander and talked to the first Sgt. And he referred the problem to the Capt. The Capt. told the 1st Sgt., you take care of this. So the 1st Sgt. and another Lt. were in fatigues and another master Sgt., in civilian clothes, went off post out to this man's house. His wife let them in and they forcibly brought him back to the post. They tried to lock him up. What they charged him with was a uniform violation. You're not allowed to wear fatigues off post. This was in this man's home. You're allowed to wear them directly from the post to your home by regulation as long as you don't stop off anywhere. But if you're just coming off post [for some other reason such as to run an errand] or going back you're not allowed to wear fatigues. Two of these men were wearing fatigues and they busted him for a uniform violation. He pressed charges against the 1st Sgt. for assault and a couple of other things. He got the paper work through, had the charges read to the 1st Sgt. But after that they put him on restriction and busted him for breaking restrictions. He's married and he's got his home off post. They put him on restriction to the company area and made him sleep there. And I guess he tried to go home to see his wife and they got him for that. They got him Article 15s for a couple other minor offenses.

Group punishment is another form of harassment that can be considered part of the treatment. An enlisted soldier commented on this potentially divisive tactic:

> The worst thing I've seen all through my Army career is the way the Army can turn one man against another. Take GI parties. We had a problem in our barracks with shoe dye sniffing. Like glue sniffing. It was all over the floor. There were only about 3 or 4 people doing it. But at the same time they took the whole barracks and made us scrape the floor. Then they start to hit us with things like, you guys tell us who these men are and give us some concrete statements and you won't be doing this. It would be in our interest to do that to keep us from having to do this work, but at the same time I'd be inclined to resist that because it breaks down the solidity of the enlisted men and that's the only defense he has against a system that's trying to turn him into a machine.

I asked, "Doesn't the Army want solidity?"

> Yeah, but it's got to be a different kind, you know what I mean? It has to be their form of solidity. In other words, if it's going to be esprit de corps, it got to be their way. You can't have it, being together, by having long hair. Or that kind of spirit. It's got to be the spirit of you fight for me, I'll fight for you. There's an attempt in the Army to create dissension among enlisted men and the threat of punishment is the most common way. They punish more than one man for something that one man has done. And when we come back and say, "Why should we do this because it wasn't our fault?" they say, "Well, inform on this man and we won't do it to you." And in our age group it's our code you can't be an informer. But at the same time you have to put up with this. And then there's a few people that say, "Well, I'm tired of this." And usually the splits are along the lines of your home state, north or south, black and white. Those are the weak points in any group like that. And the lifers just work on those points. They'll find out your weaknesses and they'll lean on them as far as they can.

As we've seen, *harassment* is a term used in the Army to refer to a variety of techniques of control. Some of these techniques seem trivial, but in a context of continued maltreatment they can irritate a soldier. I asked an exasperated soldier what he meant by harassment.

> That's really harassment when they keep moving you around. And not just moving to another unit. They say you can't work here anymore; you have to move to this other building. Then they say you can't work upstairs any more, you have to work downstairs. You move downstairs, then they say you're at the wrong end of the building, you have to move to the other end. That's harassment. I've been moved four times within this company. I was downstairs in one barracks, then they moved me upstairs. They moved me over to another barracks, upstairs; then they moved me downstairs. Now I didn't want to do any of this, but I had to because they told me to. They wanted to get us all where they could watch us. Besides the fact that you've got to carry all your stuff upstairs, get another locker set up, you have to move your bed and stuff like that, I was happy where I was. And I didn't see any real reason. If there had been some kind of reason I wouldn't have kicked too much. But there was no reason. And it was just a lot of trouble to do for nothing.

Enlisted men I interviewed sometimes thought that their Sergeant or commanding officer was trying to provoke them to go AWOL or commit some other act that is clearly illegal (and hence easy to establish guilt in a court-martial). A soldier recounted his experience during training:

> I went there [the company commander's office] and said, "I can't take any more, I'm going AWOL." And he said, "Right over the rail tracks there you're off post. So there it is—go. I don't want to see you anymore. You go AWOL or go nuts, but I don't want to see you in my office." And that's the kind of attitude you get.

For those soldiers who are mentally unstable, the treatment can have devastating effects. One case concerns a Vietnam returnee from a lower-class background who committed suicide. His roommate gave the following reasons for his friend's suicide:

> Like I said, the constant pressure from his CO [commanding officer]. They were fucking him real bad over his 212 [Army regulation 635-212 allows for an administrative discharge based on mental unfitness]. They'd hang on to it for a while and he'd go in and check on it. And finally he said that if they didn't work on that 212, he wouldn't work. Ah ha, violation of UCMJ code, article number so and so! And they put him in the stockade. He wasn't there a week and he was in solitary confinement. Just for refusing to work. Because they weren't working on his 212. But in solitary confinement a sick mind really gets worked. He was on bread and water, doesn't talk to nobody, doesn't see anybody. He's just sitting there by himself. They left him in the stockade about 8 or 9 days then gave him a leave to go home. And while he was home he blew his brains out.

It appears from my interviews that an array of harassment techniques directed at a single individual continue to be used by coercive leaders; however, I have not heard the term *the treatment* used by my interviewees, and I think the orchestration of several different officers and NCOs in the harassment is less a feature of this pattern than it was in Jones's day. I have argued previously that techniques of domination work best when used in a pattern or in concert and that each technique does not seem excessively harsh when considered by itself. Basic training and the treatment illustrate this characteristic of social control tactics.

The coercive style of control can create anti-Army and antiwar consciousness. Neutral or ambivalent recruits went into the Army during the Vietnam War and came out angry and politicized. In effect, coercive controls did more to create resistant political consciousness than any ideological program of antiwar organizers. In addition, coercive techniques caused other problems. Soldiers complained about Army life to their congressmen and their friends, thereby damaging the public image that the Army spends millions of dollars to build. Retention of personnel is hampered by coercive techniques perhaps more than any other single factor.[21] And recruitment is made difficult when young men hear so much about Army harassment. In recent years, the military spending cutbacks, reductions of the size of the military, and the ending of the draft are forcing the Army to try to solve its recruitment and retention problems. For this reason, the Army appears to have made many changes in its management policies, including curtailment of some coercive techniques.[22]

Officers and NCOs who have relied for years on coercive techniques may experience a great deal of stress as the Army limits their techniques. They feel discipline is eroding and that new soldiers will be ineffective and vulnerable to great losses in combat. A paratrooper NCO said:

> Now they more or less baby these guys out at the jump school. I don't know if they have a quota to fill or what, but that's what it seems like. Normally, for example, when you get ready to jump out of an airplane, a lot of guys are hesitating at the door. You just give them a little nudge though, that's all they need really. Most of the time when they see they don't break something, they want to go again. Now, just talking to them, they don't want to go; they don't go. So as a result they just flunk the course. I got kicked a couple times myself. While I was down there at Ft. Benning, for example, every time they made a jump at least 3 or 4 or 5 guys would get hurt on the jump. They'd jump maybe six aircraft, maybe 500 people. At least 4 or 5 of them would break a leg or something like that. The training is at fault. There was no big thing when I was out at the jump school for an instructor to come up to you and kick you or slap you or something like that. Now you can't even holler.

Comparing the Army in 1972 to the conditions that existed when he was in training in 1960, this NCO said:

> [If] you didn't have no wings [if you were not qualified], you couldn't eat in the mess hall. You went in, got a tray, got

> served, and went outside and ate in the snow. You had five minutes to eat. Now they got it set up in the mess hall you can stay there all day. I don't believe there's no discipline in the Army now.

Having lost power and status through Army modernization, he felt like the man in the middle:

> As long as you're a private you've got it made. Once you become an NCO or something like that, it's just opposite the way it used to be. The NCO is the one they hassle over here; a private has got it pretty well made.... You look at, for example, our headquarters, and these guys have all got their hair cut pretty much, compared to the trainees. Trainees don't get hassled about this stuff. . . . Actually, the Army seems to me more like a boy scout camp. You got to baby everybody in the Army now. You can't holler at nobody. You can't do nothing. And if you don't get the job done, the man who didn't do the job, they don't say nothing to the private over there. They ask the NCO why the job didn't get done.

This concern about the limitation of authority and power is focused on the military justice system, according to a War College survey. "Particularly at the lower enlisted grade levels, there was strong and pervasive animosity toward what some individual referred to as 'those long haired junior JAG [Judge Advocate General's Corps—the military lawyers] officers.' Leaders at the company commander level felt that their range of options for handling leadership problems was restricted severely by current developments in the application of military justice. Many NCO's saw this condition as a lack of downward loyalty by the chain of command."[23]

A legal officer commented on these changes and suggested how coercive leaders might misinterpret the directives:

> The whole disciplinary structure was kind of deteriorated and it turns out that a lot of company commanders feel that

> the only thing they can do is to give an Article 15. A lot of their authority has eroded. . . . The Army says this to company commanders: the more Article 15s you give the worse you look. It shows that you don't know how to take care of your company. But now, what's happened is that this concept has degenerated or else it's not understood by the local commander and they think that they got the notion of being hard nosed. The more they give, the tougher it makes them look. You know, they look sharper because they don't put up with any bullshit, they give a lot of Article 15s.

Enlisted men are sometimes able to use the disjunctures in modernization to gain bits of freedom for themselves. A soldier spoke of the ways enlisted men evade rules:

> [One way] is bypassing NCOs. Now that happens a lot. Because a lot of these Capts. have been to college. . . .And they don't require the rigid discipline. A lot of them don't care if you salute. But the NCOs care if you call them Lt., or Sir. But you can get around the NCOs by going straight to the officers. It's a breach of regulations, but it happens every day. The NCO tries to be hard core and the enlisted man says, Well, I want to hear it from an officer. And the officer says, Well, relax, take it easy, I don't think it's that serious. And the NCO's power right there is shaken. [For example] an NCO threatened me to get a haircut or else. I said you haven't got enough rank to tell me to get a haircut. The regulations at that time had been rescinded and it was left up to the commander's discretion. So theoretically speaking, the only person in the outfit who could tell me to get a haircut was the commanding officer. And I told him that. I said that until he tells me I'm not going to get one. So you can just go to hell. That really jerked him off bad and after that he just left me alone.

The Army has been experimenting with changes in the basic training process, operating with less harassment and fear and even eliminating live ammunition in the combat exercises. There is some difference of opinion about the advisability of these new training processes. At Fort Ord, for example,

> Experimental Volunteer Army Training Program (EVATP) planners searching for training hours in the program of instruction which could be used for other subjects and for "hands-on" training time, had somewhat reduced the number of hours devoted to physical training and physical-training type subjects. Hand-to-hand combat training, the confidence and obstacle courses, and speed marches had been dropped. Additionally, bayonet training had been taken from the program of instruction. Training results, observations, and command emphasis resulted in re-institution of these subjects in mid-1971 and renewed emphasis was placed on physical exercise and double-timing to and from instruction.
>
> Trainers avoid associating discipline with punishment. Rather, they emphasize the positive aspects of self-discipline, unit discipline, and teamwork.[24]

No one knows yet how effective these newly trained soldiers will be, but it is clear that the Army expects to rely on other, more manipulative, styles of control.

NOTES

1. See U.S., Congress, House, Committee on Internal Security, *Investigation of Attempts to Subvert the United States Services*, 92d Cong., 2d sess., pt. 3, May 9, 10, June 1, 20, 1972. The House Committee on Internal Security also came to the conclusion that the GI anti-war movement was ineffective. By 1969, post commanders at the larger stateside Army bases were saying that the organized dissidence was having no effect on morale. See Howard C. Olson and R. William Rae, *Determination of the Potential for Dissidence in the U.S. Army*, vol. 1, *Nature of Dissent*, Technical Report RAC-TP-410 (McLean, Virginia: Research Analysis Corp., 1971).

2. For example, see the novels by Erich Maria Remarque, *All Quiet on the Western Front* (1929; reprint ed., Greenwich, Connecticut: Fawcett Publications, Inc., 1958), and Louis-Ferdinand Celine, *Journey to the End of the Night*

(New York: New Directions Books, 1934). Even pro-Army movies, such as *Fireball Forward* and *Take the High Ground*, portray this kind of leader.

3. U.S. Army War College, *Leadership for the 1970's* (Carlisle Barracks, Pennsylvania: U.S. Army War College, 1971), p. 26.

4. Ibid.

5. Norman Mailer, *The Naked and the Dead* (New York: The New American Library, 1948).

6. Peter Bourne, "Some Observations on the Psychosocial Phenomena Seen in Basic Training," *Psychiatry* 30 (1967): 187-96. Similar accounts may be found in Donald Duncan, *The New Legions* (New York: Random House, 1967; Pocket Books, 1967) (describing Special Forces training); Peter Tauber, *The Sunshine Soldiers* (New York: Ballantine Books, 1971); Louis A. Zurcher, Jr., "The Naval Recruit Training Center: A Study of Role Assimilation in a Total Institution," *Sociological Inquiry* 37 (Winter 1967): 85-98; David H. Marlowe, "The Basic Training Process," in *Symptom as Communication in Schizophrenia*, ed. Kenneth Artiss (New York: Grune & Stratton, 1959); Anonymous, "The Making of the Infantryman," *American Journal of Sociology* 51 (March 1946): 376-79; Sanford Dornbusch, "The Military Academy as an Assimilating Institution," *Social Forces* 33 (May 1955).

7. Bourne, "Some Observations," p. 189.

8. Ibid., p. 191.

9. Ibid., p. 192.

10. Tauber, *Sunshine Soldiers*, p. 20.

11. Ibid., p. 29.

12. Bourne, "Some Observations," p. 193.

13. Ibid.

14. Tauber, *Sunshine Soldiers*, p. 29.

15. Duncan, *The New Legions*, p. 107.

16. Bourne, "Some Observations," p. 194.

17. Ibid.; Tauber, *Sunshine Soldiers*, pp. 250-54.

18. James Jones, *From Here to Eternity* (New York: The New American Library, 1951).

19. Ibid., pp. 252-87.

20. See Alvin W. Gouldner, *Wildcat Strike* (New York: Harper & Row, 1954).

21. Howard C. Olson and R. William Rae, *Determination of the Potential for Dissidence in the U.S. Army*, vol. 2, *Survey of Military Opinion*, Technical Report RAC-TP-410 (McLean, Virginia: Research Analysis Corp., 1971).

22. Harold G. Moore, *Modern Volunteer Army Monograph Project: Strengthening Professionalism and Improving Army Life*, Sixth Draft (Fort Ord, California: United States Army Training Center [Infantry], July 1972), and J. H. Hay, *Modern Volunteer Army Evaluation Report: XVIII Airborne Corps and Fort Bragg* (Fort Bragg, North Carolina: Headquarters XVIII Airborne Corps and Fort Bragg, July, 1972).

23. Army War College, *Leadership for the 1970's*, p. 26.

24. Moore, *Modern Volunteer Army*, pp. 6-3, 6-5.

3

Professional Paternalist Control

An incongruity emerged when I asked two groups of students, one ex-military and the other with no military experience, to read Norman Mailer's *The Naked and the Dead* and to comment on the appropriateness of the techniques of control described in that novel. Those without military experience condoned coercive military controls in accordance with a simple argument: assuming the country is at war, the military must have discipline; military discipline, in order to be effective, must be rigid and coercive. The nonveterans in this informal survey were mostly liberal and anti-war in their political orientation, and one might suppose that they would be least likely to support the autocratic use of authority. But those students could not bring themselves to believe that many enlisted men like being in the Army, much less be strongly committed to its objectives, and they certainly felt that most soldiers are unwilling to risk their lives and must be forced into combat.

Those who had been in the military, particularly those with some command experience, took a different view of autocratic techniques.[1] They considered Mailer's general and sergeant terrible combat leaders. Significantly, they noted that the morale of the soldiers in this novel was very poor. Generally, they believed that fear techniques should be used only when all else has failed. Because the coercive techniques lower morale, they should be the last resort. (But an essential last resort. Those who have been in command will struggle to retain the right to use autocratic techniques.)[2] They considered the general's use of officer privilege to create class hostility in the men as inexcusable. It served no military function and made morale worse. This seems to correspond with the finding that military experience decreases (or at least stabilizes) authoritarianism scores rather than increases the scores, as one might expect.[3]

Why do these ex-military people place such an emphasis on morale and de-emphasize autocratic, punishment-oriented techniques of control? As we have shown, it is because they have seen that people will do far more if they are willing to do something than if they are forced to. Forcing people is inefficient; it inevitably seems to result in resistance of some kind, such as go-slows and mistakes. Conformity is not enough in combat. In order to win, there must be enthusiasm and initiative that can come only from "willing and cheerful obedience."

These veterans reflected the intermediate style of control on my coercion-co-optation continuum, which I shall term *professional paternalism*. This style is evident in many official Army publications, such as its field manual on leadership and the widely read *Officers' Guide*.[4] From my interviews, and various published accounts,[5] professional paternalism seems to be similar to leadership techniques taught at West Point. The term *professional* can be applied to this style because it represents a kind of military ethical ideal and because it is a well-developed, coherent leadership doctrine with considerable historical continuity. A comparison of World War I generals' advice to young officers with recent articles on leadership topics shows a correspondence of techniques from the 1910s to the 1970s.[6] In this chapter, I will use the World War I generals' principles as a basis for discussion and fill in the application of the techniques with recent experiences of Army officers in their writings and my interviews. It is partly through GI resistance, recalcitrance, and accommodation that paternalistic techniques were refined and developed.[7]

Professional paternalism is the use of certain techniques to build subordinates' commitment to the organization, a sense of belonging, a sense of the overall worthwhileness of organizational objectives, and a belief that the organization is taking care of the individual. Paternalistic techniques include the manner in which officers interact with their men, the building of group solidarity as a means of control, the use of subordinates, and the great emphasis on communication. In addition to leadership techniques per se, professional paternalism is an ideology, viewable in terms of personal ethics and identity as well as an interpretation of the Army as a unique kind of organization. Group morale is central to professional paternalism.

Morale is the result of many factors, and not all of these are under military control. But the standard Army line, expressed particularly to young officers, is that good unit morale is the result of good leadership techniques.[8] According to this view, there is no such thing as an inherently bad unit. There are simply good and bad leaders.

Mutiny is probably the worst thing that could happen to a commanding officer. A mutiny, a collective refusal to obey, threatens his whole ego, and the stress the military puts on leadership as primarily responsible for morale intensifies this ego involvement. In recent military publications, such as *Military Review* and *ARMY*, mutiny is rarely mentioned except in discussions of failure of foreign militaries or remote, historical examples.[9] But as we can see in the following quotation from an interview with an Army captain, the subject is always between the lines in discussions of military leadership:

Q: What would you have done if you had a mutiny?
A: To be honest, I don't know.
Q: That's never in the books, is it?
A: No, [but] it's really one of the leadership aspects right there, sort of be able to forecast when you're going to have a mutiny and avoid the situation or take precautions to keep from having the situation. It's [using] some kind of leadership techniques to influence the men so you won't have a mutiny, such as convincing them we're doing the

right thing. Like tell [them], "OK, it would seem there [is] a problem getting in there, [but] there's no other alternative—we just have to go in there. . . . This is the way it's got to be. We're here to fight a war, we're not here to just run." And with my company I could have done it that way and I don't have any doubt they would have gone.

Q: Were there any situations where you got orders from higher up that you didn't want to do or that your men didn't want to do?

A: There was only one really specific incident [in late 1968] that I can think of. It involved a time after we got in contact with an enemy unit. We pulled back and called in an air strike and rocket artillery on [that] position. I was told that on the radio, to do that. Then I called the platoon leaders [lieutenants] together and told them this is what we'll do, and they in turn went to their platoons to give out the word to them. Then they came back again to me and said they wanted to talk to me. They told us very frankly the men don't want to go back into there and they brought up several reasons why we shouldn't, like we have to go uphill to get into enemy position, we couldn't see where we were going in, we were dug in, and that there were a lot of bad aspects to doing it the way we would have to do it. My first reaction was, well, we gotta go in there, we gotta go. But then I started considering some things, like suppose I do tell them we will go, "obey my orders!" Then if they refused to go I'd probably be in a pretty bad position. But I knew from a couple of my platoon leaders that I could have said we will go and I'm pretty sure the men would go. I don't think there really would have been that much of a problem. They would have gone reluctantly, but they would have gone on. I knew the people that well. They would really have been pissed off.

Q: You knew them all personally?

A: No, I never got to know them well enough to know each individual person, there wasn't that free enough contact there with the security situation. I knew the platoon leaders well enough and I knew the atmosphere of the com-

> pany. So that I would say that either I would really have to almost autocratically say, very forcefully, that we will go into there, and they'd all go very sullenly. And it would have changed the whole atmosphere of the company. It just called for me to step back and try to look at it and see, let me decide whether this is really the right thing to go into, do we really need to go in there? I told the tank commander on the radio I wanted to talk to him. The tank commander came down [in his helicopter] and I told him, I said, "Sir, (he was a Lt. Col.) the way we have to go into that thing . . . we're going to have to go through this extremely thick underbrush, [and] go uphill into position where the enemy is dug in up there and we can't see him. Now what I suggest is that you have another company, about 1000 meters on the other side. They can come into this thing downhill and come into them from behind and we can block them over here or whatever. They've got a clearer way to come into it and everything." He was real hesitant at first. But he could sort of see that I was convinced of the thing and it made him look at things a different way. He kind of didn't like to look at it a different way. He wanted to stay with the way he was going to do things. But then, he sort of listened to reason after a while and he said, "Well yeah, I guess it does make better sense." He in turn finally changed things to do it that way. I didn't tell him what the [real] reason was. It would have looked bad for me leadership wise. I'd have to admit . . . I probably didn't want to admit that I had a problem in that.

This incident illustrates some of the negotiations and interaction that probably typically go on between different levels during combat. The open communication, the concern about morale, and the emphasis on anticipating problems are characteristic of this style of authority. This officer tried to strike a balance between military objectives and group morale. Contrast this with a coercive leader who would simply follow orders and deal with the consequences after they arose. In this case, the officer was fortunate—and adept—in being able to talk his commanding officer into taking a different action. I asked him if there were other techniques that he had used to avoid potentially mutinous situations.

> There was one other problem one time that never really got to me to handle. It was a severe problem and I never could even completely uncover it. It was within a platoon and it was a racial problem. The platoon leader kind of let things get out of hand. One squad got to be all black in his platoon and the other two squads got to be all white. And the black squad got into some sort of power conflict and tried to dominate some things. I never really got to know exactly what happened but I think they were threatening the platoon leader and he wouldn't admit the problem. They were saying they wanted their squad all black and they didn't want any outsiders in it. "We want to say how we're going to do things." That's about all I could tell. And I don't think they wanted him interfering with their squad. I just found out there were some problems there in talking to people [because] the platoon leader wouldn't admit the problems. As a result I switched a couple of the blacks out of that squad and into squads in other platoons and put people from other platoons into his platoon and just spread out the people some so that they didn't have those little power conflicts there. And that seemed to settle it. It never got to be anything severe although it looked like it could have, that it was on the verge of getting to be a big problem.
>
> Q: What was the reaction after you transferred these guys?
>
> A: Maybe a little sullen resentment was about all.

Both of these instances show a tendency on the part of the officer to take quick, decisive action. He said at another point in the interview that he was taught that a mistake decisively carried out is better than a good idea not well executed.[10] This officer also demonstrates a nonconfrontation style of dealing with his subordinates. While this account showed the use of restructuring a situation, professional paternalism is also an interactive style of leadership.

In their writings, World War I generals told young officers to make personal acquaintance with all the men in their company.[11] They should know them all by name so the soldiers would not feel that they were unimportant to the Army.[12] Officers should try to know the men's personal problems, such as homesickness, or family problems[13] to create an impression that the officer is interested in the soldiers and that he will try to take care of them.[14] This concern will benefit the officer because he will be able to locate any morale depressants quickly, such as problems with the company mess. The soldiers will do more for an officer who looks out for their welfare.[15]

Professional paternalists are not particularly lenient. As a recent article in *Commander's Call* emphatically stated, "Care is not coddling."[16] The paternalist is severe with resisters and demands a great deal from conformists. Shils and Janowitz remarked that the German professional officer in World War II used a peculiar blend of severe domination with benevolence.[17] Perhaps in a somewhat less extreme form, this is the same contradiction that characterizes American military professionalism.

Professional paternalism is an elitist style of leadership that is based on a clear class separation between officers and enlisted men. Officers do not hesitate to dictate the behavior of enlisted men, just as parents feel justified in telling their child how to behave. Officers' manuals from World War I through the early 1960s discuss the importance of soldiers' neatness, saluting, proper language, deportment, and entertainment, and the prevention of officer-enlisted men familiarity.[18] Soldiers should have healthy entertainment and sports; no foul language or coarse behavior should be tolerated.[19] Soldiers should dress up for mess.[20] Saluting, young officers have been told in these manuals written in part by World War I generals, is a military virtue that was too often neglected by both officers and enlisted men because it represented an expression of class servility that went against the American character.[21] General Shanks, the author of much of this advice, said, peremptorily, that, on the contrary, saluting is nothing but a greeting and a mark of respect.[22] Despite the encouragement of a feeling of superiority, officers were advised to avoid "high hatting" their men.[23]

Writing at the time of World War I, Major General Stewart demonstrated an awareness of the influence of small-group expectations as he explained how discipline should be viewed and how it should be built up.[24] Discipline (meaning here willing obedience) should not be based on the club. Officers should understand that soldiers fight and do not run away in spite of their fear of the enemy because they are afraid of losing each other's respect.[25] The main control over soldiers, then, is the result of pressures from peers, not superiors, at least in a unit with high esprit de corps. This explanation is an interesting anticipation of Stouffer's findings in his group's research into soldiers' attitudes during World War II.[26]

The question that emerges from this early analysis is: How does a military officer create this very important esprit de corps? The soldier's intense desire for a sense of pride initially can be built up as a result of the humiliations in basic training and is used as a basis for creating esprit de corps. Here is one instance in which coercive techniques may support paternalist techniques.

There are several other techniques that have been recognized as capable of increasing esprit de corps.[27] Of these techniques, calisthenics and close-order drill were viewed (prior to World War II) as particularly useful for inculcating good discipline. The object was to create in each man an automatic response to orders and a sense of acting in concert with other men. The fact that actual movements and activities on a drill field were irrelevant to the confusion of a battlefield was seen as not being as important as the habit of acting in concert without thinking.

Symbols and ceremonies were specifically designed to promote discipline and morale among troops.[28] In a ceremonial review, each person identifies with his organization and becomes a part of it, similar to players practicing before a big football game. The setting, with dressy uniforms, flags, music and marching parades, was intended to inspire a feeling of group pride expressed in perfect teamwork and instant response.[29] The symbols designed to promote morale and esprit de corps include medals, unit insignia on uniforms and uniforms themselves and regi mental flags.[30]

I asked an officer what he thought was the importance for the Army of standards for hair length, sideburns, and mustaches:

> Well, because I think appearance does matter. It affects a sense of community, of belonging, and a sense of pride of self in appearance and so forth, and a sense of unity among the whole group. In combat you can't afford to have real long hair because you go for days without a bath or anything—these practical aspects. Back in garrison it's more of just what the guy is going to look [like] in uniform. It's just having certain standards to go along.

Standards for hair length created an issue of enormous conflict within the Army in recent years because hair style was a visible expression of one's political and cultural reference group. During the 1960s a GI with long hair was using one of the few visual cues remaining to a soldier to tell others that he did not identify with the soldierly role in spite of the uniform. Rather, he was signifying some identification with the anti-authority, anti-elitism, anti-regimentation, and anti-nationalism that that once implied. As we have seen, the tension between allowing cultural autonomy to soldiers and enforcing the requirements of military objectives also extends to the issue of race.[31]

Subcultures do not necessarily have to detract from military esprit de corps. Their response depends on the way the military makes use of them. For example, regional subcultures have been used to serve military objectives: in World War I and before, regiments were often drawn entirely from one state. Esprit de corps could then be built on the basis of pride in the traditions of the regiment. In World War I, however, the Army had to create several new units, which thus weakened this possible strut to esprit de corps and social control. Today, some units have a continuity and a history that are used to build cohesion.

Throwing one unit into competition with another helps to build esprit de corps within each unit. Competition can be used at a variety of levels of units, including companies and even squads. Athletic contests between units can be the basis of this competition.[32] But since some soldiers have more athletic ability than others, winning these contests may not be entirely the result of their desire to win. Thus, contests based more purely on motivation, such as paying off canteen bills or buying bonds, and not on real abilities may be better used as a basis of competition.[33]

The extensive use of subordinates was (and continues to be) encouraged.[34] NCOs should be allowed to take some responsibility in organizing the men, such as during recreation. This technique has the advantages of giving subordinates the experience in leadership they will need should the officer be missing and creates for them a more extensive sense of commitment to the unit. NCOs who take an interest in their squads have had an enormous effect in boosting morale and in creating a link to the officer.[35] NCOs are always to be backed up and never criticized in front of the men. Similarly, Evrard notes that oversupervision is to be avoided because it slackens initiative and morale.[36]

The principle of using an enlisted man (an NCO) as an intermediate level of authority over other enlisted men is an application of a technique of domination of enormous power and one that has been widely used. The Nazis used Jews as police in rounding up other Jews to be put on the trains for deportation; Jewish community leaders were used to draw up lists of their constituents talents and numbers; and Jews were even used as prison camp guards.[37] Similarly, industry uses working-class supervisors as a layer between management and the line workers.

The principle is without equal among techniques of domination. It is economical; for example, the Germans could hardly have afforded to commit thousands of troops to round up Jews and to run prison camps in the midst of a war. The technique demoralizes the oppressed; it sets them against each other. The technique redirects anger and rewards conformity and loyalty to the organization. A GI may hate his NCO, but may be more likely to trust his officers, who, according to World War II survey research, sometimes had harsher attitudes toward enlisted men.[38] The NCO knows the men more intimately, since they share similar class origins, and thus he would know what they would respond to and could control them more effectively than could officers. Officers are less subject to the normative pull of enlisted men and hence do not suffer the conflicts between enlisted men's expectations and military expectations to the extent that NCOs do.[39]

Good relations with NCOs is a mark of a professionalized officer. One such officer discussed his reliance on his NCOs:[40]

> In combat I had a First Sergeant who had been out in combat longer than me. And I would question him [extensively] about the way he thought we should do something. I even asked this of the platoon leader [a lieutenant] sometimes—some of them had been out longer than I. And I really didn't have any reservations or feel that it was bringing down my authority to ask them something like that, mainly because it is pretty well acceptable in the Army for an officer to ask the advice of an older NCO. It's kind of looked down upon if an officer is too proud to accept their advice or something. This is one of the things they keep hitting on in your training, [especially] at West Point. When you go in there you're all green and you listen to your NCOs. They're the ones who know what's going on and they can give you a lot of help. So even a Company Commander might call some of his people together and say, let's discuss how we can do this. I did do it to some extent: like I called all the NCOs together and had a talk with them and said, OK, what are the problems involved, what do you think is the best way to handle it, and so forth. Then it would come back that I would have to make the decision, and say, "Ok, this is what we'll do." I never took a vote in those kind of circumstances. But when you get into a peacetime operation, the company commander does face the men more than in combat. In combat the men are always out on security and stuff like that. You have to tell the platoon leader what to tell the squad leader to tell the men. [But] in a company on garrison duty, the company commander may get up in front of a company formation and tell them the way things will be done. This is the policy now [1972]. Or just explain something or give a class to the men. Or just going around inspecting the men or something like that. It really gives a more personal confrontation. I

> was surprised in combat: I thought I would have more personal contact with the men, but the operations and security and stuff like that prevented it. I could walk around from foxhole to foxhole and talk to the men, but it was really harder to talk.

This officer has suggested a key element of professional paternalism: the emphasis on communicating with the men.[41] Paternalism is not an "ours is not to reason why" kind of doctrine. It is based on a notion of human nature that assumes that people are more motivated when they understand why they are told to do something. Thus, paternalists argue that soldiers must be explained the purpose of the mission and perhaps why it is being done in a particular way.[42] Even a "drawdown," a term used for lowering the strength of some troops' units by not providing replacements for certain of their losses and by delaying the arrival of other replacements, must be explained to a unit, especially if some of those soldiers are going to be forced to do varied, undesirable, or unexpected jobs for which they may not have been trained.[43] Toner argues that a good officer must seriously answer such questions as "Why can't I drink in barracks?" "Why can't I wear my hair long?" "Why do I have to salute officers?" "Why do I have to wear a hat?"[44]

An important aspect of communication and leadership generally is the manner in which orders are given. A professional paternalist officer distinguishes his style of giving orders from that of others:

> I'd say you get everything from a company commander who gets up and is very dogmatic and says this is the way things are going to be, gets it over with and turns around and walks off. But I'm probably not on the other end of the spectrum either where you might see a company commander bringing in platoon leaders and platoon sergeants, saying "OK gentlemen, we have a requirement to do such and such. What are your recommendations on how to do it?" My style depends on the command relationship. Like if I [give orders] to my platoon leaders, I'll usually say, OK,

> first platoon leader you're going on an ambush, you've got an ambush tonight. Second platoon, you be ready to move out in the morning at 7:30. Or second platoon, you've got point [front position on a patrol] tomorrow. So I'm not really saying "let's do it." I'm just saying this is what it is, what you're going to do, and stuff like this, in order. About the only objections I'd get were like if I tell this platoon he's got point and he may say well, we got point day before yesterday, it's so-and-so's turn. I'd probably justify then why I'm putting him on point. I had one platoon leader who was really lazy and every time I told him to do something he'd come up with some kind of bitch about it. Sometimes I'd get to the point where I'd say, dammit, you'll do it because I say you're going to do it. Or else I'll say something like, "In order to get this done we have to do it this way and dammit you'll do it this way." It depends on the individual how I would have to handle it. I don't think I ever said things in terms of "let's go on ambush" or something like that. I'm sure I never said that. That's just too much like let's play a game of football. In order to get them to go you pretty much have to tell them. Because it was usually unpleasant. People didn't like going on ambush. They didn't like getting up at 6 in the morning and moving out at 7. You had to tell them. But it wasn't like I had to say, "Goddamn, get up on your feet, you're moving out at 7 o'clock." If they weren't ready to go I'd call the platoon leader and say why aren't you ready to go? And he'll give some lame excuse or something like that and then I'd have to chew him out or something for not having his people ready. Or maybe you prod them a little before hand, saying, come on, let's get going, it's about time to move out. There again, it depends on the individual platoon leader and all.

Clearly an officer who adjusts the manner in which he gives commands shows the importance of knowing the personality of the subordinate and the atmosphere of the unit. In general, professional American military leaders have understood that a prime requisite of being able to command soldiers, conquer other people, or even communicate with an audience lies in understanding those troops, that enemy, or that audience.[45] Generals in World War I considered the American soldier to be "more difficult to discipline than the soldier of almost any other nationality."[46] This complaint that Americans in general are not brought up with sufficient acclimatization to military types of discipline has been expressed in many different areas of American military history.

There are, however, some elements of civilian ideology that can be used to support military social control. One is the diffuse patriotism with which many young men enter the Army.[47] This can be tied to military objectives in terms of loyally carrying out established government policies. Another aspect of civilian ideology that the military uses is the masculinity ethic that Moskos described as characteristic of the soldiers he interviewed in combat in Vietnam.[48] This ethic stresses physical toughness and hardness and is transformed in a military setting where a recruit who has not experienced combat is viewed as a kind of virgin. Similarly, conformity to military expectations and demands is redefined as something that "makes a man out of you." James P. Sterba, the *New York Times*'s Houston correspondent, suggested that the permissiveness, disorder, and decadence in civilian society are partly responsible for the current success of the all-volunteer Army.[49] According to this correspondent, young men join the Army just as they might join Guru Maharij Ji's tribe or some other highly disciplined, strictly ordered group, thus reflecting some elements of conservative, puritanical civilian culture.[50]

In addition, the Army presents some ideological aspects of its own to legitimate the social role of the soldier. One source of this is the personality of the officer himself.[51] The officer should be competent at his job and should set a strong example of moral character, honor, and courage. He should be a man of honesty and integrity who deals with his subordinates in a spirit of fairness and justice.

Another aspect of the officer's moral character is the concept of duty: doing one's utmost to loyally carry out all missions and to live within the spirit of directives and regulations regardless of their source. The officer should never criticize an order he has received: he must always cheerfully accept it as his own responsibility. As a practical matter, complaining about orders, especially in front of his men, reduces the men's sense of the officer's identification with the Army and thus reduces the morale of the unit. An officer comments on the effects of criticizing orders:

> Most of [the men], I don't think, can see above the company commander. Like the company commander gets orders to do this, he relays it off. I don't go into my troops and say, "Look troops, we're doing this because the tank commander tells me and I have to tell you to do it." Because, in a way, it's not a good leadership thing because if you're not convinced on what you're telling the men to do, if you're just going up and saying I got to do this because my boss tells me I got to do it, it makes you look really half-assed as a commander. And they say, well damn, my commander doesn't believe we should do it, what's going on here? If I have reservations, I've got to reconcile that with my superior. Not bring the reservations down and pass them on to my men. That just leaves them uneasy about the whole thing. I've got to first become convinced for myself with my commander that this is what's got to be done and then I tell the men that, "men, this is what we're going to do."

Interestingly, this characteristic of unquestioning obedience (duty) is encouraged simultaneously with an exhortation to display a great deal of initiative and confidence.[52] This contradiction between initiative (or refusing unlawful orders)[53] and obedience is one of the many built-in conflicts within military ideology.

Referring to the significance of draftees' anti-war sentiments, an officer struggled with the contradiction within this ethical system:

> I think [draftees] probably have more significance than most people give them credit for. The more people you have in there who would question a wrong decision that you may

> make, the less likely you can get away with a wrong decision. You can kind of override this kind of stuff, but it still kind of influences you. If you know that the way you're going to do something isn't going to cause the men to be solidly behind you, even though you can override them and make the decision, it's going to affect the way you're going to do it. A commander is definitely influenced by the mood of his unit. And if these people in there are easily molded, easily influenced, into what you want them to do, it's very easy to get away with what you want. In any kind of situation in the Army, however hard you get, you can always get some kind of room for dissent where people can legitimately question the way you do something. They've always got some kind of chance to speak. I just look at the unit I was in and I still say that something like My Lai would have been impossible. I just can't believe that even if I had given the order to my men that they would have done something like that. I do not believe they would have obeyed me. And I would hate to think that they would have. I really would. I would much rather think that they would turn on me, before they would have obeyed an order like that. Whether they would or not makes me wonder after seeing what's happened at My Lai. I don't know.

A sense of order, honor, higher purpose, clean living, self-restraint, loyalty, and "a job to be done" are what is often meant when military men speak of professionalism. According to this doctrine, professionalism can be expected to contribute, by example, to the "character," and thus obedience, of enlisted men.[54] This effect on enlisted men, of course, assumes that officers behave according to these ideals. But, according to a former West Point psychiatrist, the promulgation of some of these ideals causes a certain amount of strain. For example, in the West Point code, honor means the soldier "does not lie, cheat, steal, or tolerate those who do." Cadets are punished or even expelled for some minor infraction of the academy rules, but they see their senior officers get away with more serious breaches of the honor code, such as lying. Similarly, some of my interviewees thought officers were hypocritical when they punished some soldiers for trivial offenses but condoned other officers' and NCOs' criminal behavior, such as stealing Army engines and installing them in their personal vehicles.

There is a tendency in the military to be rigid and absolutist about the ideals of professionalism. This may come from the nature of the military's function of violence. It seems that the more odious the task, the greater the psychological need to justify oneself with such virtues as duty and honor.[55] For example, the Nazi SS troops, who rounded up and executed civilians in advance of the German army, were said to have the highest sense of national purpose and duty.[56] They were told they were killing for Germany and that never was there to be any personal enjoyment nor private stealing involved.[57]

In addition to the officer's conception of honor and moral character, there are other agencies within the Army that can act as supports to the soldier's self-image when it is troubled by qualms over conformity, anxieties over killing, and the meaninglessness of destruction. One of these is the Army chaplain. The career chaplain, in his sermons and counseling sessions, can act as an adjunct to social control by justifying the military way to uncertain recruits.

Perhaps the most well-known social control function of the career chaplain is to help resolve conflicts over killing. Rivkin recounts the Army truism that the chaplain's first loyalty is to the Army; his second is to God.[58] Similarly, GIs, in interviews with me, criticized chaplains for their lack of support of a morally based opposition to the Vietnam War. One quoted his chaplain as saying that calling the Vietnam War immoral was a communist line.

Burchard surveyed military and ex-military chaplains in an effort to find out how they resolved the conflict between their role as ministers and as military officers.[59] He argued that there are several Christian doctrines—love, universal brotherhood, peace, nonresistance to evil ("turn the other cheek"), and the commandment "Thou shall not kill"—that might be expected to conflict with military regulations. His interviews showed that the great majority of his sample responded to the role conflict by asserting the military claim and de-emphasizing the religious claim.

In the instance where the conflict between religious doctrine and the military was most unavoidable—"Thou shall not kill"—some chaplains resolved the conflict by arguing that the commandment was corrupted in translation from its original tribalistic meaning of "Thou shalt not murder" that excluded wartime killing. Forty-five percent of his sample said that killing an enemy soldier was a righteous act, and the remainder called it a justifiable act.[60] None said that the soldier had any other responsibility in that matter except to serve his country. But the most common way to deal with these dilemmas was not to rationalize the conflicts, as Burchard had expected of educated men, but to compartmentalize their behavior, allowing the military officer's role to take precedence. Most chaplains had never before bothered to argue out the dilemmas that Burchard posed, and a few refused to do it even during his interviews. Compartmentalization may be a more successful way of resolving the role conflicts than rationalization because in the former instance one could deny that there is any ideological conflict.

Burchard showed that chaplains were not likely to oppose military authority. The great majority of chaplains were careful to define themselves as officers, *not* as champions of enlisted men's causes. For example, they would prefer to do nothing to mitigate the harshness of military justice but rather attempt to rehabilitate the prisoner after the sentence was passed by persuading him that justice was done and that it was for his own good. In counseling and in interviews, the chaplain can back up the military authority by explaining to recalcitrant troops the personal and moral consequences of not conforming. The chaplain is, incidentally, one of the officials a dissident soldier is required to see and convince in order to get administratively discharged (for example, as a conscientious objector) from the Army.

Some chaplains' pamphlets attempt to calm concerns over whether one is conforming too much and discourage various types of deviance, such as off-duty riotous or drinking behavior.[61] In his sermons, the chaplain can help the military define itself as honorable, dutiful, and self-denying by sanctifying and affirming the military virtues of cleanliness, self-restraint, reliability, and obedience.[62] The time at which chaplains are likely to be influential is during basic training when they carry out a formal "character guidance" program, which introduces recruits to these military virtues.

While the relationship of the chaplain to military authority is close and supportive, it is not apparent that the chaplain exerts a powerful influence as an "internal pacification officer." He is important because he represents a force consistent with a larger field of forces. In this connection, the chaplain helps the military to approximate the atmosphere of a community.

One of the peculiar contradictions of professional paternalism is the attempt to produce a sense of gemeinschaft, or communal solidarity, within the Army, which is, in actuality, a massive, rationalized bureaucracy. Post chapels, which often look like traditional, small-town churches, help to transfigure the garrison into a rural, small-town community. A journalist wrote of the Army bases he had visited: "The residential quarters of the larger posts invariably reminded me of a town painted by Norman Rockwell: the great, good American place protected by a white picket fence from the barbarian hordes gathered on the frontiers. I remember shade trees and station wagons, Little League football games and afternoon tea."[63] Additionally, hamburger stands, movie houses, pool halls, and so on help to create a feeling that the military is a complete society unto itself.

The atmosphere of a sequestered society isolates the soldier from civilian influences—particularly those of his peers and family—which sometimes detract from the operation of military social control and solidarity. A soldier impressed with a sense of isolation from civilian society is made more dependent on the Army, and thus the Army's definition of the situation can be more total. The professional paternalist often views himself as a patriotic conservative at odds with the rest of civilian society, which he sees as immoral, decadent, commercial, and viciously competitive.[64]

This "total society" of garrison life helps to create a sense of everyday life or ordinariness in the Army. The notion of everyday life can be in itself a form of social control. When killing becomes routinized, accepted, and integrated with a total definition of the situation—"a job to be done"—it is far more difficult to criticize than when it is viewed as unusual, abnormal, unnatural, or socially disruptive.65

Esprit de corps, morale, and honor have something of the character of a soap bubble. A soap bubble distributes and disperses surprisingly great tensions as it maintains a structure of resilience and strength. Yet this resilience is particularly vulnerable to a single, pointed assault. In a sociologist's terms, the definition of the situation is much more effective in social control when it is unanimous; even one deviant is a severe drawback to its effectiveness.[66] Thus, deviants are to be dealt with speedily and firmly. Although the Army has always recognized that paternalistic techniques are insufficient for all soldiers, it realizes that punishment must be carefully carried out.

Officers were advised in *The Officer's Guide* to avoid overusing the guardhouse and to rely more on company (nonjudicial) punishment,[67] which has the advantage of appearing to increase the company officer's power and to reduce any sense that he cannot control his men. It is also a way of communicating to other men what will be the result if they similarly transgress.

Punishment, according to this advice, should be reified as much as possible. The soldier should be made to see that military discipline is an extension of such kinds of discipline that come from touching hot objects and getting painful burns, or eating green apples and getting stomachaches.[68] One should not act like a martinet, said the early generals; this will only arouse the soldier's ire.[69] But the alternative extreme of a pushover will only cause a loss of respect from the soldier. In actual practice, the officer should take the soldier's attitude into account in meting out punishment so that it will be effective. A punishment that will correct one soldier may make another soldier transgress even more. But the soldier should not see punishment as so flexible; rather he should be brought to see punishment as sure, fair, and speedy.[70] Punishment should be meted out in such a way as to avoid resentment, just as a child does not resent the green apple.[71]

This advice, originally written decades ago, appears to be well understood today, as demonstrated by an officer's answer to the question of how to maintain order in a garrison:

> You may have somebody there objecting to just being in the Army period, but that would be more in terms of a

malingerer. You have to handle those problems with the various means of discipline that you have—your own command authority, then other means such as Article 15s, courts-martial, police authorities (the MPs) and stuff—using whatever it takes to get him to respond. If he doesn't it's usually a matter of putting him up for disciplinary action. That's deceptively simple there too, though, because it gets into a whole lot more than you can possibly explain. [For example, if] I'm the AIT company commander and something about an infraction of discipline comes up, there's a whole number of ways it may be handled. Like just the commanding influence of the squad leader on the men. Sometimes just plain disapproval is enough, if the man is conscientious. Or chewing out. Or extra duty or something like that within the squad. By his position of authority [the officer] has some influence over the actions of that man [because] he can put more or less restraints on him. Rarely it may come to strong-arm tactics that aren't legal. [But] I think it's very rare that a squad leader [would take a man] out and beat him up because he doesn't respond. It's hard to get men to respond to that any more anyway. Some other things come in, like when the company commander is presented with a disciplinary problem: it gets into an investigative thing where compound facts are involved, analyzing the guy's record so far, what he's been doing, why he did a thing wrong, what it's going to take to influence him to do a thing right. If you're doing it right, using good leadership, you can do this kind of stuff. It would be poor leadership to say the man screwed up, give him an Art. 15. Everybody who screws up, give them an Art. 15! That's when you get into such severe kinds of things where you just so over-repress to the point where they're not going to respond to whatever you do anymore. You're going to have to come up with stronger types of authority for those who break out of that. So the company commander has to consider a lot of things. And I don't think that [it is] inequitable distribution of justice to consider things other than just the fact that a wrong has been committed. [I wouldn't say that] a particular type of disciplinary action applies to this particular type of wrong. There are too many other kinds of variables involved, like how many times has the guy done something wrong, why he did it wrong, what the extenuating circumstances involved were, and then what kind of punishment, or what kind of action, will affect that particular individual or reform or to mend his ways, or whatever. And one kind of punishment isn't going to work the same on different people. But you run into problems there where you do have to watch out that you are giving equitable distribution of justice. If you give one man an Art. 15 and then another man comes up and does the same thing, you can't say that this man won't respond the same way so I won't give an Art. 15. You just about have to give the guy the same thing or you have to explain it pretty well to the unit so that they'll know what you're doing or else you'll run into a foul-up there. So there's so many ramifications of the whole thing.

Group morale is the crux of professional paternalism, the all-important variable that results in effectiveness and social control. My model is the following:

Leadership techniques ⟶ Morale ⟶ Effectiveness

But one cannot always measure effectiveness. For example, in speaking of combat effectiveness, the time of the actual battle will be too late to assess the adequacy of leadership. Thus, according to this model, it becomes important to assess morale per se rather than simply wait to measure final effectiveness. Let us look at morale assessment within the professional paternalist style.

As we've seen, in combat the officer in charge of the company, the company commander, is a commissioned officer who is likely to have little close contact with the men. He is concerned with logistics, radio contact, and artillery cover, but he is not primarily concerned with assessing morale. That information he gets from his senior NCOs, who are in close contact with the soldiers and are enlisted men themselves. This morale assessment function requires some intimacy, so there are likely to be several

NCOs for, say, each twenty men, and all know the morale of their squad or platoon. It takes considerable experience to be able to assess morale accurately, yet it is a vital function. Thus an NCO must have a great deal of experience in combat, whereas the officer need not have so much field experience. This is why the Army can function with a man in a higher command position (for example, a new lieutenant) but with less experience than men of a lower rank. (But during the Vietnam War the too-frequent rotation of officers made it particularly difficult for officers to know their men well and for loyalty to build up between the men and their commanding officers.)

Army field manuals on leadership assist the NCO (or officer) in his morale assessment function by listing some phenomena that can be directly observed in an impressionistic manner to evaluate the atmosphere of the group at any one moment. Termed *subjective indicators*, they include soldiers' appearance, personal conduct, standards of military courtesy, personal hygiene, use of recreational facilities, excessive quarreling, harmful or irresponsible rumors, condition of mess and quarters, care of equipment, response to orders and directives, job proficiency, and motivation during training.[72] Additional subjective indicators of high morale are expressions from the men showing enthusiasm for and pride in their unit, a good reputation among other units, a strong competitive spirit, willing participation in unit activities, pride in the traditions and history of the unit, readiness to help one another, the belief that their unit is better than any other in the Army, promptness in responding to commands and directives, adherence to the chain of command, and ability and willingness to perform effectively with little or no supervision.[73]

The subjective indicators require fairly close contact with the men in order to be adequately assessed. However, there are other indicators of morale that may be observed by an officer who is not an intrinsic part of the unit in question. This officer may derive some indication of the state of morale within a unit by looking at various administrative reports. The Army field manual on leadership suggests examining the following rates: arrests (military or civil), damage to or loss of equipment through carelessness, family problems, indebtedness, malingerers, men absent without leave and deserters, requests for transfer, self-inflicted wounds, sick-call rates, stragglers, and reenlistment rates.

These indicators vary in subtle ways. It is usually not an either/or kind of situation: How much quarreling is excessive? How much enthusiastic motivation during training is sufficient? The accurate assessment of morale is done comparatively; therefore it is a skill that comes with experiences in a variety of units.

The causal relationship I suggested now becomes:

Leadership (and other) techniques → Morale → Effectiveness
Morale ↔ Subjective indicators
Morale → Administrative reports

This model continues to be very important for professional paternalist social control. An officer describes his reliance on these indicators:

> [An area in which] you do get into an additional realm of problems is where you get a mass type, not insurrection, but just a mass lack of response. The whole unit is sluggish and they're not doing their job well, which indicates the dissatisfaction of that unit. A rash of AWOLs, or a rash of fights within a unit, or a rash of stealing going on: all of these are indications that there is something wrong in the unit. That's when you really have to get to the bottom of things to find out what is really wrong.
>
> Q: What kinds of things do you look for? Inequitable punishments?
>
> A: Yeah, inequitable punishments, life conditions in the unit—but usually that won't cause that big of a problem. Working conditions might be real bad where they're not getting enough time off. Their central purpose about what they're doing might be screwed up. Their knowledge about what they're doing and why they're doing it might be a factor. This is morale. They call these morale indicators. The things to look for to see if morale is good or not in the unit. If these things are lacking, it could be in a totally unrelated field seemingly. This is where the problem is, working its way over here and cropping up over there.

From the point of view of a resistance organizer, there are some intriguing relationships compressed in these multifarious lists. For example, morale building puts resistance in a most peculiar position. A unit with high morale is a happy unit. For those men, Army life is meaningful, socially involving, cooperative, and otherwise unalienating. It is difficult from the participant's point of view to see this kind of military life as a state of domination because it is associated with greater satisfaction rather than less.

According to this analysis, strategies of resistance would somehow have to be related to the lowering of morale or the restoration of a consciousness of domination. Resistance sentiment would have to feed on low morale. One might suppose that resistance should be creative and fulfilling, not only because it must be so to be effective, but because one of the objectives of resistance should be to increase one's potential for self-actualizing behavior. A paradox appears in that the development of resistance sentiment requires that people feel more miserable and unhappy before they can be made less miserable through resistance.

Resistance cannot be fulfilling if everyone is miserable, unenthusiastic, and uncooperative. This brings up a second problem. Low morale is not likely to lead automatically to counterorganization and counterconsciousness. To the contrary, low morale is far more likely to lead to infighting among subordinates. Various lines of division may appear: black versus white, rural versus urban origin, college educated versus working class, regional differences, "juicers" versus "heads,"[74] and so on. As Frantz Fanon noted among colonialized people, the oppressed are far more likely to expend their anger against each other than to send it upward against their oppressors.[75]

Not only do subordinates express their alienation against each other, but they also express it against themselves individually. Thus low morale is related to high rates of self-inflicted wounds, family problems, indebtedness, arrests, and so forth. Drug addiction is another self-destructive response to an alienated life.

This state of affairs might be considered by a resister to be absurd and tragic, and it certainly makes organizing difficult. The organizer has the dual task of battling authority and minimizing internal conflict; he must get these alienated men to trust each other, to cooperate, to defend each other, and to be committed to the goals of the resisting organization. (It is interesting that the resistance organizer faces the same problem of morale that military commanders do.)

The Army places great importance on these morale indicators. They are easily observed and thought to be valid measures of leadership abilities and are therefore important in the evaluation of officers and NCOs for promotion.[76] Thus, in order to protect themselves individually (the Army's widely used expression is "cover your ass"), and to get promoted, many officers and NCOs respond to their accountability by trying to boost the indicators while paying little attention to the proper leadership techniques. If clean and well-polished uniforms and barracks indicate high morale, then the men will clean and polish.[77] If promptness in obeying orders and snappy salutes, and "yes sir's!" indicate high morale, then the men will learn that they must promptly obey orders, salute snappily, and shout enthusiastically. Saluting, said to be a mark of respect, can hardly be expected to indicate that all-important (from the paternalist point of view) feeling when it is coerced. Nevertheless, it assures officers that their subordinates do respect them.

It may readily be seen that this pattern may operate for a vast array of "harassments." It is ironic that the very indicators that are used to detect good feelings (high morale) on the part of the men become some of the chief irritants.[78] This is one explanation for the kind of behavior that has been characterized as the coercive style of control: the routine carrying out of certain procedures and regulations with little sense of their purpose.[79]

This emphasis on these impersonal and somewhat quantifiable indicators is a manifestation of the continuing process of rationalization[80] within the Army, which is extended to many areas of military functioning. Body counts, a bizarre and morbid practice in which soldiers have to return to the scene of the battle to count the number of people they killed, is an example of this process of rationalization. Rationalization is destructive of professional paternalism in many ways:

> Almost without fail, when professionals talk about professionalism, there is the recurring theme of the "ambitious,

> transitory commander—marginally skilled in the complexities of his duties—engulfed in producing statistical results, fearful of personal failure, too busy to talk with or listen to his subordinates, and determined to submit acceptably optimistic reports which reflect faultless completion of a variety of tasks at the expense of the sweat and frustration of his subordinates."[81]

Rationalization is one aspect of modernization within the Army. I have suggested that one of the contradictions within professional paternalism is its attempt to create a gemeinschaft form of communal solidarity within a massive bureaucracy. This contradiction is increasingly becoming a problem for paternalists. The Army is too big, too bureaucratic, too technologically sophisticated, and, necessarily, too expert oriented (including enlisted specialists and outside professionals) for paternalists to be completely effective.

A second difficulty for professional paternalists is an ideological one. Paternalism requires some reciprocity: master and serf each has his own rights as well as obligations. The troops have to learn "followership": obedience, loyalty and "respect."[82] While officers are adept at handling men in "everyday" or nonpolitically heightened situations, they become increasingly ineffective when soldiers (and civilians) become more politically aware. They are insensitive to political positions other than their own[83] and are more accustomed to dealing with problems within their organization than in articulating with other institutional sectors, such as the civilian community, the family, and so forth. They are unable to understand and are hence unable to deal with racial consciousness when it shows up in the Army, or drug-oriented counterculture consciousness. The tendency, particularly at more senior levels, is to treat people who express strongly felt, but unanticipated, political views as deviants and to reject them as much as organizational requisites permit.

The style of social control emerging in the Army that can deal most effectively with these organizational problems is what will be termed co-optive rational control. The operating principles behind this style of authority will be taken up in the next chapter and further developed in later chapters.

NOTES

1. See also Tom Hamrick, "Coping with the Boob Image," *ARMY* 20 (July 1970): 26-30, for military reactions to a variety of portraits of military leaders.

2. In particular, the military's struggle to retain a traditional military justice system and command influence on the court-martial process is one of impressive vehemence. Hamilton Howze, a former commanding general of the Eighth Army and former commander of the U.S. Korean forces, has written of his difficulties in a civilianized military justice system in 1966 in "35 Years," *ARMY* 16 (April 1966): 27-44. Later, in 1971, Howze's "Military Discipline and National Security," *ARMY* 21 (January 1971): 11-15, prompted a flood of reader comment, mostly agreeing with his assertion of the impossibility of commanding an army without a military justice system under the commander's control. See the fervent agreement by Ray Hall Chittick and J. A. van Hardeveld, "Letters," *ARMY* 21 (February 1971): 2. On similar issues, see A. N. Garland, "Military Justice Before the Bar," *ARMY* 22 (January 1972): 27-29, and letters by R. G. Ciccolella, "Military Justice and the Commander: A Rebuttal to the Task Force Report," *ARMY* 23 (April 1973): 42-43; George G. Eddy, "Letters," *ARMY* 22 (March 1972): 3; and Michael J. Metzger, "Letters," *ARMY* 20 (April 1970): 4. Metzger stated that he resigned as captain partly as a result of his feelings of fear and helplessness at a lack of discipline he thought would result from the changes in the military justice system. However, see the letter by Ramon A. Nadal II, *ARMY* 21 (February 1971): 2, stating, "The excessive reliance on authority as the main base of power for the officer corps is a good shield for the incompetent officer, but not a solution to our problems."

3. Donald T. Campbell and Thelma H. McCormick, "Military Experience and Attitudes Toward Authority," *American Journal of Sociology* 52 (March 1957): 482-90; on related issues, see Richard Christie, "Changes in Authoritarianism as Related to Situational Factors," *American Psychologist* 7 (1952): 307-308; Elizabeth G. French and Raymond R. Ernest, "The Relation Between Authoritarianism and Acceptance of Military Ideology," *Journal of Personality* 24 (December 1955): 181-91; and E. P. Hollander, "Authoritarianism and Leadership Choice in a Military Setting," *Journal of Abnormal and Social Psychology* 49 (July 1954): 365-70.

4. Department of the Army, *Military Leadership*, Field Manual 22-100 (Washington, D.C.: Headquarters, Department of the Army, November 1, 1965), and *The Officer's Guide* (Harrisburg, Pennsylvania: The Military Service Publishing Co., 1942). These books are constantly being updated; however, the articles that this discussion relies upon have appeared in many editions of *The Officer's Guide*.

5. Such as Richard C. U'ren, "West Point: Cadets, Codes and Careers," *Society* 12 (May-June 1975): 23-29.

6. U.S. Army War College, *Leadership for the 1970's* (Carlisle Barracks, Pennsylvania: U.S. Army War College, October 20, 1971). See especially Omar Bradley's speech on p. 1. This study stated that "the principles of leadership listed below have been guides for many years: 1. Be technically and tactically proficient; 2. Know yourself and seek self-improvement; 3. Know your men

and look out for their welfare; 4. Keep your men informed; 5. Set the example; 6. Insure the task is understood, supervised, and accomplished; 7. Train your men as a team; 8. Make sound and timely decisions; 9. Develop a sense of responsibility among subordinates; 10. Employ your command in accordance with its capabilities; 11. Seek responsibility and take responsibility for your actions."

7. Howze, "35 Years," demonstrates how his leadership expertise developed as a result of soldiers' recalcitrance and refusals to fight.

8. *The Modern Volunteer Army Monograph Project: Strengthening Professionalism and Improving Army Life*, Sixth Draft (Fort Ord, California: United States Army Training Center [Infantry], July 1972) quotes John J. Pershing's comment, "A competent leader can get efficient service from poor troops, while on the contrary an incapable leader can demoralize the best of troops."

9. Van Loan Naisawald, "Mutiny!" *ARMY* 19 (March 1969): 36-42; Frank Kincaid, "Psywar in 1776; Why the Hessians Deserted," *ARMY* 15 (May 1965): 66-68.

10. Bradley, in *Leadership for the 1970's*, expressed a similar thought.

11. David C. Shanks, "Management of the American Soldiers," in *The Officer's Guide*, p. 450.

12. Ibid.

13. See Army Digest Staff, "Sergeant Major of the Day," *Army Digest* 24 (October 1969): 15-17; Thomas T. Jones, "Reverse the Charge," *ARMY* 15 (March 1965): 73-74; Josiah A. Wallace, Jr., "Stiffening the Backbone," *ARMY* 22 (June 1972): 28-31; and Robert F. Legg, "A Lieutenant Speaks to His Men," *ARMY* 18 (June 1968): 82-83.

14. See A. S. Newman, "Company Commanders Must Apply the Human Touch," *ARMY* 20 (May 1970): 56-57, and A. S. Newman, "Assuming Command Means Assuming Leadership," *ARMY* 20 (March 1970): 60-61.

15. See Harvey S. Bartlett II, "Letters," *ARMY* 22 (May 1972): 3.

16. *Commander's Call*, Department of the Army Pamphlet (DA PAM) 360-806, (1st Qtr Fy 1972): 30. This is a remarkably common phrase in the Army. See also Bradley, *Leadership for the 1970's*.

17. Edward A. Shils and Morris Janowitz, "Cohesion and Disintegration in the Wehrmacht in World War II," *Public Opinion Quarterly* 12 (Summer 1948): 280-315.

18. Shanks, "Management of the American Soldiers," pp. 443-64.

19. Ibid., p. 459.

20. Ibid., p. 450.

21. Ibid., p. 457.

22. Ibid.

23. See M. B. Stewart, "Discipline and Leadership," in *The Officer's Guide*, p. 475. Also see an NCO's angry response to one such occurrence in which a major wrote that a particular sergeant should be promoted to commissioned rank because of his intelligence and his understanding; John G. Stepanek's letter to the editor of *ARMY* 18 (April 1968): 8.

24. Stewart, "Discipline and Leadership," pp. 465-79.

25. Ibid., p. 466.

26. S. A. Stouffer et al., *The American Soldier: Combat and Its Aftermath* (New York: John Wiley & Sons, 1949), vol. 2, pp. 130-91. Recent studies have also emphasized the role of esprit de corps as primary in maintaining social control.

27. Stewart, "Discipline and Leadership," pp. 466-70.

28. Ibid., pp. 469-70.

29. Ibid., p. 469.

30. On medals, see H. F. Stout, Jr., "Why Not Reward Distinguished Graduates?" *ARMY* 20 (September 1970): 57, and J. Wagstaff, "A Man Among Men," *ARMY* 20 (June 1970): 25; on uniforms, see A. L. Brown, "Letters," *ARMY* 16 (June 1966): 8-9; and on flags, see Reginald Hargreaves, "A Rag on a Pole," *ARMY* 18 (July 1968): 46-52, John P. Conlon, "Letters," *ARMY* 19 (December 1969): 5, and H. T. Fincher, Jr., "Recalled Colors Can Help Up Unit Morale," *ARMY* 22 (February 1972): 54.

31. See, for example, Department of the Army, *Improving Race Relations in the Army: Handbook for Leaders*, PAM 600-16 (Washington, D.C.: Headquarters, Department of the Army, June 1973).

32. In *From Here to Eternity* Jones shows how athletic contests in the peacetime Army might become such a fetish as to occupy the entire attention of the officers commanding the units in competition.

33. One enterprising officer showed how guard duty could be turned into a competition between units. See Thomas T. Jones, "Want to Raise Morale? Do It with Guard Duty," *ARMY* 20 (September 1970): 56-57. An interviewee recounted the extremes to which competition can be put; his brigade commander sent a man out with a flashlight at night to measure the height of the letters on the sign of the adjacent brigade office so that he could order his own lettering a quarter of an inch taller.

34. See Shanks, "Management of the American Soldiers," pp. 453-54; George G. Eddy, "A Unit Is as Good as Its Noncoms," *ARMY* 18 (February 1968): 61-62; and Harold F. Stout, Jr., and Morris J. Terrebonne, Jr., "The NCO Meets His Junior Officer," *ARMY* 17 (May 1967): 66-68.

35. See Wallace, "Stiffening the Backbone," pp. 28-31, and Shanks, "Management of the American Soldiers," p. 454.

36. James A. Evrard, "Oversupervision: Its Diagnosis and Cure," *ARMY* 18 (September 1968): 82-83.

37. Raul Hilberg, *The Destruction of the European Jews* (Chicago: Quadrangle Books, 1961), pp. 664-67.

38. See Samuel A. Stouffer, *The American Soldier: Adjustment During Army Life* (New York: John Wiley & Sons, 1949), vol. 1, pp. 402-403, 408-409. This finding was contradicted by a more recent study. See Morris Showel, *Corrective Action Questionnaire: Development and Administration to Officers and NCOs*, Technical Report 66-5 (Alexandria, Virginia: Human Resources Research Office, The George Washington University, May 1966)..

39. See Robert B. Begg, "Sergeant Major," *ARMY* 16 (January 1966):

37-39; and Stouffer, *The American Soldier,* 1: 362-429.

40. For similar discussions of the problems a new officer encounters in his first command and the way a senior NCO can intervene, see Hal Simmons, "The First Months," *ARMY* 16 (February 1966): 50-53; and Stout and Terrebonne, "The NCO Meets His Junior Officer," pp. 66-68.

41. Communicating with the men is one of the tasks of not only the company commander; it is a sector of the military organization. Amos A. Jordan, Jr., in "Troop Information and Indoctrination," *Handbook of Military Institutions,* ed. Roger W. Little (Beverly Hills: Sage Publications, 1971), pp. 347-71, showed that military doctrine justifies "troop information and education programs" (that is, media and lecture propaganda) through the argument that an informed soldier is a more effective soldier. Presumably, a soldier who understands the military's reasons for a war or a particular military practice is less likely to feel coerced into it. See also Gordon A. Moon, "Information Officer or Propagandist?" *ARMY* 17 (December 1967): 58-63; and "Your Army Newspaper—Channel or Roadblock?" *Commander's Call* DA PAM 360-807 (2d Qtr Fy 72): 39-42.

42. See A. J. Sajo, "Procedure: Insulation Against Troops," *ARMY* 15 (March 1965): 72; Wallace, "Stiffening the Backbone," p. 29; Legg, "A Lieutenant Speaks to His Men," pp. 82-83; and Newman, "Assuming Command Means Assuming Leadership," pp. 60-61.

43. See Paul E. Holt, "Drawdown," *ARMY* 20 (August 1970): 22-25.

44. James H. Toner, "Leaders Must Reply When Soldiers Ask," *ARMY* 20 (August 1970): 56.

45. Robert W. Williams, "Commanders and Intelligence—The Growing Gap," *ARMY* 22 (December 1972): 21-23.

46. Shanks, "Management of the American Soldiers," p. 458.

47. John M. Gaustad, "Lessons the Book Never Taught Me," *ARMY* 22 (May 1972): 33-35; A. S. Newman, "Our Fighting Fiber," *ARMY* 18 (January 1968): 16-17. See also Morton E. Milliken, "The Pacifist Legacy," *ARMY* 22 (February 1972): 32-39.

48. Charles C. Moskos, Jr., *The American Enlisted Man: The Rank and File in Today's Military* (New York: Russell Sage Foundation, 1970), pp. 134-56. A similar ethic was noted in World War II by Stouffer et al. in *The American Soldier*; and in the Korean conflict by Roger W. Little, "Buddy Relations and Combat Performance," *The New Military: Changing Patterns of Organization,* ed. Morris Janowitz (New York: W. W. Norton & Co., 1964), pp. 195-224.

49. James P. Sterba, "In the (Volunteer) Army Now," *New York Times Magazine,* June 15, 1975.

50. Ibid., p. 38.

51. There is no shortage of descriptions of the professional soldier's moral character written by professional soldiers and their historians. Fleming describes him as no less than a cultured, humane, courageous, and anti-war man who is a quietly patriotic defender of freedom. Thomas Fleming, "Letter to a Professional Soldier," *ARMY* 21 (February 1971): 11-13. A. S. Newman lists dozens of characteristics in his monthly column, "The Forward Edge," in

ARMY; in particular, see "In Human Relations the Best Course Is Frankness," *ARMY* 22 (May 1972): 52-53, and "Combine Empathy with a Sense of Humor," *ARMY* 20 (January 1970): 52-53. Among the characteristics he lists are honesty, integrity, industriousness, humor, and loyalty. The professional soldier must also be humble, forbearing, accessible, and human. "Characteristics That Make Up Character," *ARMY* 20 (August 1970): 50-51. Similarly, Jack J. Wagstaff glowingly describes a Vietnamese commander as strong, fearless, forthright, humble, and equal in "A Man Among Men," p. 25. See for a variety of qualities, Albert N. Garland, "They Had Charisma: Marshall, Bradley, Patton, Eisenhower," *ARMY* 21 (May 1971): 26-31. See also letters by Jim Moore in *ARMY* 20 (April 1970): 8, and by Frederick L. James in *ARMY* 18 (January 1968): 4.

52. See, for example, Thomas T. Jones, "Integrity Goes Along with Loyalty," *ARMY* 20 (July 1970): 57. For a more thought-provoking discussion of this contradiction, see Zeb B. Bradford, Jr., "Duty, Honor and Country," *ARMY* 18 (September 1968): 42-44.

53. See the discussion outline in "Pride of a Pro," *Commander's Call* DA-PAM 360-803 (2d Qtr Fy 1971), in which the soldiers' moral qualities are linked to proscriptions of certain kinds of behavior in combat.

54. Ted G. Arthurs, "In Battle, the Leader Who Succeeds Is the Leader Who Knows He Can Lead," *ARMY* 19 (February 1969): 12-13; Shanks, "Management of the American Soldiers," pp. 443-64; Legg, "A Lieutenant Speaks to His Men," pp. 82-83.

55. See, for example, Bruce Palmer, Jr., "The American Soldier in an Equivocal Age," *ARMY* 19 (October 1969): 29-31, and David H. Hackworth, "Two Soldiers Named Green," *ARMY* 18 (April 1968): 64-65.

56. Hilberg, *The Destruction of the European Jews*, pp. 647-48.

57. Ibid., p. 648.

58. Robert S. Rivkin, *GI Rights and Army Justice: The Draftee's Guide to Military Life and Law* (New York: Grove Press, 1970), p. 35.

59. Waldo W. Burchard, "Role Conflicts of Military Chaplains," *American Sociological Review* 19 (October 1954): 528-35. Burchard's study was undertaken in the 1950s; however, most of his findings are probably still relevant because many of the motivations for becoming a chaplain then remain operative. An Army chaplain is often paid far more than a civilian clergyman, experiences far more doctrinal freedom, and perhaps has more of a feeling that he is performing a service in a congenial, conservative, nationalistic environment.

60. For an example of chaplains' hawkish attitudes regarding the Vietnam War, see John J. O'Connor, *A Chaplain Looks at Vietnam* (Cleveland: World Publishing Co., 1968).

61. William J. Hughes, "Leading Problem Soldiers," *Army Information Digest* (February 1961): 56-57; Rev. Edward V. Stanford, *The Serviceman and the Military Capital Sin*, Serving a Great Country Series, No. 2 (Washington, D.C.: National Catholic Comminity Service, 1968).

62. Frank A. Tobey, "Character Guidance Program," *Army Information Digest* 14 (October 1959): 2-6. See also Fr. Roger Dunn (in Melvin Zais,

"Letters," *ARMY* 18 [May 1968]: 3) describing the "modern American teen-age hood" who "took devilish delight in scaring everybody." He saw that in Vietnam these men had changed, and he said, "I bow to these men. I thought they were a lost generation, but they are redeeming themselves in Vietnam."

63. Lewis H. Lapham, "Military Theology," *Harper's* 243 (July 1971): 73.

64. Ibid., 76.

65. See a related discussion by Harold Garfinkel, "Conditions of Successful Degradation Ceremonies," *American Journal of Sociology* 61 (March 1956): 420-24.

66. S. E. Asch, "Studies of Independence and Conformity; A Minority of One Against a Unanimous Majority," *Psychological Monographs* 70 (1956).

67. Shanks, "Management of the American Soldiers," p. 451.

68. A. S. Newman, "Harsh Discipline: Balance Justice with Judgment," *ARMY* 23 (January 1973): 45-6, and Stewart, "Discipline and Leadership," p. 470.

69. Stewart, "Discipline and Leadership," p. 470.

70. Newman, "Harsh Discipline," p. 45.

71. Stewart, "Discipline and Leadership," p. 471.

72. Department of the Army, *Military Leadership*, p. 26.

73. Ibid., p. 27.

74. *Juicers* (also sometimes called "alkies") is a slang term referring to the soldiers who drink alcohol for recreation. The slang term *heads* refers to (usually younger) soldiers who use drugs, such as marijuana, for relaxation and escape. Each term represents a subculture of politics, images of man, life-styles, and responses to Army life. The juicers' robust and rowdy behavior and the heads' desire for a quite, escapist, nondemanding atmosphere often came into conflict during the Vietnam War. In general, the juicers identified with the Army, whereas the heads' culture provided a focus for anti-Army and anti-war sentiments.

75. Frantz Fanon, *Wretched of the Earth* (New York: Grove Press, 1963).

76. The *Modern Volunteer Army Monograph Project* (Fort Ord), p. 3-1, states, "Morale is much talked about in the Army and commanders are frequently judged on the basis of its relative state in their units."

77. See just such an example in Austin E. Miller, "Where Are All the Soldiers?" *ARMY* 15 (July 1965): 76-77, and Charles J. Milazzo, "Letters," *ARMY* 16 (October 1965): 6.

78. William E. Hass, "Indicators of Trouble," *Military Review* 51 (April 1971): 20-24.

79. In *Social Theory and Social Structure* (New York: The Free Press, 1957), pp. 140, 149-53, Robert K. Merton described as ritualism the bureaucratic adaptation in which institutional means are followed but societal goals are ignored or rejected. For many officers much of professional paternalism remains doctrine only and the principles are countermanded in practice. See Nadal, "Letters," *ARMY*, p. 2. In the last several years, the Army has been actively attempting to "strengthen its professionalism" in the field partly by influencing officers in the field to use professional paternalist techniques of leadership. George B. Pickett,

Jr., "Lead, Train, Administer," *Military Review* 52 (June 1972): 50. One evidence of this process is the recent publication of the *Commander's Call* pamphlet series, which contains guidance for leaders as well as speeches that can be delivered to troops. See for a view of this communication, W. C. Westmoreland's (then Army Chief of Staff) letter to officers of the Army in *Commander's Call* DA-PAM 360-803 (2d Qtr Fy 1971).

80. The term *rationality* is used here in a similar sense as Karl Mannheim viewed that he called "functional rationality" in *Man and Society in an Age of Reconstruction* (New York: Harcourt, Brace & World, 1940), p. 53. He defined functional rationality along two criteria: "a) functional organization with reference to a definite goal; and b) a consequent calculability when viewed from the standpoint of an observer or third person seeking to adjust himself to it."

81. U.S. Army War College, *Leadership for the 1970's*, p. 26.

82. Ibid.; see the speech by Franklin M. Davis on p. ii.

83. Witness the scores of angry letters and articles sent in to *ARMY* in the last few years, in which officers and NCOs bitterly rail at hippies, "long-hairs," radicals and "so-called good people" who opposed the Vietnam War. See also, Lapham, "Military Theology," pp. 73-86.

4

Co-optive Rational Control Through Behavioral Science and Management

The most nonconfrontive style of domination on the social control continuum is based on two separate, but usually compatible, principles. One is the liberal principle of inclusion and co-optation, and the other is the principle of rationalization—the application of social scientific knowledge to redesign human relations.

The co-optive principle takes no ideology seriously; it is a form of cooperation for any end. The view on dissent is that dissidence appears because there are "irritants" that alienate GIs from the military. The very word *irritant* connotes a trivial, nonfundamental response to the military and to national policy generally. The expectation is that if the Army gets rid of the irritant, the anger will disappear. For example, there would be a multifaceted response to an antiwar protest. One tactic would be to invite the protesters to sit down and talk over their views with those in charge. The sheer process of being permitted to express themselves and being listened to is often sufficient to "pull the rug out from under the feet" of the dissenters. It diffuses the anger and transforms it. Combined with this would be some attempts by the Army to improve completely unrelated conditions, by rebuilding barracks, for example. Since the co-optive policy maker or leader is not committed to any "cause," there is nothing to be lost in ideological concessions to the resisters. These modern, liberal techniques emerged in an era of affluence and seemingly unlimited money. Thus a response such as building new barracks or providing higher pay or other incentives would not be viewed as much of a cost.

As I am using the term, *co-optation* refers to a cynical approach to political commitment and values, which controls an underclass by accepting and including the opposition. In practical terms, the task is reduced to one of assessing whatever gripes GIs have and particularizing them to peripheral issues that can be reformed.

While liberal, co-optive principles may be useful in handling an opposition group, these techniques exert their greatest power by preventing such groups from gaining a following. The real target is an uncommitted but alienated mass. Hence, the liberal, co-optive principle requires a considerable degree of descriptive information about the entire population to be controlled. Intelligence must be gathered concerning soldiers' backgrounds, values, expectations, and complaints. As shall be shown, the survey research method is particularly well suited to gathering this kind of information. Survey research permits the careful choice (and timing) of improvements and other changes so they can have the maximum impact on uncommitted soldiers.

Rationalization, the other principle within this modern style of control, is based on a behavioral science that models itself after physics. This is a kind of behavioral science that sees prediction and careful measurement as key criteria in judging the adequacy of hypotheses and theories.[1] The importance of prediction is that it easily leads to practical control since the variables concerned are defined in such a way as to be readily identified and capable of manipulation. One application of this social engineering approach is the way the military matches men to machines (as well as matching some aspects of machines to men). The man is the extension of such machines as artillery pieces or weapons systems generally; he is an adjunct for some limitation the machine has due to its incomplete development. His performance is measured and predicted to a degree of precision unmatched in previous human experience. Humans' capabilities are assessed and certain important traits are identified. As Abraham Kaplan remarked, "Measurement of behavior adds immeasurably to the effectiveness of various instruments of social control."[2] This developing capacity to organize and control human behavior along predictable and efficient lines may provide a nearly unlimited potential for the bureaucratic or administrative domination of man.

Like liberal co-optation, rationalization as a method has no commitment to any values other than social order and efficiency. Anyone in power can use it, regardless of his ideology. The weakness of rationalization is its insensitivity to the vagaries of men's internal states of mind. It is basically unconcerned with interpretations of thoughts. On the other hand, this is precisely the strength of the co-optive method, which is based on an accurate understanding of men's intentions, dispositions, and so on. However, liberal co-optation suffers from its relative inability to supply specific techniques of control; it tends to be oriented to supplying descriptive and evaluative information. Thus, the two dimensions of this overarching category of domination, co-optive rational control, fit well with each other because each compensates for the other's weakness, and yet, in practice, they usually do not contradict each other. Most of the categories of controls I will discuss, such as screening, surveys, leadership, and training, display both co-optive and rational characteristics.

C. Wright Mills coined a term, "cheerful robots," which is particularly appropriate for this style of domination.[3] The ultimate result of co-optive rational controls is cheerful states of mind, with no values or beliefs other than one's own comforts, and automatic, mechanical performance.

Each area of rationalized, co-optive techniques has a history of its own, but some were conceptualized before others. Techniques of control were often first conceptualized at a psychological level where an individual's traits were considered paramount. However, as techniques developed and as unexpected information was adduced, this approach showed its limitations and a social-psychological or even sociological explanation was brought in.

Social control generally becomes more effective when the individual is viewed in larger, more social contexts. For example, testing and screening are based on a psychological view of man; attitude surveys are based on that most banal of behavioral sciences, social psychology; and systems design is characteristic of some sociological theory.

In general, with this style, social control becomes more depersonalized and imbedded in the situation. Personal leadership declines in importance as testing, attitude surveys, various utilitarian and life-style incentives, and weapons systems arrive on the scene.

The purpose of this chapter is to show how the Army has come to rely on these modern techniques of social control and how these techniques work to control soldiers. I will also suggest some of the strains in modernization as scientists[4] and other policy makers attempt to change the Army to a rationalized, manipulative, and volunteer Army.

Testing and Screening

The association of behavioral science with the United States military began with psychologists in World War I. No one asked them to get involved in military affairs; it was entirely through the initiative of the psychologists. Robert Yerkes, the president of the American Psychological Association in 1917, was the chief impetus for creating the involvement through the National Research Council, and he was the organizing force behind psychologists' main military contribution of World War I: intelligence testing. Yerkes enthusiastically began by organizing a set of twelve committees of psychologists with various specialities within the American Psychological Association. These committees were to operate through the prestigious National Research Council, which previously had not considered psychology important enough to establish even a single psychology committee. The development and importance of these areas varied somewhat.[5]

Military officers, who thought their own methods were adequate, resented the incorporation of psychological testing into their organization. But Walter Bingham, an important psychologist of this period, later wrote:

> Prior to the First World War the American Army was a small enterprise and, like other small industries, it trained its personnel pretty much by the apprenticeship system on the job. Little attempt was made to ascertain and classify by advance testing the huge range of individual differences in aptitude and experience. One man was considered as good as another until performances proved otherwise. When war was declared in 1917 we were not much farther advanced with respect to personnel classification and assignment than the British colonel in the Boer War who stood at the gangplank of a troop-ship in Capetown and tapped each descending recruit with his riding crop, diagnosing by some process of occult divination: "Infantry! Cavalry! Artillery! Er—Medical Corps!"[6]

Yerkes complained in several accounts of his difficulties in getting military officers (and, incidentally, the medical corps) to trust his tests:

> . . . My official correspondence was . . . necessarily descriptive, expository, argumentative, for my chief task, aside from making clear what we planned and proposed, was to convince military and civil officials that what we desired to undertake possessed practical value. Often it seemed that my foremost duty and obligation—one for which I usually felt myself peculiarly unsuited—was to vanquish seemingly insuperable difficulties by overcoming the passive resistance of ignorance and the active opposition of jealousy, misinformation, and honest disagreement.[7]

Military officers suspected that psychologists were using the Army as a laboratory for their own purposes.[8] Psychologists at each base had to convince officers that they had practical intentions and that they were not "pests" or "mental meddlers."[9]

Applied psychology had barely developed by 1917. The APA committee on psychological literature relating to military affairs concluded "that the psychology literature relating to military problems was not of great practical importance in connection with the emergency [World War I], because most of the tasks presented to or discovered by the committee demand [human] engineering of the pioneering sort."[10] Yerkes risked overextending his science's capabilities when he attempted to convince the military that psychology could solve many of its manpower problems. It took a man of Yerkes's persistence and boundless self-confidence[11] to initiate a pattern of "professional imperialism"[12] that continues to this day.

Yerkes had a few precedents to follow. Various psychologists had begun studies into intelligence testing several years before World War I.[13] This area was probably the most methodologically sophisticated of various fields of applied psychology. Applying these previously developed IQ tests to the military seemed a natural course to take. There were two ways the Army finally used IQ testing.[14] One way was to select cadets for officer training. A second was to eliminate from the service, or put on manual labor, those men whose intelligence was so substandard that they could not function in some military settings. These uses did not threaten military officers' prerogatives, as did some of the other uses Yerkes planned, which included applying IQ testing to promotions of officers.[15] This use would have threatened countless norms and structures of influence and control. Interestingly, field grade (majors and colonels) and general officers never had to submit to IQ testing.[16] Yerkes felt that IQ tests were closely correlated with a variety of military abilities, but the military preferred not to rely on this unproven relationship. Psychological tests were also used to measure a few separate abilities, such as mechanical abilities. Yerkes described the massive scale of testing finally attained in the military:

> After preliminary trial in four cantonments psychological examining was extended by the War Department to the entire Army, excepting only field and general officers. To supply the requisite personnel, a school for training in military psychology was established in the Medical Officers' Training Camp, Fort Oglethorpe, Georgia. Approximately

> one hundred officers and more than three hundred enlisted men received training at this special school.
>
> On November 11, 1918, the psychological personnel consisted of about one hundred and twenty officers and three hundred and fifty enlisted men. Over five hundred additional clerks were used in the examining service in the thirty-five different camps in which psychological examining had been established. The army intelligence examination had been given to 1,726,966 men; of these 41,000 were officers. Approximately 93,000 individual examinations had been given. Over 7,800 men had been recommended for immediate discharge; 10,014 had been recommended for labor battalions or other service organizations; 9,487 had been recommended for development battalions for further observation and preliminary training. Nearly 30 per cent of the 1,556,011 men for whom statistics are available were found to be unable to "read and understand newspapers and write letters home," and were given a special examination prepared for illiterates.[17]

The disclosure that 30 percent of American soldiers were illiterate shocked a nation that prided itself on its high level of education. It also enormously increased the prestige of psychology in civilian circles (although it tended to decrease the prestige of soldiers).[18] One professor was so impressed and upset with the results of Army IQ testing that he was afraid that American attitudes would shift such that democratic rights would be withdrawn and the movement for universal education would be reversed on the grounds that the "general will" would be viewed as based on a "childish mentality."[19] Yerkes was delighted with the success of his project:

> As never otherwise could have happened, military opportunities, demands, and achievements gave American psychology forward and directed impetus. . . . It will be long, however, before our profession entirely escapes from the directive influence of psycho-technological military developments or forgets that almost incredibly extensive and precious gift of professional service, which to the laity and

the military professional was the more impressive because wholly unexpected and unsolicited.[20]

Soldiers found this technique of control entirely new, but it did not take long for some of them to think of ways of counter-manipulating this technique of manipulation. Tests were usually given in a large room, and enlisted men would cheat and coach each other if they hoped to get a better score and thus a more technical assignment. The testers responded with five different versions of the IQ test, each with different questions. Other enlisted men saw, accurately, that flunking the test would get them out of the Army. A performance test was added to "prove conclusively that a man was weak-minded and not merely indifferent or malingering."[21]

Military officers criticized the psychological testing program, saying that, granted that the test might be testing intelligence or mental alertness, what did that have to do with military effectiveness? What did such military virtues as obedience, enthusiasm, patriotism, and bravery have to do with intelligence? In fact, could not higher intelligence make people less rather than more obedient? Yerkes countered by quoting numerous testimonials from officers extolling the efficacy of this testing program in selecting the best men for the jobs.[22] A later, more complex, version of the mental tests, the Armed Forces Qualifications Test (AFQT), is moderately predictive of performance in basic training today, and it is rather highly related to performance in military occupational training programs.[23] On the other hand, Yerkes found that it was not able to predict certain kinds of disciplinary offenders, such as conscientious objectors. It could do better in predicting more conventional kinds of offenders—such as those involving assault, larceny, and insubordination cases. Similarly, the newer AFQT is moderately related to disciplinary records (whether the enlisted man will finish his first tour of duty with an honorable discharge and without a court-martial conviction).[24]

Is mental alertness really so important as a requisite for success in the military? Yerkes compared the distributions of these intelligence scores with such variables as education, socioeconomic status, region of origin, and so forth and found that there were remarkably high correlations.[25] Thus, a different interpretation between these characteristics and intelligence as he measured it may emerge: the test may be actually measuring some combination of education, class, background, success in civilian society, and, perhaps, even intelligence. As such, the mental test functioned more effectively for the Army than it would have if it had provided a pure measure of intelligence.

Military personnel experts recognized this relationship between years of schooling, including success in school and success in the military (that is, no disciplinary problems). Some military psychologists have found that years of education are an even better predictor of success in the military than are AFQT scores.[26] They transmit their preference for recruits with more years of education to school counselors in journals such as *Psychology in the Schools*. Even the U.S. Marines do not want young men to join up before finishing high school. The military profits from the socialization influences of schools.

Much recent research into the background characteristics of recruits seems to bear out the general conclusion that those who are successful in civilian life turn out to be better soldiers for the Army.[27] Why might this be so? A soldier who has a bright, optimistic future is less likely to risk jeopardizing it by getting into trouble. Collaboration and cooperation are easier for the military to ensure, and officers do not have to resort to going to the hilt of the coercive dagger.

Formal education disciplines those who continue on with it. They encounter dozens of rules and learn not to fight them; a questioning attitude or a strongly committed stance only gets them into trouble. They learn to repress their impulses and not to respond emotionally as they go through school and to progressively put off gratifications for longer periods of time (spontaneous, overt resistance may be a form of immediate self-gratification). Students learn that the way to get the system "off your back" is to excel at it.[28]

Schools are bureaucracies, and bureaucracies have a distinctive rationality and narrow, defined channels for getting things done. Long years in school provide individuals with ways to manipulate bureaucracies, and they learn to be patient and persistent with large organizations. People without this experience, lacking this understanding of bureaucratic rationality, seem by contrast too unintelligent to know how to stay out of trouble. Other bureaucracies, as factories and civil services, also inculcate this discipline.

Consider for a moment Hannah Arendt's description of Adolph Eichmann's personality at his trial in Jerusalem for crimes against humanity.[29] She disputes what is probably the prevailing notion of evil: that of the machinations of demagogic monsters, of incarnations of the devil, or at least of madmen. On the contrary, Eichmann is shown to have been a simple, rather "normal" man who could not even stand the sight of killing. He had so mastered the problem of impulse control that he had no spontaneity or individuality, only self-interest and careerism. The subtitle of Arendt's book, *The Banality of Evil*, refers to the nature of the personality of the bureaucrat who can be responsible for incredible amounts of human misery. Arendt, by implication, challenges us to consider as an explanation for horror and misery not the psychopath, the sociopath, the drug addict, or the rebellious youth, but the normal, successful person.

Perhaps normalcy in a mass, postindustrial society means that beliefs are not to be taken seriously and that culture loses its character to set certain norms, standards, and principles. Birnbaum suggests that this is because we are not party to the creation of modern culture;[30] rather, that it is created for us by experts, partly in an effort to encourage consumerism and careerism and enhance conformity and to counter the rapidly slipping away social integration with external social control.

Thus one finds the peculiar contradiction that as people undergo more years of formal education they become less free, less spontaneous, and less committed to the value of their own emancipation.[31] Education, according to this argument, deradicalizes and produces conformity partly by its effect on imposing order in the classroom setting and partly through its more general failure to develop a culture that responds to the twentieth century, thereby leaving only ritualistic handing down of an outmoded and often irrelevant culture.

The problem for the military, then, is to locate and attract that segment of youthful population that conforms well in a bureaucratic setting. Many predictive tools have been developed to maximize the military's ability to identify these individuals.

To return to the discussion of the World War I mental testing program, it seems that the military officers at the time did not recognize the relationships between success in the Army and success in civilian society. Rather, their feelings that IQ had little to do with obedient soldiering and their awareness that some soldiers were faking their way out of the Army combined with their resentment at the threat to their prerogatives that the psychologists posed.[32] As a result of many complaints, the Army launched three independent investigations of the testing program by officers in the offices of the Secretary of War, General Staff, and the Surgeon General.[33] The immediate result was that the IQ testing and classification programs were terminated at the end of the war.[34] With the mass mobilization of World War II, however, the military reinstituted the intelligence testing program, this time run by psychologically trained military personnel, not by civilian consultants. This "career" of the technique of domination (testing) is typical of the transformations that behavioral-science-originated techniques of domination undergo.

Part of the importance of the mental testing program is in its role as a precedent. The testing program showed the military that behavioral science could help it organize and control its manpower, and it established the principle that men can be categorized and measured by tests. The testing program provided a precedent for the development of different kinds of tests, such as motivational tests or personality tests.

World War II saw the emergence of another form of selection based on mental characteristics: psychiatric screening. Emotional adjustment was added to mental alertness as bases for selection into the United States Army during World War II.

At the outset of World War II, government officials were concerned that the high losses due to psychiatric casualties in World War I would not be repeated.[35] Not only did psychiatric casualties reduce manpower in World War I, but they were a continuing financial burden after the war. A second personnel problem that psychiatric screening might help solve was that of AWOLs and other disciplinary offenders. Many psychiatrists and government officials at this time (1940) favored psychiatric screening of recruits to eliminate those with mental problems before they entered the military. Screening made sense at that time because the definition of common mental disorders and maladjustments was almost entirely associated with intrapsychic conflicts. Thus psychiatrists and the military hoped that those likely to have psychiatric problems in wartime might be identified early. During World War II, this expectation was put into practice in a massive psychiatric screening program, which turned out to be a failure.

Psychiatric screening went through several stages in World War II. It had little precedent to follow from World War I, since psychiatric disqualifications at, or before, induction were based mostly on such fortuitous factors as private physicians' letters rather than on any examination the military or the Selective Service system carried out.

At the outset of World War II, the military did not expect to require many troops—certainly no more than a million in all. Thus they recommended in directives sent to draft boards and induction stations that only the best men be inducted. They should reject any with even a hint of psychiatric disorder. This doctrine shifted often during the war, however, and standards were generally lowered as manpower problems became more acute, which produced some confusion. A lack of coordination between the Army personnel office and the Surgeon General's office caused more confusion.

Psychiatric screening in the early stage of World War II was carried out during the initial medical examination. It consisted of a brief interview between the inductee and the psychiatrist, who asked such questions as "Are you nervous?" and so forth. The interview usually lasted only from two to five minutes because of an acute shortage of psychiatrists available for this function. The approximately six hundred available psychiatrists acted as secondary interviewers; they were far too few for the six thousand draft boards. Sometimes a general practitioner, not a psychiatrist, would have to make the psychiatric diagnosis. Rejection rates varied greatly from place to place. Even the psychiatrists admitted they could not make an accurate diagnosis on this basis. Often the psychiatrist had no other basis upon which to make his decision than the brief interview.

This resulted in a wide-open opportunity for inductees to feign psychiatric illness. Some public outrage resulted as the high rate of psychiatric disqualifications became known. The Surgeon General's office tried to outline more carefully diagnostic states and to characterize tactics of malingerers.

The attempts to rationalize and routinize the psychiatric evaluation process produced a promising new technique of domination: a program of compiling dossiers on each Selective Service registrant to aid psychiatrists in diagnosis. The program, called the Medical Survey Program, was designed to collect information concerning each registrant's medical, social, and educational history. One form was given to the individual's former teachers who were asked for information concerning his conduct in school, adjustment to the school community, and so forth. Other forms of the dossier had spaces for information about the registrant's arrest record and his medical and social pathology. The draft board was expected to use social workers to compile and maintain the file, and to send it to the induction station with some notification for a psychiatrist to look at pertinent data in it. The information requested concerned such aspects of the recruit's background as success in school (years completed, years repeated, expulsions, suspensions, or other disciplinary problems), parents' marital status, police record (the age at which the first offense was committed was highly significant), and work experience (similarly, the age at which the boy began to work later proved to be of some significance). This predictive linkage between success in civilian society and the probability of success within the military organization corresponds with the interpretation that has already been suggested for predictive success of the mental alertness tests.

Like the brief psychiatric interview, psychiatric screening by the dossier method also turned out to be a failure in World War II. There were great variations in the percentages of forms turned in at the induction stations, varying from 2 percent to 75 percent. The majority of forms were either blank or useless. The main reason for the failure was the shortage of trained medical field agents or social workers to fill out the forms. If there was no one to research the data, the job was left undone. At induction stations, there were too few trained personnel available to open the sealed files and evaluate the material therein. The Selective Service system and the armed forces seemed to make no real effort to make the program work. After disappointed reactions from the various service commands near the end of the war, this program was ended. It had been initiated in October 1943 and was phased out in the summer of 1946.[36]

Nevertheless, several published studies have shown that the use of background characteristics (or biographical data, as they are sometimes called), when accurately described, can be of considerable predictive utility should the military decide to use them.[37] In fact, some studies have shown that background characteristics may be more predictive of success in the military than any other single test. Thus the dossier method is a technique of domination that has remained a potentially useful adjunct of military social control despite its apparent failure in World War II.[38]

The gathering of background data on recruits can be a monumental task, and such data are often not easily reduced to simple scores for making decisions. Clearly the identification of potential psychiatric casualties and other maladaptive soldiers would have to be further rationalized to produce a more convenient measure. Such a measure was produced by Samuel Stouffer's research team. It was a paper-and-pencil personality test for each recruit, and it was used as a preliminary screening device (to select men who were to see a psychiatrist for subsequent clinical evaluation).[39]

This instrument attempted to locate psychoneurotics through questions intended to elicit information about childhood fears, relations with parents, school adjustment, fighting behavior, participation in sports, and neurotic symptoms. It also asked questions concerning current attitudes and experience, such as emancipation from parents, mobility, social ability, identification with the war effort, acceptance of the soldier's role, worrying, oversensitivity, personal adjustment, and psychosomatic complaints. Other questions were later added to detect psychotics and psychopaths.

The questionnaire was developed rather late in the war and was not put into use until October 1944, when the pressure on psychiatrists was mostly relieved. The questionnaire was intended only to select inductees for psychiatrists' attention and was not in itself a predictor of Army adjustment. Since psychiatrists themselves vary so much in what they will term a rejectee,[40] there was some difficulty in establishing the validity and reliability of this instrument. However, it seemed to identify about four out of five men that a psychiatrist would have diagnosed as psychoneurotic. This adjunct to psychiatric screening was never given a real chance during World War II to prove its worth. But, like the other techniques, it demonstrated its feasibility.

Another useful and modern technique of evaluating men in military situations came about as a result of a research and training program, this time of the Office of Strategic Services (OSS).[41] During World War II, the OSS established a precedent by testing its men along a variety of dimensions while they were undergoing training. These dimensions included propaganda skills, ability to rate others, observing and recording skills, leadership, social relations, emotional stability, effective intelligence, energy, and initiative. They were measured in a variety of ways, including paper-and-pencil tests and group activities.

Like the Army's psychiatric screening program, the OSS techniques never had a chance to demonstrate their worth when they were initially employed. This was because the follow-up evaluation was based on commanding officers' reports and was much less scientific and controlled (given the wide range in jobs and locations that the trainees were placed in) than the assessment procedures in the earlier, more uniform training.[42] But, like the psychiatric screening programs, the possibilities of the new techniques were demonstrated and remained available to the military organization. Even failure can have its successes.

The World War II techniques of background assessments and personality tests continue to be researched and, in some cases, applied. There has been an upsurge in this research with the Vietnam War discipline problems and with the subsequent shift to an all-volunteer Army. In recent years personnel absences (AWOL) have become the Army's biggest manpower headache. According to one estimate, 80 percent of all incarcerated soldiers are in prison for AWOL.[43] In order to identify AWOLs, the Army predictably used techniques that it had experimented with earlier.

One avenue the Army recently explored is a paper-and-pencil personality test to identify potential AWOLs. In 1970 Fort Polk Chaplain James Berbiglia adapted the Taylor-Johnson Temperament Analysis (TJTA) for use by the Army.[44] First constructed in 1941 as the Johnson Temperament Analysis, it has been used primarily as an aid in individual, premarital, and marriage counseling. It measures nine basic personality traits and their opposites: nervous-composed, depressive-lighthearted, active/social-quiet, expressive/responsive-inhibited, sympathetic-indifferent, subjective-objective, dominant-submissive, hostile-tolerant, and self-disciplined-impulsive. According to Berbiglia, the AWOL syndrome is mainly recognized by extreme scores on the nervous, depressive, and impulsive scales and, secondarily, by extreme scores on quiet, inhibited, hostile scales. As a result of the identification of these potential AWOLs, a massive personal counseling effort was undertaken in some battalions, which caused the AWOL rate to drop to half of what it was in other battalions.

Subsequent follow-up, however, showed methodological weaknesses in these earlier studies and unimpressive reliability.[45] Fraas suggests that the "'AWOL Syndrome' does not exist."[46] Only 21 percent of Correctional Training Facility (CTF) inmates (convicted for AWOL) met Berbiglias's criteria. (ACTF is a modern, minimum security prison; see Chapter 7 for a description of the operation of this facility.) But Fraas admits that the TJTA could still be used as a tool to counsel soldiers or to identify those with problems.

Another approach to the problem of identifying potential AWOLs (and, implicitly, other maladaptive soldiers) is the construction of a profile composed of a variety of background factors and current attitudes.[47] Again, this was an update of methods developed in World War II. Recently, a profile was drawn from CTF inmates who were incarcerated for AWOL and from questionnaires drawn from four Army installations.[48] The profile included age, race, education, marital status, children, religion, parents' statuses, siblings, reasons for entry into the service, MOS (Military Occupational Specialty) training and satisfaction, rank, time in service, Vietnam experience, civilian and military arrests and convictions, drug use, and factors the AWOL soldiers felt contributed to their AWOL and what would discourage it.[49] The profile of the "absentee offenders" suggests a lower-class (or lower-working-class) background. Only one-third (32 percent) had a high-school diploma; another 17 percent had later completed the General Educational Development (GED) program.[50] During an era when the Army was still drafting many men, AWOL offenders were likely to be volunteers. Of these, 32 percent enlisted "to get away from problems," 27 percent were curious to see what the Army was like, and 26 percent were draft motivated. Twenty-one percent said their desire "to learn a skill" was important in their motivation to enlist, 17 percent agreed with the statement that "they had nothing else to do," 15 percent were "forced by a judge" to enlist, and 9 percent said they had always wanted to be a soldier.[51] Many (43 percent) had had civilian convictions. Sixty-two percent said they either used drugs or had used drugs; the age of first use varied between thirteen and twenty, averaging at sixteen.[52] A significant proportion came from broken homes.

The profile also strongly suggests that dissatisfaction with the Army motivated the AWOL behavior.[53] Of those who were MOS qualified, only half were working in their MOS at their last duty station.[54] More than half (53 percent) were not satisfied with their MOS.[55] Many (29 percent) had served in Vietnam, for about twelve months on the average.[56] Other data suggest that these men felt that they had done their duty and were not very tolerant of having to continue to endure the petty use of power in garrison, in contrast with the looser authority in Vietnam. According to the AWOL soldiers, much of their motivation to leave the Army centered around their lack of satisfaction with Army life, in terms of their work and the quality of leadership (other reasons were marital and related financial problems and personal problems).[57]

A pamphlet drawn from this study and written for officers describes these men as "problem prone," failure prone, and escapist: "They have continued creating problems for themselves because they can't cope with responsibility. They refuse to accept our standards, often because experience has taught them they'll only fail in an effort to achieve them."[58] There is probably some truth to this explanation for certain AWOL soldiers. Undoubtedly a wide range of motivations exists for AWOLs and similar acts that are defined as disciplinary infractions.

An additional interpretation for some lower-class soldiers is that they are more likely to rebel at alienating conditions in contrast to soldiers from higher-class backgrounds.[59] Whether they go AWOL, desert, fight back, sabotage, or commit self-destructive acts depends on the circumstances and the individual's style. The point is that there is a great deal of resistance to bureaucratic domination and unsatisfying work present in lower-working-class youth. This is just as apparent in automobile factories as it is in the Army.

In 1967 and 1968, when the GI anti-war movement was growing, there was some alarm about the potential of this movement. The Army could be expected to identify dissidents by turning to some of the tools—such as the construction of profiles—that it had developed earlier.

In 1969-1970, a contract research corporation for the Army constructed such a profile of political dissidents from information from Army personnel files.[60] A file of 1,092 known, active dissidents was maintained by the Army Counterintelligence Analysis Detachment (CIAD) and of these, complete "201 files" (including DA Form 20: Enlisted Qualification Record, DD Form 398: Personal History Statement, and DD Form 98: Armed Forces Security Questionnaire) were available on 152 of the more serious cases of dissidence (such as organizers and members of protest groups.[61] They examined the following characteristics: component (entitled or drafted), race, state of birth, religious preference, level of education, Army Classification Battery Test scores, and primary MOS.[62]

A slightly higher proportion of volunteers (Regular Army [RA]) (53 percent) than draftees (Army of the U.S. [AUS]) (45 percent) appeared in the sample.[63] At that time, the Army was composed of 63 percent RA, 35 percent AUS, and 2 percent Reserves and National Guard.[64]

About 11 percent of the sample was black, which is about equal to the proportion of blacks in the Army.[65] Hence, race is not part of this profile.

In terms of state of birth, marked differences appear. The West South Central states and the Mountain states have a much smaller proportion of dissidents per unit of population than do the Pacific and East North Central states.[66] The other regions fall in between. The ratio of extremes is almost four to one.

Religious preference showed little in the way of outstanding differentials when compared to the U.S. population.[67] (Army proportions were not available.) The authors report that their sample of dissidents contains a slightly smaller proportion of Roman Catholics, slightly higher proportion of Protestants and Jews, and a lower proportion of unaffiliated than one would expect.[68] They commented on the fact that dissidents listing no religious preference tended to be involved in more serious dissident acts whereas Protestants tended toward somewhat less serious activities.[69] Soldiers who listed a Catholic preference did not seem highly politically motivated but rather inclined to what the authors called humanistic motivations.[70]

In educational background, dissidents are more likely to have had college training than typical Army soldiers.[71] Those having college training were most often listed as organizing dissident activities, whereas high-school graduates tended toward less serious dissident activities.[72]

Dissidents can also be identified through the Army Classification Battery Tests, which consist of a group of eleven tests that measure various aspects of mental ability, perceptual speed, interests, and knowledge in several subject areas. Dissidents test significantly higher than Army averages, except in the test of automotive information, for which there is no significant difference.[73] They tended to score a little lower than average on shop mechanics.

The Army combines scores on the berbal and arithmetic reasoning tests to develop a general intelligence score. Dissidents scored high on both of these tests, but scored significantly higher on verbal reasoning than on arithmetic reasoning.[74] In fact, 10 percent of the 152 dissidents had the maximum possible score in verbal reasoning. "The relation between these tests, i.e., Verbal and Arithmetic Reasoning both high, but Verbal significantly higher than Arithmetic, may prove to be a useful selection and classification technique for isolating potentially dissident personnel."[75]

Among the MOS, which are grouped into ten broad areas, three are useful for identifying dissidents. Dissidents tend not to show up in "Tactical Operations" and "General Electronic Maintenance," but are overrepresented in "Clerical and Graphics."[76] "Further examination of the Clerical area shows that these assignments are mostly in general administration and supply. Such assignments, however, may augment the problem, as persons in the administration and supply areas often have access to supplies, equipment, and information which can facilitate dissident activities."[77]

The greatest problem of all of these identification tools is the use to which they are put. If they are used as bases for selection, they will exclude many men who would make adequate soldiers. McCubbin estimates that six out of seven soldiers who fit the AWOL profile will never go AWOL.[78] Similarly, the psychiatric screening program during World War II screened out thousands of soldiers who would almost certainly never have "broken"—because they might not have ever been put in such a stressful situation (as combat) for very long.

On the other hand, if these tools are used as an adjunct to leadership, they can be very useful for the Army. Commanding officers can make special efforts to carefully handle soldiers whom they expect may some day cause them trouble.[79]

Officers could monitor potential dissidents or transfer them to some position where they would have little responsibility or contact with other soldiers. They could be kept out of power or sensitive positions, such as intelligence, aviation, or military advisers to foreign nations.[80]

My impression, however, is that the dissident profile was not widely distributed or acted upon at lower levels. It was published after it was apparent that the GI anti-war movement was declining and clear that dissidence had exerted relatively little influence. However, the AWOL profile appeared to be widely distributed. The findings of the AWOL study were rewritten into homespun language with suggestions indicating how officers could reduce their AWOL problems.[81] The pamphlet also explained how officers can identify and understand potential AWOLs. The authors of the original study recommended the use of training films, posters, circulars, pamphlets, leadership seminars, service schools, NCO and drill instructor academies, ROTC courses, and service academies to disseminate the findings.[82]

In an interesting recognition of the fact that going AWOL is largely contingent on the soldier's experience in the Army, this study details different programs for combat, support, and training units.[83] In combat units, leaders were advised to emphasize "Problem-solving, flexible policies concerning leaves and AWOLs."[84] For example, they could make frequent referrals to various assistance agencies to help their men solve their problems (such as financial, personal, or whatever).[85] While officers should emphasize the importance of the mission, the study asserted that stopping the Vietnam War would not have reduced AWOLs (whereas ending the war might have in training units).[86]

In contrast, support units suffer from lack of meaningful work for many soldiers, especially those who are not working in their MOS.[87] Multiple missions and diffuse structure of many support units exacerbate the problem.[88] "Young, well-educated leaders and men who are relatively new to the service do best in these conditions. In the absence of meaningful work, leave policy, open door policies, referrals to social service agencies and the like are only palliative measures and not very effective at that."[89]

In training units the study recommends "firm discipline and strict policies" because soldiers are in a "time of transition and stress."[90] "The image of the 'Old Army' Sergeant with the 'heart of gold' is far from inappropriate in a training unit."[91]

The overall theme of this study was on "placing emphasis on the individual," reducing harassment, developing a more lenient pass and leave policy, improving leadership, making work meaningful, and lessening "personnel turbulence."

Testing and screening demonstrate both co-optive and rationalizing principles in practice. The potential deviant's characteristics are translated into a set of variables that can be identified, predicted, and controlled.[92] The application of co-optive principles is also apparent as these studies assist the commanding officer in "understanding" his lower-class soldiers. The fuller application of co-optive principles comes with the development of survey research.

Attitude Surveys

The history of attitude surveys in the Army, which began in World War II, displays some of the characteristics of the earlier experience of testing. Samuel Stouffer, the director of the Army's first major attitude survey program, wrote of the initial resistance of Army officers to this new form of what he called social engineering. He commented that in early 1941 the Secretary of the Army announced that polls would not be permitted in the Army. The secretary reasoned that polls are anonymous, and any anonymous criticism would be destructive of the cohesion of the Army.[93]

The survey researchers in the research branch (within what was successively called the Morale Division, Special Services Division, and Information and Education Division) were able to develop a large-scale attitude survey program partly as a result of some high-level support.[94] One source of support was Frederick Osborn, "an influential businessman and author of two social science books" who received a direct commission from a civilian to a general and became head of the Information and Education Division.[95] Army Chief of Staff George C. Marshall also lent considerable support to the survey researchers. And significantly, G-2, the Intelligence Division, was interested in the work of these behavioral scientists and provided some additional support.[96]

The social scientists, especially Stouffer, were anxious that their researches be sought and used by the Army. Stouffer took pains to avoid allowing their work to be academic or scientific at the expense of being practical.[97] He developed a team that could, on very short notice, generate survey results on a variety of topics of interest to policy makers.[98] Stouffer emphasized personal contact with policy makers within the divisions and within the Army generally. The survey researchers encountered resistance at lower levels and frequently used officers as official escorts for their interviewers who were often enlisted men or civilians.[99]

During World War II, Stouffer's team questioned over a half million soldiers in all parts of the world. They administered more than 200 different questionnaires; some contained 100 or more separate items.[100] Parts of this massive program were reinterpreted and published in *The American Soldier* volumes under the general editorship of Samuel Stouffer. The World War II volumes showed several uses of attitude measurement, most of which remain in use today. In general, this study looked at morale and the factors that affect it, such as soldiers' personal adjustment and experiences and Army policies, such as those concerning propaganda, support services, combat duty, and so on.

Morale is the cornerstone of professional paternalist control, and paternalists have ways to assess morale; the NCO's function and the use of indicators come to mind. But with attitude surveys, the Army has a morale assessment tool that goes far beyond these traditional sources. Attitude surveys can be highly specific and they can pinpoint irritants. They can also generate an aggregate measure, which is beyond the capabilities of the NCO because his perception and memory are selective. Attitude surveys provide a kind of internal intelligence function for the Army—which explains the interest Army Intelligence has had in survey research.

Why is such detailed information so important? Subordinated people have complex attitudes: they may, at the same moment, hold contradictory conceptions of themselves.[101] For example, if a GI is continually told he is lowly and worthless and it is always demonstrated to him what an incompetent bumbler he is, then he begins to accept this image and to view himself in the same terms his "superiors" use to define him. He may indeed feel that he could not run the Army any better than it is already being run, and that he really is not enough of a man to measure up to Army traditions. Repression produces a feeling of worthlessness in the repressed. But simultaneously, repressed people are often conscious of their powerlessness, and they resent those who have power over them. They respond angrily, if not always collectively. Many soldiers during the Vietnam War felt that the Army was a uselessly repressive, poorly managed, and generally incompetent organization, which had no business pushing them around.

The proportion of each side of the self-image varies. It depends on literally dozens of factors, such as what rewards the Army has just bestowed, other GIs' expressions, and the state and length of the war. At the extreme there is a possibility of a revolt of striking intensity, the character of which an ideologically motivated response such as an anti-war argument could never match. The intensity is due to the fact that the oppressed person is attempting to resolve contradictions within his own mind. Hegel argues that the most important struggle is within the slave's own mind, rather than between the master and the slave.[102] I think this interpretation of reactions to oppressive conditions is what is missing when idealism and psychopathology are given as the only possible reasons for resistance.

Self-image questionnaires are less useful than one might suppose in detecting this sort of internal conflict because there is a tendency to look for a single or unitary measure of a complex and divided phenomenon. Morale or attitude surveys, on the other hand, can indirectly detect the balance of sentiment that is present beneath appearances without presuming to distill a measure of so complex a mixture as a person's self-image. For example, the Military Morale Inventory simply asks soldiers to respond to eighty words, including *agreeable, confident, cross, disgusted, downcast, fit, good, lonely, offended, relaxed*, and *suffering*.[103]

A comparison of the introductions to two survey questionnaires on similar topics—dissent by American soldiers—reveals some reasons why attitude surveys are such a useful way of gathering information on an underclass. The version given to Army post commanders read:

POST COMMANDER QUESTIONNAIRE FORMAT

Installation __________

Questionnaire completed by __________

Questionnaire for Post Commanders on RAC Study 011.180, "Future Impact of Dissident Elements Within the Army on the Enforcement of Discipline, Law, and Order," sponsored by the Office of the Provost Marshal General.

The nature and extent of dissidence in the Army are matters of concern. In particular, the interest of the Government and the public in the maintenance of an effective and disciplined Army for the purpose of national defense justifies certain restraints on the activities of military personnel which need not be imposed on similar activities by civilians.

In January 1970, a survey was conducted at 17 installations in CONUS to obtain information related to a study "Determination of the Potential for Dissidence in the US Army." The attached questionnaire is in large measure based on the responses to that previous survey. Please respond to the questions as objectively and candidly as possible. Add sheets if more space is required.[104]

Contrast this rather descriptive introduction to a questionnaire given to enlisted men:

Post

ARMY PERSONNEL SURVEY — MARCH, 1971

This survey is a part of a study of significant importance to the Army and to the country as a whole. Your answers

> are *anonymous*—there is no way to determine who filled out the questionnaire. Honest, seriously considered answers will substantially contribute to the value of the study's findings.
>
> Please read each question carefully, take as much time as needed, and use the back of the page if more room is needed.[105]

One difference that suggests the usefulness of survey research in social control is that the enlisted men's questionnaire is anonymous. Many GIs have an overly particularized notion of social control. They think in terms of specific individuals getting caught for committing specific illegal acts, and they think that social control consists simply of these individuals being brought to trial or being otherwise harassed. So when a questionnaire is handled anonymously, these GIs feel safe. They do not understand that co-optive social control is based on controlling the state of mind of an entire class, not on punishing certain individuals. Thus, these soldiers do not have any notion that they are "squealing" or informing on the general state of their class when they answer attitude questionnaires. If they saw the survey as a technique of intelligence work, they might be less cooperative or might use it as a "hustle"—to influence the Army to allow them an easier life.

Another difference between these two questionnaires is the clarity of what is being measured and to what use the information is being put. It is not apparent to the enlisted men that this questionnaire is sponsored by the military police, nor is it immediately clear that the study is being used to assess the effect of dissidence on the enforcement of discipline, law, and order.

Another reason attitude surveys might work where more traditional, inquisitorial methods, such as spying or interrogations, might fail is that the questions are often written in such a way as not to expose what is being measured. Sociologists are experts at using a set of oblique questions to get at some attitude without ever asking a direct question. For example, a study entitled "Determination of the Potential for Dissidence in the U.S.

Army" asked questions such as "What is something you like about the Army?" "What is something you dislike about the Army?" "What is something not now done that would improve the Army?" This study also asked "What . . . would be the likelihood of [your] reenlisting?" and "What would be the likelihood of reenlisting if the improvements you suggested had been made in the Army?"[106] Another example of oblique questions is the military morale inventory mentioned previously.

There are other strategies to gain acceptance from soldiers filling out the survey. For example, the first questions on a questionnaire might be innocuous; the more important questions, which might reveal some kind of intent, follow later in the questionnaire. For example, the Army personnel survey for the military police begins with questions about easily answered biographical data. The questionnaire then asks about the respondent's race and religion, stating:

> Since a person's race, religion, and nationality may have a strong influence on his thoughts and behavior, it is vital to have this information to properly understand the answers received in this questionnaire. This is the *sole purpose* of requesting this information.[107]

It is never pointed out that this information is useful for constructing dissident profiles. Later this questionnaire asks soldiers if they have ever *seen* certain kinds of dissident acts. Then it asks soldiers if they have ever been *asked* to participate. Finally, it asks if they ever had personally participated in any of these acts, and it even asks what the motivation for participation was: "If you answered that you have *participated* in any protest activity, please describe what you were protesting about and what the Army should do to correct the situation."[108] The questionnaire also asks: "If you answered that you have never *participated* in any protest activity, please tell us why not."[109]

There is a scientific aura to a survey that almost compels collaboration.[110] In general, sociologists have found that you can ask anything of anyone if the asking is done well.

The surveys asking about the prevalence and motivation for

dissidence are relatively unusual uses of survey research. They represent the way the Army turns to established techniques in its repertoire to deal with new and worrisome problems. But many other descriptive surveys have been carried out by Army researchers, informing officers of the nature of enlisted men's attitudes and their definition of the situation.[111]

Surveys have consistently found that soldiers are much less ideologically oriented than their officers think they are. Officers in World War II assumed that soldiers fought for ideological and political reasons. It seems that they did not. They fought, according to Stouffer, because the small group, or their buddies, supported them and maintained a level of aggressiveness that kept them winning.[112] They fought to defend their buddies and because the small group expected it of them.

Soldiers fight out of concrete necessity, and they resist out of concrete necessity. A recent survey on dissidence shows that, as was the case almost thirty years ago, officers believe that soldiers resist the Army for ideological reasons.[113] Officers, reflecting their more educated backgrounds, feel that since soldiers are resisting the Army, they must be highly political and ideological and opposed to imperialism and to United States policy.

The real explanation is precisely the reverse. Soldiers resist the Army because they find it oppressive. They do not like regimentation, petty uses of authority, constant, useless formations and marches, and, to them, ridiculous constraints on their life-style. Once they express their hatred of the Army, *then* they are predisposed to think in more ideological terms. They begin to search for a justification to legitimate their feelings because they feel no civilian would support their resistance in merely the kinds of terms that preserving their own humanity would require.[114] Thus they find the ideology available, and they take it for their own. Once having resisted, they also may be more interested in an analysis of why they are soldiers for a country at war. So being anti-war or anti-imperialist is often the consequence of being anti-Army.

If officers had acted on the basis of their belief that soldiers resisted for ideological reasons (a kind of projection of their own feelings), they might have responded by stepping up ideological indoctrination and suppressing criticism. This response would have been completely inappropriate. In fact, in light of the above analysis, it would act precisely to exacerbate the sense of oppression and manipulation that was beginning to develop among enlisted men. But the policy-making officers had that powerful surveillance instrument, the attitude survey,[115] at their disposal and they found that the GI's response is mostly in terms of how the troops are treated as individuals. Those few who responded originally in entirely ideological terms were in the minority and may have been unassimilable anyway. However, it should be pointed out that the Army's reluctance to present strongly ideological propaganda to its troops is a result of a variety of forces in addition to survey research, such as the civilian furor resulting a few years ago from General Edwin A. Walker's extreme right-wing ideological indoctrination programs.[116]

There are many survey research studies that are mostly descriptive in their approach to morale and soldiers' attitudes. However, morale is usually looked at as a consequence of something else, especially something that is under Army control.

These studies can loosely be divided into two categories. One includes theoretical studies, which identify the techniques (such as leadership style) that work best in general, and assessment studies, which ask how well a given policy (such as refurbishing barracks) is working at a certain time.

Many studies of the theoretical, or generalizing type, were carried out in World War II. Some attempted to ascertain the most effective leadership techniques. This part of the research compared high morale companies with low morale companies in terms of leadership practices of the company officers. Within the military community, this has been one of the most widely disseminated parts of the entire *American Soldier* research. The researchers found the following practices to be present in companies with high morale and usually absent in low morale companies:[117] officers are interested in men; officers understand men's needs; officers are helpful to men; officers recognize men's abilities; officers are willing to back men up; officers give fair shares of off-duty time to men; men given authority to do their jobs; best use made of training time; fair furlough and pass policy; fair promotion policy; good selection of NCOs; officers give talks on importance of outfit's job; personal talks of officers on men's progress; men given opportunity to know the reasons for their work; and punishment meted out fairly. Many GIs wrote comments on the questionnaire explaining how the Army could become more effective by changing officers' practices in certain directions, such as becoming more fair, less privilege oriented, and more co-optive generally. Thus different leadership styles could be experimented with and tested for effectiveness, using the survey instrument as an indicator.

Survey instruments (and similar measures) were used in World War II to evaluate the effectiveness of propaganda appeals (propaganda is the prototype of psychological warfare).[118] Social psychologists learned which techniques of presenting propaganda worked best, such as the order of presentation of arguments, the issue of two-sided versus one-sided arguments, the length of presentations, and the use of audience participation in gaining attitude changes. By measuring intelligence, motivation, and other attributes, they learned how certain types of soldiers responded to certain types of appeals. They also learned what specific topics soldiers liked and responded to, such as realistic military action scenes (popular) versus speeches by politicians, documentaries on civilian workers, and women working in factories (disliked). Questionnaires were supplemented with polygraphs and with push buttons, which soldiers pushed during a film when they liked something. The research showed that some of the propaganda movies were relatively ineffective, and the authors attempted to explain why soldiers would be unconvinced at too slick propaganda. Thus survey research can exert a subtle effect on improving propaganda effectiveness or test co-optive strategies.

There are many recent studies that develop generalized relationships between Army practices and policies and social control. While many do use the concept of morale as a dependent variable, others use closely related concepts. For example, one study generated a measure of military unit discipline (composed of unit performance, appearance, and conduct) and demonstrated the relative effects of some predictor variables, including esprit de corps, leadership, and satisfaction with the work role and with the quality of living quarters.[119] The effect of these variables was assessed in combat, support, and training units. According to this study, esprit de corps is usually the best predictor of discipline, followed by leadership and satisfaction with work role. The authors argue that discipline can be better understood by these "environmental" variables (that is, esprit de corps, leadership, role satisfaction, and so forth) than by individual variables, such as those generated by the Taylor-Johnson test or background profiles.[120] The environmental variables in turn are affected by unit competition and team training, the quality and continuity of leadership, task structure, recreation, living quarters, and so on. On the basis of the differences between the three categories of units, this study advocates an earlier suggestion of a two-part Army: a combat Army and a support army, which would operate on separate organizational and social control principles.[121] This could have tremendous implications for social control, generally isolating the effects of future antiwar activity.

These generalizing studies also have a feedback aspect. For example, one of the objectives of this survey study just cited was to "develop demonstrably reliable measures of unit discipline and its predictors that may be used to help Army leaders empirically assess and manage discipline in their commands."[122]

Stouffer's World War II group felt it could accurately predict combat efficacy with a survey instrument.[123] If a relationship could be established between an attitude score for a unit prior to combat and its subsequent performance during combat, the Army would have a powerful predictive tool. A commander could compare the scores of two companies and decide which one he should send into combat. Although Stouffer's researchers could make this kind of correlation with some degree of success, the Army has made little use of this principle.

The other major use of survey research is in policy development, both in assessing the effect of policies and in predicting what new policies soldiers will support. An example of the latter approach appears in the *American Soldier* as the survey researchers provided a little of what they called "democracy" in the Army when soldiers were asked to rank categories of who should be discharged first, once the war was over in the Pacific. The "point system" was developed along the lines of priority of withdrawal that the soldiers themselves listed as preferences.[124] A GI received points for time in combat, for his family responsibilities (if he was a father, for example), and so on, and these determined how soon he would be sent home. This attempt at gaining acceptance of the slow withdrawal of soldiers may have minimized the already massive demonstrations by soldiers at the end of World War II.

Survey research is an important direct assessment technique and is emphasized in virtually all written evaluations of Modern Volunteer Army (MVA) actions (in contrast, commanders' reports, reenlistment statistics, crime rates, AWOL rates, dissidence rates, and other indicators of morale seem less prominent in these studies). In some commands, such as basic training companies at Fort Ord, morale surveys are carried out on a biweekly basis.[125]

Survey research is not a neutral tool, and it can even distort traditional military culture. For example, survey questions are usually written (or at least scored) in as specific a form as possible. This can particularize the milieu to bits or elements to which attention may be directed. The result may be that it is easier or more natural to focus on some areas that can be specified, such as barracks conditions, pay, and work hours, more than others, such as leadership. Another way survey research affects the military is that it is particularly suited for cost-effectiveness studies, another form of rationalization. Many MVA projects involve considerable cost. At Fort Bragg, for example, they ranged from $2.4 million for civilian KPs to $4,000 for the "Inscape" coffeehouse.[126] During VOLAR experiments at Fort Bragg, twenty-eight projects were evaluated for their cost effectiveness in terms of their impact on soldiers' satisfaction.[127] Each project was given a cost-effectiveness index and ranked on the combined bases of effect on soldiers' attitudes and dollar cost. Barracks partitioning and free sewing service had high cost effectiveness, while renovating, repairing, and maintaining buildings such as theaters and clinics had low cost effectiveness. In this way the Army can make choices on which projects to pursue and which to dispense with. This can be a misleading measure because some highly popular services, such as civilian KP and garbage pick-up, appear only in the middle of the cost-effectiveness ranking due to their high expense.[128] Of course, the point of this approach of modernization is maximum impact for dollar spent. The direction or nature of the changes is in a very real sense, irrelevant to this sort of assessment strategy.

Because surveys are conducted mostly on enlisted men, they help to transmit the specifics of enlisted men's resistance and discontent to the military organization. In this way, this research tool cannot help but usher in co-optive forms of social control. This shift to co-optive control has quickened with the need to rely on an all-volunteer force and as a result of the recent massive discipline and troop control problems (such as racial conflict, dissidence, nonresponse to orders, and crime). The Army also relies on surveys of civilian public opinion as guides for designing a volunteer Army that will draw recruits. Such surveys, coupled with similar research on soldiers, have deeply affected the nature of the direction of the volunteer Army changes.[129]

One such study of civilian youth was conducted by Opinion Research Corp. of Princeton, New Jersey, for the Army's advertising agency, N. W. Ayer & Sons.[130] Completed in 1971, it showed that the Army's main attractions were self-development and training, and, of lesser importance, dignity, patriotism, adventure, and travel. The main deterrence to enlistment was the threat of being sent to Vietnam. Another study showed that for a substantial percentage of civilian youth, military service was seen as interfering with their "freedom/life-style."[131] However, a large percentage saw military service as offering a "secure/steady job." A fully paid college education was the most preferred enlistment incentive, except for poorer youth (under $8,000 family yearly income). Many studies emphasize the role of pay in drawing volunteers.

Reenlistments are similarly strongly affected by actions related to job assignment, growth and experience, health care, and pay and benefits.[132] In particular, the ratio of military to civilian earnings strongly affects the reenlistment rate.[133]

The results of these studies (and earlier ones with similar findings) appear to be put into practice with the MVA changes.

Generally, MVA changes can be categorized into four areas: instrumental incentives, life-style improvements, leadership modernization, and training modernization. The instrumental changes and life-style changes appear to be most directly related to the results of survey research. Leadership and training modernizations seem to be a consequence of broader, earlier, and more long-term developments. Let us look first at the instrumental inducements.

Utilitarian Incentives

Utilitarian incentives include pay and education. The military pay structure has been upgraded extensively by Congress to the point where a young man in the Army can make as much money as his civilian peer working at a similar skill level,[134] and, if he is quite young, he can make considerably more. The Army provides a range of educational opportunities, even to the point of paying 75 percent of college tuition for some soldiers, according to an Army recruiter. Soldiers can learn a trade in the Army through their MOS training as well as through supplementary courses.[135] The importance of adequate pay, security, and the assurance of a career upon return to civilian life are enormously important inducements in a civilian economy with a high rate of unemployment for this youthful age group. As part of a system of positive gratifications within the Army, their effects cannot be underestimated.

These utilitarian incentives are not unique to co-optive rational controls except insofar as they are a direct result of pinpointing by attitude surveys, and they will continue in force if later surveys show that they are cost-effective. In other words, they must have a maximum impact per dollar spent in comparison with other techniques.

Segal suggests other modernizing consequences of these incentives.[136] He observes that the United States is now one of the few Western nations whose military pay scale is comparable to civilian employment. Pay for military personnel had lagged for years behind civil-service salaries, but it is now roughly equivalent to them. One result of this increase in pay is a decreasing support for post commissaries (in terms of price discounts), which, Segal suggests, will reduce the fraternal and communal nature of the military and increase the similarity to a business corporation with its weaker solidarity, loyalty, and commitment.[137]

Life-Style

The life-style changes in the Army are among its most widely publicized developments. They include the increased use of civilians to do some of the menial work, barracks renovation, easing of restrictions, post services improvements, and a few other co-optive strategies.[138]

Probably the most important of the changes in the soldier's mind is the use of civilians in KP and garbage collection and as armed guards in crime prevention.[139] KP was one of the most onerous of soldiers' duties. It was sometimes used as a punishment like "policing the grounds" (picking up scraps of paper and other debris) and other menial tasks not related to one's MOS. These tasks tended to reduce the soldier's dignity.

Barracks renovations, another expensive modernization, are also important to soldiers, especially permanent party soldiers. Old clapboard barracks have been torn down and replaced by structures similar to college dormitories in which two to four soldiers share a small room. The older barracks that still remain have been partitioned to offer more privacy.[140] In some cases, new furniture has been supplied for dayrooms and for the sleeping areas.

Soldiers have been relieved of many of the "Mickey Mouse" restrictions for which Army life has been notorious for so many years.[141] Now soldiers do not have to wear hats in privately owned vehicles (the hats could not fit on with the low roofs), and they can wear civilian clothes on post at certain times, such as when they are off duty and on the weekends. They are allowed in some cases to decorate their barracks walls with posters and other paraphernalia. The Army has also moved in the direction of a five-day work week.[142] Pass restrictions, which previously included mileage limits have been eased. Now the soldier can drive as far from the post as he wishes. Bed checks, reveille, and other formations have been eliminated or reduced in number.[143] At Fort Ord, basic trainees are now allowed to leave the company area (they had been restricted for the entire time of basic training, ostensibly as a disease prevention technique).[144] All these changes are in response to the results of survey research that indicated the irritating nature of Army restrictions.

Co-optation is more than passive in the volunteer Army. Training posts have a service that not only welcomes the incoming soldier but his family.[145] The dependents of the soldier receive increased benefits at health-care clinics.[146]

Some other post services have been expanded. Bus service on post, and sometimes to nearby towns, has been provided.[147] Some posts now have a free sewing service (to sew on Army patches and to make minor repairs), free laundry for some items, and more sports equipment.[148] Post exchange and commissary services have been expanded both in terms of the hours they are open as well as the variety of items they carry (soul food, cosmetics for blacks, and so on).

The Army gives the impression of earnestly trying to co-opt soldiers in every way it can. While reading brigade on post accounts of Army modernizations, I occasionally ran across disappointed comments, such as "beer in the mess halls and in the barracks, one of the most publicized innovations, has met with an almost alarming disinterest."[150] Similarly, soldiers just do not find the on-post coffeehouses (at many posts) to be quite the same as the old off-post ones, and they tend not to frequent them.

There are other, perhaps more effective, changes that receive little publicity. Some posts make an effort to "stabilize" commands so as to reduce the oft-noted "personnel turbulence" that caused leaders to hardly know who the men in their command were. Discipline is improved by the simple expedient of removing troublemakers through administrative discharges.[151]

Publicity is a continuing problem for the Army. Some commands, such as the 197th Infantry Brigade at Fort Benning, try to popularize their units in nearby towns through civic-action programs, such as building playgrounds[152] (this was a strategy that worked well for the U.S. military in Third World countries). Other strategies include using neighborhood councils, having roving speakers from a certain division give public talks, or inviting civilians to tour a base.[153] In 1971 and 1972, the Army's enthusiastic—and premature—publicity caused difficulties internally as recruits arrived with high expectations of the liberalization of the Army and were subsequently disappointed and resentful, feeling that they had been sold a bill of goods.[154]

Overall, these policies seem to provide a rather broad system of positive gratifications for young men going in the Army, but they sometimes create strains for company level officers and NCOs.[155] As a report from a large basic training post stated in its discussion of barracks decorations, "It was always easy to spot the drill sergeant—he was always the one who was gritting his teeth."[156] Some officers have felt a loss of control by the liberal pass policy, because, they claim, they do not know their soldiers' whereabouts.[157] This resistance has sometimes resulted in retrenchment in certain areas. At Fort Ord, no more posters are allowed on the walls, because "one man's art is another man's graffitti." Also at Fort Ord, previous uniform and haircut policies have been reinstated.[158]

While it is undoubtedly true that some of the tools of lower level control have been removed from the leader, the leader is expected to use some new techniques to control his men.

Leadership

How different are these new, co-optive leadership techniques from the professional paternalist approach? The Army apparently does not expect its leadership doctrine to change fundamentally. In its study *Leadership for the 1970's*, the Army War College emphasized that the traditional leadership doctrine is sound and will continue through the 1970s.[159] Nevertheless, it appears that leadership doctrines are shifting subtly away from the professional paternalist ideal. The change is one from a fatherly role to a role closer to a counselor, therapist, or labor-relations expert. The change is partly one of a different attitude toward soldiers. Since many soldiers seem unwilling to learn "followership," the leader cannot deal with them as dependent, loyal, but errant children but, rather, must see them as a potentially oppositional class.

In the first chapter, I showed how traditional police measures (identifying dissidents, monitoring activities, and so on) are supplemented with what I later called professional paternalist and co-optive rational techniques. The paternalist tactics include the clarification of regulations and dissemination of propaganda on soldierly character, and co-optive techniques center around the careful management of hostile attitudes. The co-optive leader must draw antagonistic sentiments out in the open in a setting that allows him to "cool them out," rather than allow them to coalesce in a counterorganization, such as along dissident or racial lines. As the post commander's reports in Chapter 1 indicate, there are several strategies for accomplishing this.

One strategy is counseling, on a one-to-one basis, in the commander's office. According to a West Point leadership text, *Taking Command: The Art and Science of Military Leadership*,[160] nondirective counseling is the best approach for this open-door counseling. In this way, the soldier should not feel that anyone is trying to manipulate him or sway him. Nondirective counseling allows a wide range of sentiments to be expressed and many kinds of complaints can be aired. An officer could give the impression that he will redress these grievances or otherwise correct the problem, or he could deal with the soldier as a therapist, helping him surmount his maladaptive behavior and feelings. Clearly this latter approach requires some degree of behavioral scientific training on the part of the leader. The emphasis on understanding social psychological processes is apparent in *The AWOL Soldier—A Challenge to Leadership*,[161] which includes a profile of the typical AWOL soldier and emphasizes that with proper leadership, he (and other potential AWOLs) still can become a good soldier:

> Command emphasis [on AWOL prevention] is productive only when a thorough understanding of the problem is developed. The issue is infinitely more complex than it may appear: effective guidance demands study, patience, honesty and accuracy.[162]

The officer is advised in this pamphlet to present himself to his men as an "insurance agent" and guarantee them that he will listen; that he will do everything in his power to make sure the man finds an acceptable answer to his problems; and that "every resource of . . . the Army will be brought into play. On his side!"[163] Finally the officer must guarantee that he will personally follow through to make sure everything possible is done to resolve the situation. If this program were taken seriously, it would require a great deal of personal attention in evaluating and following through each AWOL case. This pamphlet is typical of many recent Army leadership documents that de-emphasize punishment and emphasize getting the men to set standards for themselves through exploiting knowledge of their motivations.[164]

Another way of dissolving the development of counterconsciousness is through open discussions and classes, or perhaps informal question-and-answer sessions at an on-post coffeehouse. This provides the officer with a good opportunity to present the rationale for Army policies and to air some grievances in a manner that he can engage with.[165] This strategy involves some risk, but an officer with self-assurance, poise, and presence can be remarkably effective with this technique. This kind of open seminar is useful in discussing race relations issues; however, the officer must be well informed about the bases for the hostility many black soldiers harbor for white soldiers and officers, not to mention the hostility many whites have toward blacks and black politics. *Improving Race Relations in the Army: A Handbook for Leaders* provides just this sort of information.[166] This fifty-page pamphlet discusses several typical views of race conflict held by both whites and blacks and explains in straightforward language how to deal with complaints by blacks and reactions by whites. In general, the pamphlet urges commanders to get the issue out in the open and to make extra efforts to deal with complaints, such as off-post discrimination.

This understanding of political undercurrents among enlisted soldiers is one of the strengths of co-optive leadership. It can also be seen in the approach to understanding drug usage, another activity connected with the extent of alienation from Army life.

Enlisted men's advisory councils and drug advisory councils are useful ways of transmitting these undercurrents to the officers, and they usually result in suggestions for taking the most appropriate actions. This increasing participation by enlisted men in leadership, albeit in an advisory capacity, is one application of the modern approaches to management discussed in *Taking Command.*

Taking Command is an interesting document from the point of view of Army modernization. This text presents many of the issues that are current in business management schools. Particularly odd in the military context is the discussion of the many advantages of democracy at the workplace. Democratic, decentralized organizations have high morale, respond well to changing conditions, and are quite productive in certain kinds of tasks. Instead, with co-optive techniques, the Army tries to create an illusion of the unity of officers and men but not the reality. Without a true unity of purpose and a diffusion of power, co-optive techniques can be only a smokescreen for class relationships.

Lower level commanding officers vary in terms of their evaluation of whether professionalism, motivation, and discipline have improved as a result of these changes. But in 1972, many seemed less impressed with MVA changes than glowing reports from higher levels would indicate.[167] A Signal Corps commanding officer wrote: "The feeling on discipline since the inception of MVA differs according to the category of personnel. Career-oriented personnel are distressed and feel discipline has deteriorated, while the opinion among the younger, lower ranking personnel is that discipline is now based on logic and reasoning rather than fear of rank or indiscriminate power."[168] The commander of the John F. Kennedy Center for Military Assistance wrote that "senior NCO's and unit commanders felt that MVA had made their jobs more difficult by taking away many of their prerogatives and tools of leadership, such as passes, extra training, inspections, etc."[169] Another commanding officer felt that "the soldier in the MVA atmosphere feels entitled to more freedom than he is getting. Therefore discipline is weakened and the Chain of Command is weakened by Awareness Councils and Dragon Messages."[170]

Some officers think the changes lower standards and, in some cases, make the Army look hesitant and equivocating. An airborne battalion commander wrote, "Some actions make the Army look indecisive, for example, the haircut policy. The first set of pictures and the verbal description did not agree. Then those pictures were cancelled and a new set published. Also the saluting policy has changed so many times every one is confused."[171] Such officers would like to see a tightening up of certain regulations (such as haircut and uniform standards), and less permissiveness in courts-martial so that AWOLs would not think they would merely get a "slap on the wrist" (Article 15) for going AWOL.[172] Some suggest that there be more emphasis on professional paternalist topics, such as "Our Moral Heritage."[173] A field artillery commander wrote, "A few programs pointed toward the career soldier (Officers and NCO's alike) would go a long way in gaining some much needed support."[174]

One commander observed that "attitudes seem to have changed from reluctant compliance to most any directive, condition or situation, to one where soldiers now almost expect to be treated as any civilian employee."[175] And another officer glumly said, "Even though the Army is trying to improve Army life and professionalism, the young soldiers still don't like the Army."[176]

Some of the changes in Army policies seem to coalesce at the company commander level. The recent emphasis[177] in dealing with deviant soldiers results in requiring increased attention of the company commander to race relations (classes, counseling, rap sessions, and the "balancing" of units), alcohol and drug control programs (urinalysis, counseling), and military justice problems (Article 15s, court-martial charges, "serious incident" reports, contacts with military police and the Criminal Intelligence Division, admonitions, and flaggings). The increased complexity and expense of material and systems requires many reports and other information, which are typically collected at the company level. This comes in addition to the company commander's normal duties of company administration (such as morning reports, inspections, commanders' meetings, mess management, open door policy), personnel actions (administrative discharges, letters of indebtedness, counseling, efficiency reports, promotion recommendations, awards), supply inventory, unit security, training, and equipment maintenance. Demands from a variety of sources seem to converge at the company commander's desk: the company commander has to sign laundry deduction authorizations, repair parts requests, bank loans, separate ration requests, meal cards, ad infinitum.

One result of this degree of overwork at the company commander level is "selective neglect" of certain functions, such as race-relations seminars. Thus, while co-optive mechanisms are present in the Army, there is some question about whether they are utilized.[178]

Leadership is one area where the co-optive and rational dimensions of social control may not always be compatible. According to General Willard Latham, who in 1971 used some co-optive strategies in adapting his brigade to the all-volunteer Army:

> For some years, there has been a dialogue going on in the Army concerning the relationship of leadership to management. The military leader has been characterized as the charismatic man on horseback, whereas the manager has been typified as the cool, efficient, emotionless man of statistics. The Army has generally taken the position that a good commander must be a good manager. However, over the past few years, particularly with the advent of the systems analysis technique, there has been an ever growing acceptance and respectability for the manager image in military affairs.
>
> The increasing admiration for the cost effective analysis in dealing with problems and concurrently the managerial approach put less stress on the shoulder-to-shoulder, eyeball-to-eyeball contact by the leader-manager. This situation, combined with the use of highly efficient communication and transportation resources such as the helicopter, has allowed commanders to directly influence operations without being personally involved. This trend started a chain reaction, for as brigade and battalion commanders tended to operate from helicopters and charts and thus to

> see less of their troops, company commanders, platoon leaders, first sergeants, and even platoon sergeants—taking their cue from this example—also began to see less and less reason to be personally involved. Avoidance of personal contact became fashionable.
>
> As evidenced by the current [1971] major personnel problems, the Army is now reaping the whirlwind of this condition. As leaders no longer felt obliged to involve themselves personally with their troops, soldiers soon began to feel that they were unimportant cogs in the "great green machine." By definition, there is little inspiration in management, but the necessity to inspire is an organic part of leadership.[179]

David Segal argues that if the military relies on those organizational principles and incentives that are characteristic of civilian corporations, it can expect to be faced with soldiers' unions (similar to other federal employees' unions) and labor-management negotiations.[180] I might add that if the Army follows the pattern set by other sectors, many discipline functions will simply be transferred to the union. In the United States, there is no reason to assume the emancipation of the individual will result, because such individual freedom could threaten the union as well as management. However, the question of the contribution of soldiers' unions to individual freedom may become moot if Congress prohibits military unionization—a prospect that appears likely at this writing.

Basic Training

Rationalization of military social control underlies many changes in basic training. What was once a process of transforming identities into a uniform mold of a soldier has changed in the direction of an individually managed learning of discrete skills.[181] The theoretical basis of the new direction of basic training is reinforcement and learning theory, especially according to B. F. Skinner's principles.[182] According to the theory of operant conditioning, specific behaviors will be learned if rewards result from their enactment. The rewards must be carefully scheduled in response to the behaviors. For example, intermittent rewards produce more long-term learning of behavior in the absence of subsequent rewards after training. A reward should be given immediately after the desired behavior occurs. The person or animal being trained learns to associate certain behaviors with rewards (reinforcements), which he desires. While punishments will act as reinforcers to eliminate certain behavior, behavior shaping is best carried out through rewards.

In order for this process to work in the Army, certain preconditions should be met. Using co-optive strategies, these include removing "irritants" and "unnecessary" details, such as guard and burial details, so that attention may be focused upon those behaviors to be reinforced.[183] Similarly, potential AWOLs among recruits should be identified and either removed or given special leadership attention.

The bits of behavior that are to be learned must be identified.[184] This process is similar to what is called job analysis in civilian circles. The existing job (for example, infantry, rifleman, cook) is analytically broken into very specific acts and each of these acts can be learned in training. This process is a legacy of Frederick Taylor's scientific management and shares with it a relative disregard for the overall attitude of the worker involved. But in the Army's case the simultaneous use of co-optive principles precludes the discontent that could come from such rationalization.

In order to be effective as a reinforcer, the rewards must be highly valued by the subject to be trained. While pigeons may be trained with food, more careful research must be used to identify reinforcers for soldiers, and survey research is particularly suited for this.[185] Through this method, promotions and time off were identified as the rewards most highly valued by recruits.[186] But in the Army, there are many behaviors to be rewarded; only a limited amount of time off is available, and even fewer promotions are possible. One way the Army psychologists solved this problem was to break up the promotions and time off into bits.[187] At one point each soldier had his own card with thirty or so spaces to be punched by his drill instructor as he performed each behavior proficiently.[188] Some soldiers at Fort Ord now graduate from Basic Combat Training-Advanced Individual Training (BCT-AIT) (now combined into one sixteen-week program) with the rank of E-4 (corporal), a rank that previously took months or even years to attain.

In order to reward recruits for performance, basic training must be transformed into an individualized process.[189] The basic training method used from World War II until 1971 was a "group oriented socialization effort" with many lectures and lecture-based demonstrations. All recruits were given the same training, which concluded with a test at the end of the process.[190] Those few who failed the final examination were recycled through the process. Reinforcement theory, however, necessitates self-paced instruction. Many of the recruits could already pass some of the tests,[191] particularly in the physical proficiency area. Lectures were replaced with more "hands-on" training, and there were several tests along the way for particular skills. The individualized process used some traditional rewards in a more systematic way. Those trainees who had shown highest skills became "peer instructors," teaching fellow trainees some of the skills at which they excelled.[192] This gave some of the most skilled trainees a leadership role, which is useful for co-opting possible dissidents. (High aptitude scorers generally did better in this training.)

As I have suggested, high morale is considered essential for the operation of a positive reinforcement-based instructional program. Morale in the training companies was assessed regularly at biweekly intervals.[193]

This new training process, based on an individualized reward system for learning certain skills, can be expected to transform the role of drill instructors.

> The task force anticipated considerable resistance on the part of the drill sergeants and in this anticipation they were not disappointed. MRS [merit reward system] called for a reordering of the priorities in the drill sergeant role and a fundamental change in the drill sergeant-trainee relationship. Under the new system, the challenge to the drill ser-

> geant would no longer be how, as a father surrogate, he could motivate men by personalized giving and taking; rather, the challenge became one of operating in a system wherein the motivational elelments were already established. To the extent that leaders prefer to apply their own personal, and sometimes arbitrary, consequences to the behavior of the men in their charge, executing the leadership role within the confines of the MRS system could be unpalatable. In effect, the MRS shifts the locus of power from the more personal reward/punishment decisions of the drill sergeant and embodies this power in a formalized, institutionalized set of rules. The drill sergeants were, in effect, being ordered to expand their father figure position to include more actions of a coach, an instructor, and a technician. . . . The idea of "punching someone's ticket" [with a railroad conductor's punch on a color-coded merit card] did not conform well with the drill sergeant's image. Additional problems were caused by the excessive time spent punching cards (40-50 trainees per drill sergeant) and some confusion about how to run the system. In order to deal with this, cards were replaced by a roster and bulletin board, and rules and rationale of the system were published in detail in a "drill Sergeant's manual" for the merit reward system. [Recruits were given a similar, abreviated version.]194

There was still some resistance to the new program, and in 1973 some retrenchments were made, such as including more instruction on discipline, military courtesy, and military appearance;195 saluting, precision marching, and proper uniforms were reemphasized. More authority was given to NCOs (and more leadership training was instituted), and the training system was somewhat more decentralized.

The MRS is employed in all training companies at Fort Ord196 but not throughout the Army, perhaps because of drill sergeant resistance to the excess paperwork and the limitations on face-to-face leadership.

Again, the Army has, through behavioral science, a powerful

social control device in operant conditioning, but the new technique faces certain organizational resistance to its institutionalization. We can expect this system to be reinstituted when pressures on the military arise but without behavioral scientists' continuing participation.

Like other co-optive rational techniques, this method is far better at removing resistance than it is at creating loyalty. In professional paternalist fashion, John Faris deplores the changes in BCT because he feels it reduces the tendency of young recruits to identify with their drill sergeants as role models.[197]

Systems Design and Simulation

Social control is more effective when it is embedded in the totality of a situation rather than in a specific individual. In contrast, personalizing social control makes resistance more possible because one can get angry at a person more readily than at a situation.

Two developments have emerged somewhat simultaneously that have elements of this type of situational or nonpersonalized social control. One is a result of technological development in weaponry. As weaponry gets more complex and is based more on hardware than on manpower, the interaction of various components becomes emphasized and is termed a system or a weapons system. The weapons system becomes, perhaps in an unanticipated way, a new and effective technique of domination. It elicits obedience and makes resistance appear senseless. The other development associated with the modernization of weaponry and hardware is the principle of training men who operate weapons systems through simulating the environment with a computer. These two new developments, one a method of warfare and the other a method of training, will be considered together and illustrated in a single example in this section.

Technological developments in warfare tend to be thought of as simply bigger bombs, better planes, and guided missiles, but among military technology developers the key to understanding major technological developments since World War II is the systems concept. A system is a concept referring to a set of interacting components with some specific purpose and some boundary that adapts to its environment by taking in and analyzing information coming from the environment. The components include men and a variety of machines such as sensors, computers, and bombs. The emphasis is on interactions of components and on processing information. The boundary is an arbitrary construction, which, depending on the analyst's purpose, can include more or fewer components. A guided missile is thus only a part of a system; essential to its functioning is the capacity to locate and identify targets and to take into account and interpret large amounts of varied data that might affect its deployment. (The terms *system* and *systems analysis* or *operations analysis* have been used to refer to a wide range of phenomena, including small groups in Antarctic posts, interpretation of data about trends in AWOL rates,[198] weapons systems,[199] large-scale battle plans,[200] and so on. In this section, systems design and analysis will be used only to refer to a weapons system.)

The full reasons for the increasing development of the technology of warfare and the consequent uses of systems analysis are beyond the scope of this book, but a few suggestions can be proposed to explain why these changes might take place. The most obvious is that the more technologically developed weapons become, the more effective they are in terms of firepower and accuracy. The use of more technologically sophisticated hardware, such as enemy sensors and detectors (heat, smell, vibration, sound, and radar) and weapons such as guided missiles and death rays (including lasers and low-frequency sound), and computerized intelligence information increasingly requires that system design principles by used. The use of the hardware is in iteself a force for change because these technological elements of warfare require new capabilities to operate and integrate them.

There is another set of considerations that encourages the use of higher technology and the systems approach in warfare. Like the impetus behind developments in industrial production and automation, the military develops its technology to eliminate manpower difficulties. Personnel is always a problem; not only does one have to take care of the personality and social needs that a large aggregate of men might have, but their tendency to refuse to cooperate is well known in military circles. Military officers are well aware of S. L. A. Marshall's finding that in the Normandy invasion in World War II only an average of 15 percent of the men in the front lines actually fired their weapons.[201] They may also be aware of the problems encountered early in the Korean War when foot soldiers confusedly retreated.[202] Or they may even be aware of the conventionalized restraints on fighting aggressiveness in World War I.[203]

The Vietnam War in particular may have been a strong inducement to use more technology in warfare. Military men infatuated with the new weapons systems had been debating among themselves during the 1950s and 1960s about the desirability of deemphasizing the importance of the foot soldier.[204] For a while, especially during the Kennedy years, the advocates of the foot soldier seemed to be winning as the United States was facing an increasing number of small guerrilla wars. The foot soldiers would be more useful than the missile, given the political and diplomatic international considerations and the fact that guerrillas are often peasants themselves and rather difficult to conquer with missiles. But the technology advocates seem to have had the last word, at least at this writing, because that undependable factor, the morale of the soldier, has borne out their position. When the American soldier seemed to refuse to fight in Vietnam, the ground war was transmuted into an air war. In my opinion, manned bombers (and artillery) were used in Vietnam partly because foot soldiers would not fight.

Why were the men who manned the bombers more dependable than foot soldiers? Part of the answer may be found in the operation of the modern weapons system and in the way these particular men were trained. A variety of weapons systems operate along basically similar principles. One example of a system is the Rand Corporation's studies of air defense facilities.[205] This is one of the first extensive attempts at systems design and simulation. This approach considers a group of men and machines as an interacting unit and tests their ability to function effectively as a unit.

This weapons system is a radar tracking and reporting facility with about twenty-eight men. Some men watch the radar screen for aircraft coming into their area, which consists of several hundred square miles. These scope watchers report each aircraft they spot, along with information about its speed, direction, location, and so on, to other men who plot the location of the aircraft on a large board. Yet other men assist in identifying the aircraft as friendly or enemy, partly on the basis of information received from outside of the facility, such as flight plans filed with civilian authorities. Another function is carried out by different men who are in contact with outside information sources in the Washington defense hierarchy in order to get information as to the state of emergency or war in which the country might be involved. And finally, other men are responsible for notifying the nearby air base to send up interceptor planes to force the enemy aircraft to land or to shoot it down.

These men and machines are considered to be one system because they are analyzed while they are operating with each other and examined in the course of their action in concert. Systems advocates contrast their viewpoint with the previous analysis that considered each component virtually by itself. For example, during World War II, radar scope readers were trained and selected on the basis of their ability to make identifications with the scopes accurately and quickly. But this technical ability, however easily measured and manipulated, may not be the only ability or attribute that would be involved in a system. There is often no way to tell if other attributes are needed until the real event occurs and then it may be too late.

In contrast, if the men, each with their different skills and roles, are put into an environment that is close to the actual environment for which they are being trained and use realistic information to perform the tasks in concert with other men in the team, problems that could have remained unanticipated thus become apparent during the training. Boguslaw noted, for example, that one scope reader who was particularly fast and accurate did not produce the most efficient operation because his communication skills had never been measured or improved in training. In the hubbub of the operation of the team, some of this scope reader's fast-paced and mumbled reports were missed by the plotters. Presumably, there is a myriad of unpredictable difficulties that could not be identified in the individualized training but could be easily spotted during frequently simulated situations.

Simulation here refers to a training exercise that approximates real conditions that a system may ultimately expect to face. The best simulations are those that are most similar to the variety of real conditions that are possible and those that take in the largest number of components—that is, the system with the widest boundaries. Modern simulation has been made possible with the use of high-speed computers. For example, a computer handling the simulation of the air defense unit would transmit information to the system representing incoming aircraft, flight plans, and military orders. Following the system's response, the computer would return information quickly and inform the team of the results, based on such information as the number of interceptors the team had ordered into the air and the number of enemy bombers that would have gotten through to a city had the situation been a real one. The enhancement of learning by providing quick knowledge of results is, of course, a basic principle of learning theory. At first, Rand's simulation was done with one team of twenty-eight men. Later the simulation was expanded to the entire U.S. Air Defense Warning Operation, consisting of 6,000 to 8,000 men at varying times.[206]

Harman suggests five rules for effective training through systems simulation: (1) train a functionally complete unit; (2) simulate the real environment of the system; (3) train the system to operate under stress conditions; (4) exercise the system frequently; and (5) provide the system with knowledge of the results.[207]

Some of the reasons the personnel of a modern weapons system may be more effective than infantry soldiers can be seen by contrasting the concepts of the small group (representing an infantry unit) with the concept of the systems team. A small group is characterized by a loose or indefinite structure that allows a high degree of variance in each member's performance, which depends on his personal characteristics. Since the degree and kind of participation by members is not known beforehand, it is difficult for authorities to set down specific orders for specific tasks. A systems team, on the other hand, is characterized by a rigid structure and communication network in which each member has a well-defined task and his performance can be anticipated. The coordinated participation requires little overlap, since each member has his own area of proficiency. Decision making is narrower, and the tasks usually involve some perceptual-motor activities connected with technologically developed equipment.

In a situation with a high division of labor and a well-defined communication network, any individual who is resisting can be easily located and replaced. The systems approach does not tolerate resistance. Each member's accountability is thus markedly increased. In the infantry, on the other hand, a GI who feels that the war or killing is wrong can simply not shoot, or he can shoot to miss. A GI pinned down on a battlefield is rarely called to answer for insufficient aggressiveness under fire. In contrast, a GI in a systems team would be caught if he chose to resist the Army by noncooperation at his job.

Ideally, resistance could be culled out in advance in a simulation. A GI who wanted to resist might unknowingly do so at a time when there was a simulation going on; he would thus be ineffective at his operation and would be identified and removed. On the other hand, those who did not resist might find that their attitude would become increasingly adjusted to their roles and would make the next time, perhaps the real thing, easier. Some simulations are carried out in special training rooms, but even in those simulations carried out in actual installations there is probably a subtle, special intensity that would give away the difference between the real thing and a practice session.

The very training as a team builds a kind of informal group social control. As the paternalist theory of morale points out, men in cohesive groups control each other to a great extent. Even though these few men have differentiated functions, the team is small enough to create many opportunities for face-to-face interaction, so some solidarity is likely to grow. The fact that the men undergo a series of experiences together also helps to build a sense of solidarity.

This solidarity is likely to operate against the possibility of any anti-Army resistance, since the solidarity is aligned with

Army values as a result of the task structure. Groups with well-defined and differentiated task structures (high division of labor) tend to be more cooperative because there is less basis for internal competition. In contrast, an emphasis on individual skills could be divisive; each man might try to improve, say, his own score often at the expense of the overall output of a work group. But in a weapons system under simulation, individualism does not make much sense; the indicator is the output of the team, not of each individual. In other words, the team gets a score on the basis of its cooperative activity. After the results of the simulation are presented to the team members, they often talk it over together and work out whatever difficulties they might have in attaining high efficiency. This interaction also supports group cohesion as well as identification with military objectives.

The division of labor itself creates an automatic justification of authority because the leader is the key decision maker in the system's output. Authority based on function makes more sense than authority invested in someone who has merely spent more time in the Army or has managed to cajole some superior into a good efficiency report. Thus authority depends less on coercion and the leader's personality attributes.

Harman has asserted that a simulation serves as a means of indoctrination, since it exhibits the feasibility of a complex system.[208] Each man's job makes a little more sense than if he were trained individually without seeing his skills interact with others. Simulations are deliberately varied to increase student interest and motivation. Biel asserted that traditional basic training and advanced individual training left theindividual unintegrated into a team or a system.[209] The weapons system concept clearly is designed to avoid this difficulty.

The functionally interdependent nature of military operations is considerably increased in the systems situation. Even in a traditional military setting, resisting the Army by refusing to kill the enemy can endanger other GIs' lives. Consider an artillery unit that refused to fire when asked to do so by some other unit trapped by hostile forces. Few artillery men would refuse to cooperate under these conditions. But these soldiers might be so isolated from other aspects of the war that they would have almost no idea of the consequences a given action might have for fellow GIs. In the Rand example, with its mission of protecting cities from attack by enemy missiles or bombers, resisting would be unconscionable. A manned bomber might appear to be a different situation. The crew might not always know whether they were supporting their own men or carrying out a purely aggressive action. When trained as part of a system, their sense of supporting other soldiers is increased.

Team functioning diffuses responsibility for killing. No one person seems to be responsible for any act. Who is more responsible for bombing civilians in North Vietnam: the navigator who announces when the aircraft is over the position, the pilot who puts it there, or the bombardier who drops the bombs? And this includes only the men who are up in the air; there are hundreds of men involved at some point in the dropping of bombs.

The very operation of a complex and expensive machine seems to be rewarding for many soldiers. There is an informal prestige system within the service linking one's own prestige with the firepower of the weapon he handles. A bomber pilot garners more prestige than an infantryman does. That prestige system is, of course, not inherent to the system's functioning per se, but in practice it is a powerful support of it and an impetus for soldiers to try to become a part of it. For GIs who have no training for civilian jobs, participating in a modern weapons system suggests the possibility that their skills may bring them a good job once out of the Army.

Additionally, as Blauner pointed out, working in a technologically sophisticated environment in the commonly associated absence of severe regimentation seems to create greater satisfaction at work.[210] Regimentation inevitably would have to be reduced in the weapons system, since immediate mindless response to officers' commands has little place in a system where the machines have taken over those automatic aspects of functioning. Similarly, when workers and other functionaries (such as soldiers) become more professionalized with greater training, greater skills, and greater responsibility, there is less need for regimentation and close supervision. The need for professionalization increases as the technology develops.

The systems technology of warfare provides a kind of isolation from a phenomenon that may have restrained destructiveness in previous warfare. The soldier is now isolated from the enemy. The bomber pilot never sees the bodies of the people he has killed. War is made "clean" at the site of killing. Interestingly, artillery men have a slogan that artillery adds dignity to war, which would otherwise be a bloody brawl. This alienation from the products of one's decisions makes the decision making easier.

Team functioning occurs in another context of isolation. The team is likely to be isolated from some of the political undercurrents that would ordinarily pass quickly among soldiers. Team units are likely to be small and physically isolated at any single location. Of course, personnel selection effects add to this insulation.

Thus the structuring of a situation through the use of technologically developed equipment and realistic team training can produce a degree of conformity and effectiveness of a far greater level of magnitude than that which may be elicited by leadership techniques alone. It is very difficult for the individual to sense the degree to which this form of domination can control his behavior. Perhaps this is what Sartre and other existentialists were foretelling when they wrote that "the situation" drastically, but imperceptibly, limits freedom.

NOTES

1. Gerard Radnitzky, *Contemporary Schools of Metascience* (Sweden: Scandinavian University Books, 1970).

2. Abraham Kaplan, *The Conduct of Inquiry: Methodology for Behavioral Science* (San Francisco: Chandler Publishing Company, 1964), p. 210.

3. C. Wright Mills, *The Sociological Imagination* (New York: Grove Press, 1959), pp. 171-76.

4. Military behavioral scientists (often with military rank) have been viewed with considerable suspicion and some contempt by military professionals. See Robert Leider, "Must the Professionals Step Aside Again?" *ARMY* 22 (June 1972): 39-45. Leider suggests that behavioral scientists have their own criteria for success, their own value structures, and their own political persuasions, all of which made conflict with professional military officers.

5. The military psychology committees that might be of interest here, on recreation, morale, training and discipline, never developed much past the planning stage. The War Department was so opposed to psychological analysis of discipline that it refused to fund the project. But a precedent had been suggested, and World War II saw its fuller development. See Robert M. Yerkes, "Psychology in Relation to the War," *The Psychological Review* 25 (March 1918):85-115, and his "Report of the Psychology Committee of the National Research Council," *The Psychological Review* 26 (March 1919): 83-149.

6. Walter B. Bingham and James Rorty, "How the Army Sorts Its Man Power," *Harper's* 185 (September 1942): 435-36. Copyright by *Harper's* Magazine, 1942. Quoted by permission of the publisher.

7. Robert Mearns Yerkes, *A History of Psychology in Autobiography*, ed. Carl Murchison (New York: Russell & Russell, 1961), vol. 2, p. 398.

8. Daniel J. Kevles, "Testing the Army's Intelligence: Psychologists and the Military in World War I," *Journal of American History* 55 (December 1968): 574.

9. Ibid.

10. Yerkes, "Report of the Psychology Committee," p. 87.

11. See his self-congratulatory comments in Yerkes, *A History of Psychology in Autobiography*. See also Richard M. Elliott, "Robert Mearns Yerkes: 1876-1956," *American Journal of Psychology* 69 (September 1956): 487-94; and R. M. Yerkes, "Psychology and National Service," *Psychological Bulletin* 14 (July 1917): 259-63.

12. See Yerkes, "Psychology and National Service," and Robert M. Yerkes, "Man-Power and Military Effectiveness: The Case for Human Engineering," *Journal of Consulting Psychology* 5 (September-October 1941): 205-209.

13. See Harry F. Harlow, "Robert M. Yerkes," *International Encyclopedia of the Social Sciences*, ed. David L. Sills (New York: Macmillan Co. and The Free Press, 1958), 16: 588; Elliott, "Robert Mearns Yerkes," p. 488; and Loren Baritz, *The Servants of Power* (New York: John Wiley & Sons, 1960).

14. Robert M. Yerkes, ed. "Psychological Examining in the United States Army," *National Academy of Sciences, Memoirs* (Washington, D.C.: Government Printing Office, 1921), vol. 15.

15. R. M. Yerkes and C. S. Yoakum, *Army Mental Tests* (New York: Henry Holt & Co., 1920), p. xi.

16. The acceptance of mental testing by Army officers was furthered by "the general observation that commanding officers and others usually received the highest of ratings." Yerkes, *Memoirs*, p. 96.

17. Yerkes and Yoakum, *Army Mental Tests*, p. 12.

18. Harlow, "Robert M. Yerkes," p. 588.

19. Percy E. Davidson, "The Social Significance of the Army Intelligence Findings," *The Scientific Monthly* 16 (February 1923): 183-94.

20. Yerkes, *A History of Psychology in Autobiography*, p. 399.

21. Yerkes and Yoakum, *Army Mental Tests*, p. 10.

22. Yerkes, *Memoirs*, pp. 104-14.

23. See Edmund F. Fuchs, "Screening Potential Enlisted Men," *Psycho-*

logical Research in National Defense Today, Technical Report S-1 (Washington, D.C.: U.S. Army Behavioral Science Research Laboratory, June 1967), p. 12; John A. Plag and Jerry M. Goffman, "The Armed Forces Qualification Test: Its Validity in Predicting Military Effectiveness for Naval Enlistees," *Personnel Psychology* 20 (Autum 1967): 323-40

24. Fuchs, "Screening Potential Enlisted Men," pp. 10-16.

25. Yerkes, *Memoirs*, passim.

26. See John A. Plag and Jerry M. Goffman, "A Formula for Predicting Effectiveness in the Navy from Characteristics of High School Students," *Psychology in the Schools* 3 (July 1966): 216-22; and N. H. Barry and P. D. Nelson, "The Fate of School Dropouts in the Marine Corps," *Personnel and Guidance Journal* 45 (September 1966): 20-23.

27. For a general discussion, see P. D. Nelson, "Personnel Performance Prediction," in *Handbook of Military Institutions*, ed. Roger W. Little (Beverly Hills: Sage Publications, 1971), pp. 91-119.

28. Peter Tauber, *The Sunshine Soldiers* (New York: Ballantine Books, 1971).

29. Hannah Arendt. *Eichmann in Jerusalem: A Report on the Banality of Evil* (New York: Viking Press, 1964).

30. Norman Birnbaum, *The Crisis of Industrial Society* (New York: Oxford University Press, 1969), pp. 106-66.

31. The New Left movement emerged as a reaction to this development in higher education and mass culture, not as a consequence of it. It opposed much of the university culture and the mass culture generally.

32. Kevles, "Testing the Army's Intelligence," pp. 574-75.

33. Yerkes, *Memoirs*, p. 45; and Kevles, "Testing the Army's Intelligence," p. 576.

34. Kevles, "Testing the Army's Intelligence," p. 578.

35. This discussion of psychiatric screening is drawn largely from a history of "Selection and Induction," by Ivan C. Berlein and Raymond W. Waggoner, in *Neuropsychiatry in World War II*, vol. 1: *Zone of Interior*, ed. Robert S. Anderson (Washington, D.C.: Department of the Army, 1966), pp. 153-91.

36. Albert J. Glass noted that while World War I experiences with psychiatric casualties provided much of the impetus for World War II screening, the neuropsychiatric casualty rate in World War II was much higher than in the earlier war. This was particularly embarrassing in light of the fact that a much higher proportion of men were rejected for military service for neuropsychiatric reasons in World War II than were during World War I. Rejections for psychiatric disorders ("mental disease") were 15.3 times as high in World War II compared to World War I. The comparison for mental deficiency and neurological defects was less extreme but still dramatic at 4.6 and 2.3, respectively. The overall rate was 20.3 rejected per 1,000 examined in World War I and 115.4 per 1,000 in World War II. Yet the discharge rate (that is, of soldiers, rather than registrants) for neuropsychiatric reasons (including neurological, psychotic, psychoneurotic and other psychiatric disorders) was 11.1 men per 1,000 per year in World War I and 23.5 per 1,000 per year in World War II.

See Albert J. Glass, "Army Psychiatry Before World War II," in *Neuropsychiatry in World War II*, pp. 3-26; and Albert J. Glass, "Lessons Learned," in ibid., pp. 736-60. See also Bernard D. Karpinos and Albert J. Glass, "Disqualifications and Discharges for Neuropsychiatric Reasons, World War I and World War II," in ibid., p. 761.

37. Nelson, "Personnel Performance Prediction," pp. 98, 102.

38. The background check is regularly used by the Army for officer candidates. Military secrecy requires that background checks on officers be conducted by an investigative agency, such as the FBI. However, the traditional police use of dossiers should be distinguished from the behavioral scientific construction of dossiers discussed in this chapter. For a review of studies relating to *Motivational Prediction and Selection Procedures*, AFHRL-TR-71-19 (Brooks Air Force Base, Texas: U.S. Air Force Human Resources Laboratory, January 1971). Available through National Technical Information Service (NTIS), Department of Commerce, as AD 728625.

39. Berlien and Waggoner, *Neuropsychiatry in World War II*, pp. 185-91.

40. See John A. Aita, "Efficacy of the Brief Clinical Interview Method in Predicting Adjustments," *Archives of Neurology and Psychiatry* 61 (1949): 170-76; and Robert J. Stoller and Robert H. Geertsma, "The Consistency of Psychiatrists' Clinical Judgments," *Journal of Nervous and Mental Disease* 137 (1963): 58-66.

41. OSS Assessment Staff, *Assessment of Men: Selection of Personnel for the Office of Strategic Services* (New York: Rinehart & Co., 1948).

42. See Leland D. Brokaw, "Noncognitive Measures in Selection of Officer Personnel," in *Psychological Research in National Defense Today*, ed. J. E. Uhlaner (Washington, D.C.: U.S. Army Behavioral Science Research Laboratory, June 1967)

43. H. McCubbin and L. Fox, "Influence of the Counter Culture on AWOL Behavior," paper presented at Conference on Current Trends in Army Social Work, Fitzsimons General Hospital, Denver, Colorado, September 1970.

44. James C. Berbiglia, *The AWOL Syndrome: A Study in the Early Identification of Potential AWOLs by the Use of the Taylor-Johnson Temperament Analysis Leading to the Development of a Preventive Program* (Los Angeles: Psychological Publications, Inc., 1971).

45. Louis A. Fraas and Lawrence J. Fox, *The Taylor-Johnson Temperament Analysis "AWOL Syndrome": A Further Evaluation* (Fort Riley, Kansas: Research and Evaluation Division, U.S. Army Correctional Training Facility, May 1972); and Louis A. Fraas, *Taylor-Johnson Temperament Analysis as a Predictor of AWOL Recidivism* (Fort Riley, Kansas: U.S. Army Correctional Training Facility, November 1972).

46. Fraas and Fox, *The Taylor-Johnson Temperament Analysis*, p. ii.

47. Samuel A. Stouffer et al., *The American Soldier: Adjustment During Army Life* 1 (New York: John Wiley & Sons, Inc., 1949), 1: 105-54.

48. H. McCubbin et al, *Leadership and Situational Factors Related to AWOL: A Research Report* (Fort Riley, Kansas: U.S. Department of the Army, U.S. Army Correctional Training Facility, 1971).

49. See the "profile of absentee offenders" and the summary on pp. 22-29 in ibid.

50. Ibid., p. 22.

51. Ibid., p. 23.

52. Ibid., pp. 24-25.

53. Ibid., p. 36.

54. Ibid., p. 24.

55. Ibid.

56. Ibid.

57. Ibid., p. 25, and Department of the Army, *The AWOL Soldier: A Challenge to Leadership*, Pamphlet 600-14, (Headquarters, Department of the Army, September 1972), p. 4.

58. Department of the Army, *Personnel Absences: The Absentee Soldier*, Pamphlet 630-1 (Headquarters, U.S. Army, Europe, and Seventh Army, May 24, 1972), p. 6.

59. Their predisposition to rebel may be related to the fact that it is difficult to threaten people with limited life chances. In this study, AWOL offenders were asked to evaluate "reasons which might discourage others from going AWOL." They felt that only the desire for an honorable discharge might have any significant effect, but even this factor was not perceived as particularly important. A majority (65 percent) strongly disagreed with the suggestion that it would be difficult to get a job after a court-martial. Most of these men felt that even a bad conduct discharge would not cause them problems in civilian life. McCubbin et al., *Leadership and Situational Factors Related to AWOL*, p. 26.

60. H. Olson and R. Rae, *Determination of the Potential for Dissidence in the U.S. Army*, Vol. 1: *Nature of Dissent*, RAC-TP-410 (McLean, Virginia: Research Analysis Corporation, March 1971). Available from NTIS, listed as AD 884031.

61. Ibid., p. 37.

62. Ibid., p. 39.

63. Ibid.

64. Ibid., p. 40.

65. Ibid., p. 41.

66. Ibid., pp. 41-42.

67. Ibid., p. 44.

68. Ibid.

69. Ibid., pp 44-46.

70. Ibid., pp. 45-46.

71. Ibid., p. 46.

72. Ibid., pp. 46-47.

73. Ibid., pp. 46, 48.

74. Ibid., p. 49.

75. Ibid.

76. Ibid.

77. Ibid.

78. Department of the Army, *Personnel Absences*, p. 2.

79. This use of profiles and other tools of identifying troublemakers is urged in many recent studies. See, for example, McCubbin et al., *Leadership and Situational Factors Related to AWOL*; Ronald G. Bauer, Robert Stout, and Robert F. Holz, *Developing a Conceptual and Predictive Model of Discipline in the U.S. Army* (U.S. Army Research Institute, n.d.); and Berbiglia, *The AWOL Syndrome*.

80. See Brokaw, "Noncognitive Measures in Selection of Officer Personnel," pp. 35-47. The term *noncognitive* is a euphemism for probing, psychological tests. See also Francis F. Medland, "Psychological Factors in Selection of Special Forces Officers," Report of the Eleventh Annual Army Human Factors Research and Development Conference (Washington, D.C.: Department of the Army, October 1965), pp. 147-54; and A. J. Drucker and Harry Kaplan, "Predicting Success in Army Aviation Courses," *Report of the Tenth Annual Army Human Factors Research and Development Conference* (Washington, D.C.: Department of the Army, October 1964), pp. 276-83.

81. Department of the Army, *The AWOL Soldier*, and Department of the Army, *Personnel Absences*.

82. McCubbin et al., *Leadership and Situational Factors Related to AWOL*, p. iii.

83. Ibid., pp. 41-42. The study identifies factors that affect AWOL in different kinds of units and these factors are written into the pamphlet, *The AWOL Soldier*, in the form of accounts of successful programs that had been tried by various units.

84. Ibid., p. 41.

85. Ibid.

86. Ibid., p. 44.

87. Ibid., p. 56.

88. Ibid.

89. Ibid.

90. Ibid., p. 57.

91. Ibid.

92. We have looked at a sample of the wide range of researches conducted in the area of military personnel prediction. Nelson groups various tests into five general categories: Task proficiency, emotional adjustment, motivational effectiveness, interpersonal effectiveness, and systems effectiveness. P. D. Nelson, in "Personnel Performance Prediction," *Handbook of Military Institutions*, pp. 91-119. Nelson briefly comments about studies that use peer ratings as a predictive tool. For example, trainees (such as those at West Point or in special forces officer training) are asked to periodically rate one another's interpersonal skills, emotionality, enthusiasm, assertiveness, responsibility, conformity, need for social support, and so forth. Another predictive tool that is similarly not based on a paper-and-pencil self-disclosure test is to put a whole group in a demanding situation and to score individuals on the basis of their actual behavior.

93. Stouffer et al., *The American Soldier*, 1: 12.

94. Ibid.

95. Ibid., p. 13.

96. Ibid.
97. Ibid., pp. 14-18.
98. Ibid., p. 19.
99. Ibid., p. 20.
100. Ibid., p. 12.
101. See G. W. F. Hegel, *The Phenomenology of Mind*, trans. J. B. Baillie (New York: Harper & Row, 1967), pp. 228-40. See also George P. Rawick, *The American Slave: A Composite Autobiography, vol 1: From Sundown to Sunup: The Making of the Black Community* (Westport, Connecticut: Greenwood Press, 1972).
102. Hegel, *The Phenomenology of Mind*, pp. 228-40.
103. Department of the Army, *Fort Ord Final Project VOLAR Evaluation* (Headquarters, United States Army Training Center, Infantry and Fort Ord, California, August 1972).
104. R. William Rae, Stephen B. Forman, and Howard C. Olson, *Future Impact of Dissident Elements within the Army on the Enforcement of Discipline, Law, and Order*, RAC-TP-441 (McLean, Virginia: Research Analysis Corporation, January 1972). Available from NTIS, listed as AD 891558, p. 177. CONUS refers to Continental Army of the United States, or stateside bases.
105. Ibid., p. 121.
106. Howard C. Olson and R. William Rae, *Determination of the Potential for Dissidence in the US Army, vol, 2: Survey of Military Opinion*, RAC-TP-410 (McLean, Virginia: Research Analysis Corporation, May 1971), pp. 96-102. Available from NTIS, listed as AD 724165.
107. Rae, Forman, and Olson, *Future Impact of Dissident Elements*, pp. 107-22.
108. Ibid., p. 126.
109. Ibid.
110. See related experiment by Stanley Milgram. "Behavioral Study of Obedience." *Journal of Abnormal and Social Psychology* 67 (1963): 371-78.
111. The various services run hundreds of attitude surveys each year on a variety of personnel topics, including retention, pay, working conditions, housing, duty preferences, and "interpersonal values." A look at any one issue of the Air University Library Index (the main interservice reader's guide) on the topic of "surveys" will reveal perhaps fifty or a hundred survey reports.
112. Stouffer et al., *The American Soldier*, 2: 105-91.
113. Olson and Rae, *Determination of the Potential for Dissidence*, 2: 1-5.
114. For a related discussion about blue-collar workers, see Alvin W. Gouldner, *Wildcat Strike* (New York: Harper & Row, 1954).
115. Some survey researchers are very explicit about the use they intend for their surveys. The careful scaling of dissent activities from most severe to least severe categories can assist commanders in devising strategies that are most appropriate to each category. "It is possible that official reaction against dissent in these low severity categories may in fact serve to exacerbate dissent. In other

words, an action such as a locker search in barracks to uncover the possession of dissident literature may create more dissent than is represented by the mere possession of literature." Olson and Rae, *Determination of the Potential for Dissidence*, 1: 31.

116. See Amos A. Jordan, Jr., "Troop Information and Indoctrination," *Handbook of Military Institutions*, p. 348.

117. Stouffer et al., *The American Soldier*, 1: 387.

118. Carl I. Hovland, Arthur A. Lumsdaine, and Fred D. Sheffield, *Experiments on Mass Communication* (New York: John Wiley & Sons, 1949). This study is the third volume of *The American Soldier* series.

119. Bauer, Stout, and Holz, *Developing a Conceptual and Predictive Model of Discipline*.

120. Ibid., pp. 3-9.

121. Ibid., p. 71. The suggestion for a two-part Army is from Zeb B. Bradford, Jr., and Frederic J. Brown, *The United States Army in Transition* (Beverly Hills: Sage Publications, 1973).

122. Bauer, Stout, and Holz, *Developing a Conceptual and Predictive Model of Discipline*, p. iii.

123. Stouffer, *The American Soldier*, 2: 6-30. The researchers correlated a battle-nonbattle casualty ratio with willingness for combat, confidence in combat stamina, and confidence in combat skill. A nonbattle casualty rate is a measure of how many GIs went out on sick call for reasons not associated with getting wounded in battle. Large numbers of such men on sick call would be indicative of a unit's low fighting efficacy.

124. Stouffer, *The American Soldier*, 2: 520-48.

125. Department of the Army, *Fort Ord Final Project VOLAR Evaluation*.

126. J. H. Hay, *MVA Evaluation Report* (Headquarters, XVIII Airborne Corps and Fort Bragg, Fort Bragg, North Carolina, July 1972). This is a semiannual evaluation report. The term *VOLAR* (an acronym for volunteer Army) refers to field experiments conducted at several Army bases from 1970 to 1972. This project consisted of assessing some modernizations, liberalizations, and other incentives. MVA (Modern Volunteer Army), a more general term, refers to the Army-wide program of incorporating some of these changes. The goals of the MVA program include reducing the reliance on the draft, raising the number and quality of enlistments and reenlistments, increasing service attractiveness and career motivations, and making provisions for a stand-by draft law. Willard Latham, *The Modern Volunteer Army Program: The Benning Experiment, 1970-1972* (Washington, D.C.: Department of the Army, 1974), pp. iii-9.

127. Hay, *MVA Evaluation Report*, pp. C-4-1 to C-4-11.

128. The cost-effectiveness rating is only one assessment technique. The Fort Bragg evaluation study also includes an "integrated analysis of MVA/VOLAR action impact." See Latham, *The Modern Volunteer Army Program*, pp. C-5-1 to C-5-47.

129. Ibid., pp. 3-7.

130. Opinion Research Corporation, "Attitudes and Motivations of Young

Men toward Enlisting in the US Army" (Princeton, New Jersey, May 1971). Abstracted in W. L. Clement et al., *Evaluation of the Modern Volunteer Army [MVA] Program, Volume IV, Studies and Surveys Relating to the Modern Volunteer Army*, RAC-R-147 (McLean, Virginia: Research Analysis Corporation, November 1972), pp. 3-7.

131. HumRRO Report, "Attitudes of Youth Toward Military Service: A Comparison of Results of National Surveys Conducted in May, 1971 and November, 1971," April 1972. Abstracted in Clement, ibid., pp. 2-7 to 2-8.

132. System Development Corporation Report, "Analysis of MVA/VOLAR Actions Impact on Soldiers' Attitudes Toward the Army and on Retention," July 1972. Abstracted in Clement, ibid., p. 2-2.

133. Gary R. Nelson, "An Economic Analysis of First-Term Reenlistments in the Army, Research Paper" (Arlington, Virginia: Institute for Defense Analyses, June 1970). Abstracted in Clement, ibid., pp. 3-17 to 3-18.

134. David R. Segal, "Convergence, Commitment, and Military Compensation," paper prepared for presentation at the 70th Annual Meeting of the American Sociological Association, August 25-29, 1975, p. 4.

135. With "unit-of-choice" recruiting, recruits now have more freedom to choose what unit they want to serve with and what kind of MOS they want to train for. Furthermore, education opportunities have widened; at Fort Ord, for example, "On post education opportunities were expanded to include offerings from four colleges and universities in addition to a full range of high school subjects. For the first time, four year college and graduate programs were offered on post. At the same time, the opportunities for trainees and cadre to further their civilian education through on duty and off duty attendance at education center classes were increased and enrollment procedures in the program simplified." Soldiers also can get much of their tuition paid by the Army. See H. G. Moore, *Modern Volunteer Army, Monograph Project: Strengthening Professionalism and Improving Army Lift* (United States Army Training Center and Fort Ord, Fort Ord, California, June 1972), pp. 5-22, 5-16.

136. Segal, "Convergence, Commitment, and Military Compensation," pp. 5-14.

137. Ibid., pp. 13-14.

138. Moore, *Modern Volunteer Army, Monograph Project*; Hay, *MVA Evaluation Report*; and Latham, *The Modern Volunteer Army Program.*

139. Hay, *MVA Evaluation Report*, p. D-3-2, and Moore, *Modern Volunteer Army*, p. 5-21.

140. Moore, *Modern Volunteer Army*, pp. 5-19; see also Latham, *The Modern Volunteer Army Program*, p. 47.

141. Moore, *Modern Volunteer Army*, pp. 5-10. At Fort Benning, planners are considering eliminating coercion in fund drives and savings bonds campaigns as well as quotas for the suggestion awards program. In addition, commanders are prevented from requiring individuals to buy two sets of personal items, one for display and one for use; clerical workers are now permitted to make pen and ink changes in typewritten paperwork; soldiers no longer have to stand at attention at the beginning of each class (until a report is rendered and

they are given a command to take seats); and wives should no longer be pressured to join wives clubs and attend coffees. Latham, *The Modern Volunteer Army Program*, pp. 107-11.

142. Hay, *MVA Evaluation Report*, p. D-3-2. See also Latham, *The Modern Volunteer Army Program*, p. 45.

143. Moore, *Modern Volunteer Army*, p. 5-20. See also Latham, *The Modern Volunteer Army Program*, p. 43.

144. Moore, *Modern Volunteer Army*, pp. 3-9.

145. Hay, *MVA Evaluation Report*, pp. D-3-8 to D-3-9. The primary purpose of "family orientation" was to convince the wives that their husbands are important as individuals to the division.

146. Moore, *Modern Volunteer Army*, pp. 5-16.

147. Ibid., p. 5-21.

148. Ibid., p. 5-16.

149. Latham, *The Modern Volunteer Army Program*, p. 48, and Moore, *Modern Volunteer Army*, p. 6-26.

150. Evaluation letter by Earl K. Keesling in Hay, *MVA Evaluation Report*, p. D-5-2.

151. Hay, *MVA Evaluation Report*, p. D-3-11. According to General George S. Blanchard, commanding general of the 82d Airborne Division, "In parallel with our efforts to raise the quality of our new troopers, we are continuing an active campaign to eliminate substandard personnel, and calendar year 1971 shows a 14 percent increase in eliminations over calendar year 1970."

152. Latham, *The Modern Volunteer Army Program*, pp. 74-9. "Domestic actions were a means of presenting the Army in a favorable light before the public's eyes." These rograms were shrewdly designed: "Projects were carefully selected in order to prevent the program from becoming an extension of government welfare."

153. Moore, *Modern Volunteer Army*, p. 6-23.

154. Hay, *MVA Evaluation Report*, p. D-5-1.

155. Moore, *Modern Volunteer Army*, p. 6-2.

156. Ibid., p. 5-20.

157. Hay, *MVA Evaluation Report*, p. D-5-2.

158. Moore, *Modern Volunteer Army*, p. 6-21. Also reinstituted were pass forms and sign-out rosters in basic training.

159. U.S. Army War College, *Leadership for the 1970's* (Carlisle Barracks, Pennsylvania: U.S. Army War College, 1971).

160. Samuel H. Hays and William N. Thomas, *Taking Command: The Art and Science of Military Leadership* (Harrisburg, Pennsylvania: Stackpole Books, 1967).

161. Department of the Army, *The AWOL Soldier*. A similar version is Department of the Army, *Personnel Absences*.

162. Department of the Army, *Personnel Absences*, p. 4. See also Department of the Army, *The AWOL Soldier*, p. 9.

163. Department of the Army, *The AWOL Soldier*, pp. 10-11.

164. Military psychiatrists are one of the sources officers can rely on to help

them further understand their soldiers. General W. C. Westmoreland, the former Army Chief of Staff, was particularly energetic at incorporating the results of psychological, social psychological, and communications research, and he showed great sensitivity to what psychiatry can offer the Army. In November 1962, Westmoreland, then commandant of West Point, delivered the William C. Porter Lecture at the sixty-ninth annual meeting of the Association of Military Surgeons of the United States. In his talk, "Mental Health—An Aspect of Command," Westmoreland expressed his desire to see the role of psychiatry expand to include dealing with problems of morale, as well as "breakdowns," and he emphasized the unity that he felt psychiatrists should have with troop commanders.

> The psychiatrist who is educated and trained in the behavioral sciences may find additional work in a personnel management consultant type role. For example, he might work with personnel staff in the development of over-all policies, regulations on morale, esprit, and motivation. One of the main things a commander can do in order to utilize more fully his Mental Hygiene Staff is to bring it closer into his own headquarters and thus closer to the troops where the real problem lies. I understand that the psychiatrist has a rule of thumb in therapy that states, "you must start where the patient is." To me this seems to say that you start where the problem is. It is not at the station hospital—it is in the barracks, the ship, the shop, the unit training areas, the ranges, the troops at the front. . . .
>
> Remember your mental health people (psychiatrists, psychologists, and social workers) are a part of the command, and as such are vitally involved in the unit mission. . . . We are not operating separately—we are not in business for ourselves. . . . Your mental health staff can help the unit commander get the most efficiency out of the normal men who represent the greater part of the unit. . . . Those of you schooled in the medical science of human behavior can help the commander get rid of the few abnormal men that the unit cannot use. . . . The psychiatrist can help the commander learn how to tell the difference between normal and abnormal behavior. . . . You can all sell the idea that mental health services can help men accomplish their part of the unit mission. . . . Your psychiatrists should be encouraged to socialize every opportunity they get with the commander, the lower unit commanders and the other members of the staff. Let them see he is not the "weirdo" the comic books sometimes lead us to believe. [W. C. Westmoreland, "Mental Health—An Aspect of Command," *Military Medicine*, March 1963, pp. 211-213. Quoted by permission of publisher.]

Psychiatrists can assist commanding officers in combat situations. They can help them anticipate increases in psychiatric casualties—which tend to occur just before units are moved into the field and just after they return. They can also identify problem soldiers, such as high-school dropouts, "short timers," and those who are not readily assimilable into a unit (such as foreign soldiers during the Korean War). Psychiatrists can use their patients as a guide to advise commanders about unit morale. This function is called "primary prevention" of psychiatric casualties. See Douglas R. Bey, "Division Psychiatry in Viet Nam," *American Journal of Psychiatry* 127 (August 1970): 148-49.

165. Seminars are also useful in "exposing unproductive social attitudes" and continually treating them. Latham, *The Modern Volunteer Army Program*, p. 38.

166. Department of the Army, *Improving Race Relations in the Army: Handbook for Leaders*, PAM 600-16 (Washington, D.C.: Headquarters, Department of the Army, June 1973).

167. Hay, *MVA Evaluation Report*. See Tab D. "Commander's Evaluation of the MVA Program."

168. Ibid., p. D-7-1.

169. Ibid., p. D-5-1. This problem of removing the "traditional tools of NCO authority" is a serious concern and is frequently mentioned in discussions of the MVA. For example, "The platoon sergeant no longer was the recommender of class A passes, and thus his disapproval was no longer a threat to the platoon members. Many platoon NCO's thought themselves without leverage for correcting minor infractions of discipline. Other than nonjudicial punishment, there seemed to be little left but counseling as a tool for correcting substandard appearance, punctuality, or responsiveness. In short, the NCO had the feeling that the rug had been pulled out from under him." Latham, *The Modern Volunteer Army Program*, p. 53.

170. Hay, *MVA Evaluation Report*, p. D-6-15.

171. Ibid., p. D-6-14.

172. Ibid., p. D-6-8.

173. Ibid., p. D-4-2.

174. Ibid., p. D-6-9.

175. Ibid., p. D-7-2.

176. Ibid., p. D-6-16.

177. Latham, *The Modern Volunteer Army Program*.

178. Even professional paternalists' standards frequently go unmet by officers at various levels according to a discussion of "shortfall" (falling short of standards). U.S. Army War College, *Leadership for the 1970's*.

179. Latham, *The Modern Volunteer Army Program*, pp. 138-39.

180. Segal, "Convergence, Commitment, and Military Compensation," p. 13.

181. Moore, *Modern Volunteer Army*, pp. 3-10 to 3-18.

182. Ibid., p. 3-11.

183. Ibid., p. 3-9. This also included the establishment of company trainee councils, which were conceived as a means by which a trainee could communicate with a company commander.

184. Ibid., p. 3-14.

185. Ibid., p. 3-12.

186. Ibid.

187. Ibid., p. 3-13.

188. Ibid., p. 3-14.

189. Ibid., pp. 3-14, 4-21.
190. Ibid., p. 1-19.
191. Ibid., p. 2-11.
192. Ibid., p. 4-29.
193. Ibid., p. 6-15.
194. Ibid., pp. 3-11, 3-16, 3-17.
195. Ibid., pp. 6-20 to 6-21.
196. Ibid., p. 3-18.
197. John H. Faris, "The Impact of Basic Combat Training: The Role of the Drill Sergeant in the All-Volunteer Army," *Armed Forces and Society* 2 (Fall 1975): 115-127.
198. See Thomas T. Jones, "Systems Analysis Can Help the Small-Unit Commander," *ARMY* 20 (June 1970): 56-57.
199. Lynn D. Smith, "Facts, Not Opinions," *ARMY* 19 (December 1969): 24-31.
200. Eric C. Ludvigsen, "Lifting the Fog of War," *ARMY* 22 (July 1972): 29-34.
201. S. L. A. Marshall, *Men Against Fire: The Problem of Battle Command in Future War* (New York: William Morrow & Co., 1966).
202. See Hamilton Howze, "35 Years," *ARMY* 16 (April 1966): 27-44.
203. A. E. Ashworth, "The Sociology of Trench Warfare 1914-1918," *British Journal of Sociology* 19 (December 1968): 407-23.
204. For an example of the resistance of some Army officers to this new form of warfare, see John C. Burney, Jr., "Yessir, Computer, Sir!" *ARMY* 19 (September 1969).
205. This example is drawn from a description provided by Robert Boguslaw and Elias H. Porter in their article, "Team Functions and Training," in *Psychological Principles in System Development*, ed. Robert M. Gagne (New York: Holt, Rinehart & Winston, 1965), pp. 387-418.
206. Although the Rand example is an application of simulated systems training for teams whose main function is the handling and interpreting of information (perhaps the most common use), there are other possible applications. See for some current applications of systems design and simulation, with artillery, missiles, and field command decision making: Robert Sadacca, "Information Processing in Advanced Computerized Surveillance Systems," *Report of the Twelfth Annual U.S. Army Human Factors Research and Development Conference* (Fort Benning, Georgia: U.S. Army Infantry Center, October 1966), pp. 157-67; John A. Ely, "Systems Development and Research Needs—Human Factors in ADSAF Design," *Report of the Thirteenth Annual U.S. Army Human Factors Research and Development Conference* (Fort Monmouth, New Jersey, October 1967), pp. 97-102; and Ludvigsen, "Lifting the Fog of War," pp. 28-34. For applications with riflemen and machine-gun squads and helicopters, see Smith, "Facts, Not Opinions," pp. 24-31. For uses with tanks and again missiles, see John T. Burke, "Machines Don't Fight," *ARMY* 22 (August 1972): 24-31. For a general review of the operation and areas of experimentation of the Army's Combat Developments Command Experimentation

Command, see John H. Hoye, "Introduction to U.S. Army CDCEC," *Report of the Fifteenth Annual U.S. Army Human Factors Research and Development Conference* (Fort Ord, November 1969), pp. 205-16; and Warren F. Sutherland, "Instrumentation of U.S. Army CDCEC," *Report of the Fifteenth Annual U.S. Army Human Factors Research and Development Conference* (Fort Ord, November 1969), pp. 217-31.

207. Harry H. Harman, "Designing and Implementing the System Model," in *Psychological Research in National Defense Today*, ed. J. E. Uhlaner (Washington, D.C.: U.S. Army Behavioral Science Research Laboratory, 1967), pp. 287-303.

208. Ibid.

209. William C. Biel, "Planning for Team Training in the System," in *Psychological Research in National Defense Today*, ed. Uhlaner, pp. 279-86.

210. Robert Blauner, *Alienation and Freedom: The Factory Worker and His Industry* (Chicago: University of Chicago Press, 1964).

5

Psychiatry in War and Peace

There are, of course, many soldiers who are not controlled by the collective techniques analyzed in the last three chapters. These men are processed by a variety of deviance-controlling sectors, including military psychiatry, the military justice system, and military prisons. Although there are differences in histories and methods among the deviance-controlling sectors, the trends toward rationalization, co-optation, and civilianization (including a reliance of behavioral scientific experts) appear to underlie these parts of the Army as well.

In my view, two general principles underlie modern methods of handling deviance within the Army. One is to preserve manpower by returning as many deviant soldiers as possible to duty. This requires some transformation of these soldiers' deviant responses as well as certain adaptations on the Army's part. But there are some soldiers whom the Army cannot reintegrate under any conditions, and this fact suggests the second principle: these soldiers must be punished or expelled from the Army in such a way as to maintain the legitimacy of the Army in other soldiers' (and civilians') eyes. The balance between expulsion (through discharges or incarcerations) and resocialization (or therapy) depends on the manpower needs of the Army. During wartime or other manpower shortages, the Army will refuse to allow recalcitrant soldiers to leave the Army and will put pressures on its deviance-control sectors to keep these soldiers in active duty. In this chapter, I will argue that psychiatrists in garrison situations as well as those who deal with combat neuropsychiatric casualties have a strong tendency to define as ill as few soldiers as possible so the Army will not lose manpower.[1]

The psychiatrist's role in garrison situations requires him to assess GIs for the possible presence of mental illness for administrative discharge and to provide certification in court as to an accused soldier's sanity (and ability to stand trial).[2] During the Vietnam War there was considerable pressure to prevent GIs from getting out of the Army (both in combat and in garrison) for psychiatric reasons because the potential for great losses of manpower would be too great. Similarly, a commander bringing charges against a defiant GI is likely to resent a psychiatrist's giving the accused a mentally ill label because the soldier would be able to evade trial and punishment.[3] These pressures are transmitted to the psychiatrist, and the result is a minimal tendency to define a GI as mentally ill. Daniels cites an estimate that only two in 1,000 referrals are diagnosed as mentally ill.[4]

Why would a psychiatrist succumb to these organizational pressures? Wouldn't one expect his professionalism to be more durable and well defined than that of other "servants of power" (such as chaplains, psychologists, social workers, and sociologists)? There are several explanations for the accommodations that many psychiatrists make to military requirements.

To begin with, the structure of the psychiatrist's tasks makes long-term therapy impossible. The Army places so many demands on a psychiatrist's time that he cannot function in the therapy role for which he may have been trained as a civilian.[5] A visit and a diagnosis usually take less than fifteen minutes.[6] The psychiatrist may be called out on special assignments, or may be transferred, which would cause appointments to be juggled.[7] Patients similarly have demands on their time each day and are also likely to be transferred. A military psychiatrist at a stateside base reported in an interview that if the Army gave him the opportunity, he could easily cure, within a few weeks, frequent complaints among combat veterans, such as nervousness, insomnia, violent overreactions, and nightmares, all of which arose from guilt from what they had seen and done in combat. He asserted that this kind of therapy is discouraged by the Army and is rarely accomplished, or even attempted, in garrison settings. This may perhaps be as much because of organizational limitations (such as the Army's making no effort to set up treatment programs) as the view that mental symptoms are at best transient[8] and at worst evidence of malingering.[9]

Another source of difficulty is the fact that military psychiatrists do not enjoy the close relationship with their patients that most civilian psychiatrists do. Their communications are not privileged, and what a soldier tells a psychiatrist may be held against him in court.[10] For example, during the Vietnam War many symptoms that soldiers complained of were related to combat violence and atrocities or violent attitudes toward superior officers. If a soldier troubled in this way went to a psychiatrist to talk about his work problems, one of two conditions would have to prevail for psychotherapy to continue: either the psychiatrist would have to (illegally) tell the soldier he would not reveal or record anything that occurred in interviews, or the soldier would have to be able to withhold his "illegal" thoughts or acts from his conversation with the psychiatrist.[11] Ungerleider reports that few soldiers go to mental-hygiene clinics on their own initiative for relief of symptoms.[12] The great majority of referrals come through line officers or from administrative reasons.[13]

During the Vietnam War with the accompanying widespread anti-war sentiment among soldiers, how would a liberal, anti-war psychiatrist have resolved the role conflicts inherent in his position as an "internal pacification officer"?[14] There are probably as many resolutions as there are psychiatrists, but I think the response of one politically liberal psychiatrist is instructive. In 1970, I asked him if he would support resisters in the Army. Surprisingly, he said it never was a problem for him because he did not think there were any. This psychiatrist, however, held rather narrow standards of what constituted resistance; to him, a definition seemed to require a commitment to pacifism or some other "ism" and therefore had to be articulated, explained, and maybe even justified in philosophical terms. His view restricts the term *resistance* to those who can speak in middle-class terms, particularly college-educated terms.

The majority of resisters, however, are from working-class and lower-class backgrounds. If not from an urban ghetto or industrial section of a city, they are from some small town. They resist the Army as they have always resisted oppression: immediately, physically, and nonideologically. If court-martialed, they will not likely be accused of illegal distribution of a newspaper, or of uttering disloyal statements but rather be accused of going AWOL, disrespect toward an officer, refusal of a direct order, and similar disciplinary infractions. They do not have an articulate explanation for their resistance; they do not have an articulate explanation about most things, for that matter. They are not adapted to living in bureaucratic societies, and they do not comprehend bureaucratic rationality; but what they do understand of bureaucracy they immediately dislike. They have a different kind of rationality.

Thus this psychiatrist did not share this group's view of the world and rationality. Their inability to adapt to the institution seemed to this specialist to be simply stupidity. (This lack of sympathy with lower-class soldiers was shared by many college-educated enlisted men who themselves resisted the Army by organizing and writing anti-war newspapers.)

This value for manipulating bureaucracies even came down to manipulating the psychiatrist. This psychiatrist had some contempt for soldiers he thought were too inept to know how to manipulate him properly. According to the psychiatrist, one proper way might be a forthright request to get him out of the Army.[15] Another way might be a really effective job of acting. But the middle position, that of feigning psychiatric symptoms poorly so that the psychiatrist recognizes it as a blatant "put-on," causes a difficult interactive situation. If the psychiatrist went along with the act, he would look like a fool. The very attempt, therefore, is an insult to his own competence. This psychiatrist interviewee said he might respond to this ploy by using the psychiatric technique of giving the soldier "permission" to go insane—daring him to do it, knowing he could not.

This kind of resister, with his minimal experience with bureaucracies, does not understand the rationality of his psychiatrist. If he had more experience, he would know that he must allow the psychiatrist to save face. He cannot let the psychiatrist look incompetent or appear to be a "fall guy." And if he wants to be political and open about it, he must play on the psychiatrist's liberal, political conscience and let him think he is doing a legitimate or sanctified act, that is, "resisting the war machine."

This whole problem of incompatibility is a class phenomenon. The two classes do not appreciate each other's rationalities, and they do not appreciate each other's peculiar weaknesses. The Army is the overall winner in this one of many splits and antagonisms, in spite of the fact that it is probably not aware of the whole mechanism. It should be pointed out that while this class incompatibility may exist between resisters and various professionals (such as lawyers) in the Army, it was a rare psychiatrist who would have considered resisting the Army and the Vietnam War by helping GIs to escape.

If need be, such liberal (usually drafted) psychiatrists can be controlled by putting pressure on their superior medical officers (rather than on them directly). The superior medical officer, almost always a career officer in the Army, is dependent on efficiency reports for his promotions. Senior medical officers function more as administrators than as physicians. The result is that the administrator's main contact, and thus his reference group, is with senior line officers who are strongly disposed to measure competence in terms of quick recoveries and unfilled wards. Additionally, high sick-call rates reflect badly on the physician, making him appear too lenient in his definition of illness.[16]

Daniels argues that military psychiatrists' definition of what constitutes mental illness has adapted to the organizational needs of the military.[17] As a result, there is a tendency to stress adjustment rather than introspection or self-awareness. There is also a tendency to view adaptability as both a voluntary act of the soldier and a result of psychiatrist's denial of symptoms.[18]

This approach to mental disorders is transmitted to individual line officers. Some of my interviewees have asserted that their commanding officers refer soldiers whom they do not know how to handle ("troublemakers," for example) to the psychiatrist. The psychiatrist typically will simply send them back to their unit after minimal counseling. Some psychiatrists tell commanding officers not to refer them *any* mental cases unless they want to (1) discharge the soldier under AR 635-212 (unfitness and unsuitability) or 635-89 (homosexuality), or (2) court-martial him and require certification of sanity, or (3) evaluate him for security clearance.[19] In this manner, psychiatrists and line officers can cooperate in denying illness (and treatment) except in those cases where they want to get rid of the soldier.[20]

Many of these intractable—or faint-hearted—soldiers are, of course, not mentally ill. But the question comes to mind, how can this denial of symptoms and refusal to engage in serious therapy be extended to combat disorders? Let us look at the kinds of prevention and treatment that Army psychiatrists offered during the Vietnam War.

According to Glass and others, the prevention of psychiatric casualties can be divided into three approaches or levels.[21] "Primary prevention" consists of attempts to influence living, working, or fighting conditions to minimize the likelihood of disabling maladjustment and is a recognition of various influences upon morale and the experience of combat.[22] "Secondary prevention" is the early recognition and prompt management of emotional or behavioral problems that some individuals might develop.[23] This is carried out on an out-patient basis, so the individual remains a member of his unit. "Tertiary prevention" is used for persistent and severe mental disorders that require hospitalization.[24] Here, milieu therapy is the main therapeutic tool.[25] As in secondary prevention, this technique is oriented to rehabilitation back into military duty and the reduction of chronic disability.[26]

The secondary prevention level is the most relevant in a discussion of how psychiatrists prevent soldiers from escaping combat. This approach is based on years of experience of the many problems that arose from hospitalizing soldiers in wards far from the fighting areas.[27] It was discovered that the "fixing" of psychiatric symptoms (or their becoming permanent, like an image on a photographic plate) would occur less frequently if the soldier were treated as close as possible to his own unit.[28] This allows other, functioning, soldiers to exert a social control function over the soldier-patient.

A second principle is one in which the soldier is not allowed to develop an ill role by being treated as soon as possible after he develops the incapacitating symptoms. The Army's use of Medevac helicopters can make this factor one of minutes. A third principle is to deny the seriousness of the response by the psychiatrist's communication of his expectation that the soldier will respond favorably and return to duty within a short time. These three principles have been termed *immediacy*, *proximity*, and *expectancy*."[29]

Since the Korean War, the Army has been placing psychiatrists at the division level, which keeps them closer to the front.[30] In 1968 and 1969 there were seven infantry divisions in Vietnam. To each division, comprising around 18,000 men, was assigned a psychiatrist and his staff, which included a social work officer and six to eight medical corpsmen who were trained in psychiatric social work.[31] The division psychiatrist and the social work officer usually operated from the division's base camp, while most of the corpsmen were located at forward base camps that were closer to actual areas of fighting.

The corpsmen themselves treated most of the less serious cases of psychiatric (combat) breakdown.[32] If they could not handle a case in a matter of hours, the patient would be sent back to the division psychiatrist, who treated the soldier but on an out-patient basis.[33] If the division psychiatrist decided that the soldier-patient was seriously ill or psychotic and could not be treated on such a casual basis, he sent this individual to a hospital.[34]

As the following example demonstrates, the enlisted medical corpsmen were able to treat what would appear to be debilitating psychiatric illnesses with surprising ease and swiftness:

> Example 1. An infantry man was brought by dust-off (medical evacuation) helicopter to one of the division's

clearing stations with symptoms of combat exhaustion. He complained of nightmares in which he saw eyes coming closer and closer to him. When the eyes were upon him a gun pointed at him appeared and he would awaken in a cold sweat. He would then force himself to think out the end of the dream in which he would get his weapon or grenade and destroy the frightening apparition. Specialist A talked with the soldier and learned that he had previously been in an ambush patrol and had been wounded. The infantryman related that he had found himself in close proximity to the enemy, "so close I could see the whites of their eyes," but had remained cool at the time and radioed for help. His report resulted in his being discovered and wounded before assistance arrived. As he recovered from the injury, he became increasingly troubled by his nightmare. He began to have trouble falling asleep, lost his appetite, and was unable to concentrate.

The infantryman was extremely apprehensive about returning to the field. Specialist A consulted with a company physician who, as a result, hospitalized the soldier for 24 hours and ordered tranquilizing medication (100 mg. of chlorpromazine four times daily). The specialist told his patient he had observed that as his physical wound healed his psychological problems seemed to increase. He pointed out that the dreams were probably the soldier's way of gradually working out his anxiety about his stressful experience, which would have immobilized him had he experienced it at the time of the incident. Specialist A observed that just as the infantryman had done the right thing during the crisis and at the end of the dream, he could be assured that he would do the right thing in future times of stress. The infantryman went back to the field, and subsequent follow-up from his unit indicates he has been on patrol and is functioning effectively.

Example 2. Another example of the ingenuity of the technicians was demonstrated by Specialist B, who evaluated and treated a new man in the field unit who had developed conversion symptoms in his first fire fight. The

> patient was brought to the clearing station mute and seemingly oblivious to his surroundings. Specialist B enlisted the assistance of a wounded combat veteran on the ward, who talked to the patient about his own apprehension with regard to coming to Viet Nam and going into the field. The technician then discussed the situation with the man's unit, which sent two enlisted men from its squad to express their concern about his welfare and further reassure him about their having experienced similar feelings in their first contact with the enemy. The patient asked Specialist B for permission to return with his fellow squad members to the unit. Follow-up indicates that he has functioned effectively in his unit since this time.[35]

Medical corpsmen during the Vietnam War did not undergo extensive training in the recognition and treatment of psychiatric disorders.[36] They might thus be expected to have been less sensitive to serious mental problems underlying certain symptoms. The fact that they were enlisted men themselves puts them in a position closer to that of the soldier-patient. Some of the small-group expectations of the soldier-patient's unit would be reflected in the enlisted corpsmen's own attitudes. The corpsmen were likely to view neuropsychiatric casualties as normal reactions to combat rather than as mental aberrations.[37]

This use of medical corpsmen appears to communicate certain things to the soldier-patient and his peers. For example, the fact that he is being treated by enlisted corpsmen rather than by a psychiatrist suggests that neither the Army nor the psychiatrist takes very seriously the soldier's "psychotic" behavior. If the corpsmen do not view the soldier-patient as seriously ill, then the patient should similarly not view himself as ill.

Even when division psychiatrists saw these patients, they did not carry out lengthy therapy.[38] Their direct services were limited mainly to crisis intervention and evaluation,[39] and their inpatient treatment consisted mostly of drugging the soldier to sleep for a day or so, followed by fairly brief consultation.[40] My belief is that the brief treatment and quick reappearance in the company of a psychiatric case communicates to other soldiers that they will not be able to use psychiatric symptoms as a way out of the Army. They may learn that if the Army will not take their problems very seriously, there is no point in seeking treatment. According to this view, this phenomenon of the quick reappearance of the GI and the cursory treatment that he receives is probably the most important explanation for the low psychiatric casualty rate of the Vietnam War.

Even at the tertiary level, diagnosis and treatment seem to have been casual and brief. During the Vietnam War, tertiary treatment, or more extended clinical psychiatry, was carried out by two neuropsychiatric teams.[41] One team operated a ward in the northern half of the republic of Vietnam and the other served the southern half. These teams consisted of three to five psychiatrists, a neurologist, a clinical psychologist, two social work officers, a psychiatric nurse, and twenty to thirty enlisted corpsmen.[42] The enlisted corpsmen worked either in ward management or in clinic work, such as taking social histories and administering psychological tests. A few other Army hospitals in Vietnam had single-staff psychiatrists who might have admitted patients to their medical wards for a week or so, but they too referred patients to the neuropsychiatric teams. The psychiatric wards carried out "intensive," though brief, treatment of psychiatric cases, maintaining the principles of immediacy, proximity, and expectancy.[43]

The approach of military psychiatrists was essentially "oriented toward intervention in the interpersonal dimension of patients' problems."[44] Like psychiatrists in garrison, they were concerned with returning the patient to duty and were thus not particularly concerned with "underlying internal emotional conflicts,"[45] which would take "much longer periods of time to resolve."[46]

Milieu therapy has the dual advantage of treating interpersonal problems as well as treating several patients at once. Group norms are mobilized in channeling behavior into ways that the Army can use. All ward patients, even the most ill, got up together and dressed and cleaned up their ward together.[47] The group decided about each patient's privilege status (such as freedom to go off the ward) and went to group therapy together five days a week.[48] Thus, the objective was to use a "highly structured program geared toward much group activity" while still trying to increase "individual patient responsibility."[49] The underlying assumption of this treatment practice seemed to be that even seriously disturbed soldiers can be effective individuals in a structured atmosphere, hence should also be able to function well after being returned to duty.[50]

The following examples, including the psychiatrist's comments, help to convey an idea of problems that were handled at this level as well as the techniques for handling them.

> Case 1. Moderately severe combat exhaustion. A 21-year-old rifleman was flown directly to the hospital from an area of fighting by a helicopter ambulance. No information accompanied him, he had no identifying tags on his uniform, and he was so completely covered with mud that a physical description of his features was not possible. His hands had been tied behind him for the flight, and he had a wild, wide-eyed look as he cowered in a corner of the emergency room, glancing furtively to all sides, cringing and startling at the least noise. He was mute, although once he forced out a whispered "VC" and tried to mouth other words without success. He seemed terrified. Although people could approach him, he appeared oblivious to their presence. No manner of reassurance or direct order achieved either a verbal response or any other interaction from him.
>
> His hands were untied, after which he would hold an imaginary rifle in readiness whenever he heard a helicopter overhead or an unexpected noise. The corpsmen led him to the psychiatric ward, took him to a shower, and offered him a meal; he ate very little. He began to move a little more freely but still offered no information.
>
> He was then given 100 mg. of chlorpromazine (Thorazine) orally; this dose was repeated hourly until he fell asleep. He was kept asleep in this manner for approximately 40 hours. After that he was allowed to waken, the medication was discontinued, and he was mobilized rapidly in the ward milieu. Although dazed and subdued upon awaken-

ing, his response in the ward milieu was dramatic. This was aided by the presence of a friend from his platoon in an adjoining ward, who helped by filling in parts of the story that the patient could not recall. The patient was an infantryman whose symptoms had developed on a day when his platoon had been caught in an ambush and then was overrun by the enemy. He was one of three who survived after being pinned down by enemy fire for 12 hours. His friend told him that toward the end of that time he had developed a crazed expression and had tried to run from his hiding place. He was pulled back to safety and remained there until the helicopter arrived and flew him to the hospital.

Within 72 hours after his admission the patient was alert, oriented, responsive, and active—still a little tense but ready to return to duty. He was sent back to duty on his third hospital day and never seen again at our facility. It should be noted that he had no history of similar symptoms or emotional disorder.

[Psychiatrist's] Comment: One should note the use of chlorpromazine for sleep and the value of sleep (or perhaps chlorpromazine-induced sleep) as restitutive therapy in people who have been under great physical and emotional strain. Patients with combat exhaustion are mobilized for return to duty very rapidly, it is well known that the longer one waits, the harder it is for men to accept the idea of going back into life threatening situations.

Case 2. Probable marijuana-induced psychotic episode. A 26-year-old Negro boat operator with three and a half months in Viet Nam was referred to the neuropsychiatry team by his dispensary physician because of violent behavior and inappropriate speech that morning. The referring note indicated that this soldier had presented behavioral problems in his unit previously. At the time of his admission no meaningful history could be obtained from him. Mental status exam revealed an agitated, unshaven man whose speech was vague and disjointed, with markedly loosened associations. His attention span, recall, and orientation were severely impaired. He was posturing, seemingly with religious connotation, frequently staring heavenward and acknowledging direct communication with God. He was extremely suspicious, with apparent ideas of reference and influence, and struck the psychiatrist when he was being sedated with intramuscular medication, he thought an experiment was being performed on him.

The patient was given a 48-hour course of sleep therapy with chlorpromazine in the manner indicated in case 1, except that the drug was administered intramuscularly until he agreed to take it orally. Following this his agitation, unusual behavior, belligerence, posturing, and manifest paranoid ideation abated markedly. The chlorpromazine was discontinued and he was placed on trifluoperazine (Stelazine) and mobilized in the ward milieu. Over the next several days he was somewhat vague at times and always a bit tense; he claimed that this was his usual emotional state.

An anamnesis taken at that time revealed a history of behavioral problems during his growing years including difficulties with civilian authorities in his preservice life. He denied previous psychiatric hospitalization or psychotic symptomatology. When questioned about the use of drugs and specifically about the use of marijuana prior to the onset of his symptoms, he initially denied this but subsequently acknowledged it in a veiled manner. His condition remained unchanged over the next few days. He was discharged to duty on his fifth hospital day with instructions to take 10 mg. of trifluoperazine, plus trihexphenidil (Artane), four times daily for approximately two weeks.

[Psychiatrist's] Comment: Brief psychotic episodes, usually with predominantly paranoid symptoms, are a syndrome that psychiatrists and other physicians in Viet Nam have come to associate with marijuana usage there, although such syndromes are reported only infrequently with marijuana usage in the United States. The relative incidence of such reactions compared with the incidence of marijuana usage in Viet Nam is unknown, and a definite, clinically proven relationship between marijuana usage and psychosis has not been documented by a research protocol there. Nevertheless, any unusual symptom complex developing in previously healthy (though often character-disordered) men has come to make physicians in Viet Nam strongly suspect marijuana usage.

Case 3. Anxiety reaction in a recent arrival. A 20-year-old private, an artillery observer with six months of active duty service, was referred by his division psychiatrist during his first week in Viet Nam following an overnight admission at the small division hospital for an anxiety reaction. On admission to the psychiatry ward the youthful-looking soldier was observed to be tremulous, hyperventilating, to clutch himself and rock back and forth, and to become tearful and uncommunicative. This behavior abated with a firm approach by the interviewer. The patient communicated the following history: He had been a tense and anxious person for years, but these traits had been more prominent since he entered the service. Particularly since preparing for his tour in Viet Nam he had been aware of tremulousness, nervousness, and phobic symptoms, as well as obsessional-type thoughts and nightmares about his mother, fiancee, and brother coming to horrible violent deaths. He yearned for them, fearful of the separation. During his Army training, these symptoms had been eased by visits from his mother. However, during the week since his arrival in Viet Nam, when he was waiting to be assigned and was essentially unoccupied, the symptoms exacerbated markedly and he began to develop fearful suicidal ideas. He sought psychiatric help.

Anamnestic data revealed that he was the middle of three children raised by a nervous, histrionic mother and a much-loved stepfather. From the age of 13 he had harbored strong, unrealistic feelings of guilt and responsibility for the stepfather's accidental death and his mother's presumed near-death when she slashed her wrists after the funeral. Afterwards he became a model, compliant lad and never again experienced anger—only "nervousness" at times when anger would be appropriate. Associating to more recent events, he noted that in the setting of his impending assignment to Viet Nam, his mother's behavior had been reminiscent of the way she had shaken and trembled at the stepfather's funeral before she "went out of her mind" and cut her wrists.

This material gave rise to a working psychodynamic formulation that his concerns were like those of the phobic patient with separation anxiety who could not let persons toward whom he felt much unconscious rage out of his sight for fear that they would die because of his own hostile impulses.

During the first day of the patient's hospitalization these underlying issues were clarified with him as he experienced anxiety in the psychiatrist's office. His feelings and the issues were related both to his condition at the time of the interview and to similar experiences of anxiety in the past. Following this interview he was worked with intensively in the ward milieu. After about a day and a half of relative apathy and social isolation he began to respond rapidly to the milieu and thereafter maintained himself well. He continued to experience some anxiety but reported spontaneously that its quality as well as his ability to cope with it had changed. He still had some difficulty sleeping but no longer worried about this. He was eager to return to duty. Occasional sleeping pills were the only medications utilized during his hospitalization. He was returned to duty on the fourth hospital day after arrangements had been made with the division psychiatrist for him to be assigned to a unit without further delay.

[Psychiatrist's] Comment: Although this case might have been managed successfully by milieu therapy alone, it is one in which the intrapsychic components seemed prominent enough in the man's incapacitation to warrant the use of individual psychotherapy aimed at clarifying aspects of internal emotional conflicts in an effort to impart some insight to enhance the patient's capacity to tolerate anxiety. This case was included as a contrast to the previous two to

> illustrate the distinction between intervention aimed at intrapsychic rather than the interpersonal dimensions of a man's illness. In addition, it illustrates two other phenomena—the readiness with which patients under stress will share and associate meaningfully if urged to do so, and the use of an insight-clarification technique in a somewhat didactic manner to teach a patient about his symptoms as a way of helping him become less frightened and consequently less influenced by them.[51]

Apparently, even at the tertiary level, treatment is remarkably brief and appears to be singularly oriented to returning the soldier to duty. Case three is somewhat unusual in that the soldier himself sought psychiatric help. However, while this young man might have been able to benefit from some in-depth psychoanalysis, it is not clear that he received it. Simply telling a patient what the sources of his problems are is not the same as having him incorporate that explanation and truly understand it.

Treatment in cases one and two seems to rely heavily on drugs. These drugs have had a significant effect in reducing the psychiatric casualty rate and are especially effective for those psychiatric casualties resulting from shock and exhaustion. (I would expect the reliance on various mind-affecting drugs to increase in the future, perhaps to be included in training to enhance learning.)

Milieu therapy, on the other hand, is of particular value in handling problems of interpersonal adjustment, such as hating Army life.[52] Psychiatrists have been influenced by small-group cohesion-building techniques and effective leadership techniques that the Army itself has generated, and they have combined these approaches with research from their own professional fields. Military psychiatrists are trained in community psychiatry by the Army as residents.[53] Residents are given some specific knowledge of Army customs and procedures, and they are introduced to some of the operations in a military post.[54] Medical corpsmen are also trained both as military personnel and as paramedical personnel. The result, milieu and group therapy, is a collectively oriented treatment in which the GI cannot help but feel that he is important to the military psychiatrist, and thus to the Army, only as a soldier, not as an individual.

I have argued in this chapter that military psychiatrists tend to refuse to define soldiers' aberrant behavior as psychiatric casualties or mental illness. In terms of the Army's overall rate of psychiatric casualties, these efforts have been very effective. Neuropsychiatric casualties dropped from an all-time high in World War II to a moderate level in the Korean War and finally to a surprisingly low level during the Vietnam War.[55]

This trend toward much lower psychiatric casualty rates is particularly interesting in light of many forces that would suggest the opposite. For example, morale among soldiers has been steadily dropping at least since World War II. The strong unit solidarity[56] that characterized that war degenerated to dyadic buddy relations during the Korean War[57] and then to a rather atomized, almost utilitarian, kind of relationship among combat soldiers in the Vietnam War.[58] The Vietnam War was, of course, the most unpopular war the United States has carried out in recent years, and there was much more anti-Army and anti-war resistance of Vietnam-era soldiers than during previous, recent wars. It can also be assumed that contemporary soldiers have a greater knowledge of mental illness that could contribute to their skill in feigning mental illness in order to get out of combat. All these lines of evidence would suggest a high psychiatric casualty rate for the Vietnam War.[59]

In part, the recent lowering of the psychiatric casualty rate is related to the shift away from policies used in World War II and earlier. The Army relied heavily on screening out potential psychiatric cases prior to induction and seemed to neglect some of the conditions of combat and the organizational situations generally.[60] Toward the end of World War II, it was discovered that unit morale, length of combat experience, leadership, and even training had an effect on the psychiatric casualty rate.[61] Since the end of World War II, these factors have been somewhat altered by the use of a shorter tour of duty, the rotation system, and more frequent rest and recreation.[62]

But the most important change is in methods of handling

psychiatric disorders after they arise. In World War I and In World War II, soldiers were treated in hospital wards far removed from combat areas, and often they never returned to their unit. Clearly, significant changes have been made in these methods of treatment.

The current treatment style is a result of the discovery of the importance of labeling (or more accurately, the refusal to label) small-group normative pulls (and exploiting them by treating soldiers close to the front) and the tendency for soldiers to get attached to their symptoms (preventable by the onset of treatment immediately after symptoms appear). And finally, the Army makes it apparent to soldiers that they will not be able to avoid combat by becoming neuropsychiatric casualties.

The Army can maintain its legitimacy as a responsible and paternalistic organization by having psychiatrists in garrison and in combat. It can simultaneously maintain its manpower level by structuring the situation in such a way that the psychiatrists do not detract from the numbers of soldiers that can be committed to combat and combat support. In this way, the Army can refuse to recognize mental problems in the context of a modern society that is very aware of the reality of mental illness. Thus the paradox can be explained that, in combat and in garrison, psychiatry functions best for the Army when it does not do in-depth therapy at all.

NOTES

1. The motto of the medical corps, "to conserve fighting strength," appears to be a guide for the Army psychiatrist and is frequently mentioned in their articles. See J. Thomas Ungerleider, "The Army, the Soldier and the Psychiatrist," *American Journal of Psychiatry* 114 (March 1963): 875; Donald B. Peterson, "Discussion" of "Army Psychiatry in the Mid-60s" by William J. Tiffany and William S. Allerton, *American Journal of Psychiatry* 123 (January 1967): 819; and H. Spencer Bloch, "Army Clinical Psychiatry in the Combat Zone—1967-1968," *American Journal of Psychiatry* 126 (September 1969): 289. Ungerleider commented on the oft-repeated medical corps phrase, "You are an [Army] officer first and a doctor second," and added, "and a psychiatrist third" (brackets in the original).

2. Arlene K. Daniels, "The Captive Professional: Bureaucratic Limitations in the Practice of Military Psychiatry," *Journal of Health and Social Behavior* 10 (December 1969): 258-60. See also Martin B. Giffen and Herbert Kritzer, "An Aid to the Psychiatrist in Military Forensic Medicine," *Military Medicine* (November 1961): 838-41; Robert L. Pettera, "Mental Health in Combat," *Military Review* (March 1971): 74-77; Arlene K. Daniels, "Military Psychiatry: The Emergence of a Subspecialty," in *Medical Men and Their Work*, ed. Eliot Friedson and Judith Lorber (Chicago: Aldine-Atherton, 1972), pp. 145-62; and Roy E. Clausen, Jr., and Arlene K. Daniels, "Role Conflicts and Their Ideological Resolution in Military Psychiatric Practice," *American Journal of Psychiatry* 123 (September 1966): 280-87.

3. See Daniels, "The Captive Professional," pp. 260-61. Daniels observed that a conscientious objector may encounter more serious disciplinary measures if a psychiatrist labels him "NPD" (no psychiatric disease).

4. Daniels cited E. L. Maillet, "A Study of the Readiness of Troop Commanders to Use the Services of the Army Mental Hygiene Consultation Service" (D.S.W. diss., Catholic University of America, 1966), p. 168. See Daniels, "Military Psychiatry," p. 161.

5. Clausen and Daniels, "Role Conflicts and Their Ideological Resolution," p. 281. Clausen and Daniels mentioned that in addition to the lack of time available to the psychiatrist, the psychiatrist must delegate a considerable amount of authority to his psychiatric team.

6. Daniels, "Military Psychiatry," p. 153.

7. Ungerleider, "The Army, the Soldier and the Psychiatrist," p. 876. Daniels argues that psychiatric therapy in the sense of a series of vis-à-vis sessions in a private office is largely confined to major military medical centers and is practiced by residents as part of their training. See Daniels, "Military Psychiatry," p. 156.

8. Arnold Rose, "Conscious Reactions Associated with Neuropsychiatric Breakdown in Combat," *Psychiatry* 19 (February 1956): 87-94. See also Arnold Rose, "Neuropsychiatric Breakdown in the Garrison Army and in Combat," *American Sociological Review* 21 (August 1956): 480-88.

9. A military psychiatrist told his fellow officers that in many instances a young man "has a hard time facing decision and responsibility" because of his immaturity and "what is needed here is a firm hand from the fatherly type of person who refuses to protect him, but insists on the individual taking charge of himself and accepting responsibility for his own actions." Pettera, "Mental Health in Combat," pp. 75-76.

10. Daniels, "The Captive Professional," pp. 255-65. Ungerleider, "The Army, the Soldier and the Psychiatrist," p. 876, suggested that the lack of privileged communication explains why so few officers ever see a psychiatrist. They fear their career would be put in jeopardy.

11. Ungerleider, "The Army, the Soldier and the Psychiatrist," p. 876.

12. Ibid.

13. Daniels, "The Captive Professional," pp. 255-58. Clausen and Daniels, "Role Conflicts and Their Ideological Resolution," p. 282, stated that "referrals

may regard the psychiatrist-officer with suspicion, thinking the officer's responsibility to the service makes him a 'company man' and not a man genuinely interested in their welfare."

14. I am indebted to Mark Selden for this characterization.

15. Ungerleider, "The Army, the Soldier and the Psychiatrist," p. 876, reported that some soldiers quite frankly ask the psychiatrist for discharges, compassionate transfers, or changing of overseas orders—and not for relief of symptoms. He said he frequently heard the remark, "I heard this was the place to get my orders changed (or to get out of the Army)."

16. For a discussion of the informal pressurs on physicians generally, see Roger W. Little, "The 'Sick Soldier' and the Medical Ward Officer," *Human Organization* 15 (Spring 1966): 22-25. Little observed that even in a basic training company, word would get around about the leniency of various medical ward officers. If a nonsympathetic doctor were on duty, only the most seriously ill soldiers would go to him. Sometimes a soldier who was rejected on the night shift at the ward would come in again on the day shift. Thus the rates of soldiers on sick call corresponded closely with which doctor was on duty.

17. Daniels, "The Captive Professional," p. 257, and Daniels, "Military Psychiatry," p. 160.

18. For a discussion of neuropsychiatric casualties as a failure in adaptation, often of a temporary nature, see Peter Bourne, "Military Psychiatry and the Viet Nam Experience," *American Journal of Psychiatry* 127 (October 1970): 125, 129.

19. Pettera, "Mental Health in Combat," pp. 76-77. On the difficulties involved in screening for security purposes, see Tiffany and Allerton, "Army Psychiatry in the Mid-'60s," p. 813.

20. Daniels, "The Captive Professional," pp. 255-65, argues that psychiatrists in the military shift from a counseling role to more of a controlling role whereby they become agents for eliminating deviants.

21. Albert J. Glass, Kenneth L. Artiss, James J. Gibbs, and Vincent C. Sweeney, "The Current Status of Army Psychiatry," *American Journal of Psychiatry* 117 (February 1961): 673-83.

22. Ibid. See also Chapter 4, n. 164, above.

23. Ibid.

24. Ibid.

25. Ibid.

26. Ibid.

27. For a discussion of this history, see Albert J. Glass, "Army Psychiatry Before World War II," in *Neuropsychiatry in World War II, vol. 1: Zone of Interior*, ed. Robert S. Anderson (Washington, D.C.: Department of the Army, 1966), pp. 3-23.

28. Glass et al., "The Current Status of Army Psychiatry," p. 675. and Albert J. Glass, "Advances in Military Psychiatry," *Current Psychiatric Therapies* 1 (1961): 159-67.

29. Bloch, "Army Clinical Psychiatry in the Combat Zone" p. 289.

30. The Army did occasionally asign psychiatrists to divisions in World War

II (See Douglas R. Bey, "Division Psychiatry in Viet Nam," *American Journal of Psychiatry* 127 [August 1970]: 146), and in World War I (see Glass, "Advances in Military Psychiatry," p. 159). See also Glass, "Army Psychiatry Before World War II," pp. 3-26. However, the emphasis on immediacy, proximity, and expectancy clearly did not emerge until the end of World War II when it became well known that the course of psychiatric illness was highly responsive to variations in treatment methods and attitudes.

31. See Bloch, "Army Clinical Psychiatry in the Combat Zone," pp. 289-90; and Bey, "Division Psychiatry in Viet Nam," p. 147.

32. Bloch, "Army Clinical Psychiatry in the Combat Zone," p. 290, and Bey, "Division Psychiatry in Viet Nam," p. 147. Bey stated that the corpsman (social work/psychology technician) always discusses the case with the referral source and may consult with the psychiatric or social work officer.

33. Bloch, "Army Clinical Psychiatry in the Combat Zone," p. 290, and Bey, "Division Psychiatry in Viet Nam," p. 147.

34. See Bloch, "Army Clinical Psychiatry in the Combat Zone," p. 290. According to Bey, the statistics for the direct services of the division psychiatrist staff, of which he was a part, were as follows: "We average 180 new clients per month. Diagnostically the population is comprised of five percent with psychotic reactions (which include toxic psychosis secondary to drug abuse), ten percent with psychoneurotic reactions, 20 percent situational stress reactions (combat exhaustion, 'short timer's syndrome,' etc.), 25 percent with no psychiatric diagnosis, and 40 percent with character and behavior disorders. We hospitalize ten percent for two to three days in one of our clearing stations. One-half to one percent of our 180 new clients have to be sent to an evacuation hospital in order to be sent out of country; 14 percent are cleared for administrative separation from the Army; and 80 percent are returned to duty." Douglas R. Bey, "Division Psychiatry in Viet Nam," *American Journal of Psychiatry*, 1970, Vol. 127, p. 230. Copyright 1970, the American Psychiatric Association.

35. Douglas R. Bey, "Division Psychiatry in Viet Nam," *American Journal of Psychiatry*, 1970, Vol. 127, pp. 228-232. Copyright 1970, the American Psychiatric Association.

36. See Edward M. Colbach, "Morale and Mental Health," *Army Digest* 25 (May 1970): 9-11.

37. According to Bloch, "Army Clinical Psychiatry in the Combat Zone," p. 293, many cases of character and behavior disorders are not considered by the Army to represent psychiatric illness; hence, soldiers with these disorders who are not responsive to rehabilitation efforts are discharged through administrative channels rather than medical channels.

38. Ibid., p. 290.

39. Ibid.

40. Ibid.

41. Ibid., pp. 289-98.

42. Ibid., p. 290.

43. Ibid., p. 291.

44. Ibid., p. 292.

45. Ibid.
46. Ibid.
47. Ibid., p. 291.
48. Ibid.
49. Ibid.
50. Ibid., p. 292.
51. H. Spencer Bloch, "Army Clinical Psychiatry in the Combat Zone—1967-1968," *American Journal of Psychiatry*, 1969, Vol. 126, pp. 289-298. Copyright 1969, the American Psychiatric Association.
52. See Glass, "Advances in Military Psychiatry," for a brief discussion of milieu therapy in the Army.
53. Tiffany and Allerton, "Army Psychiatry in the Mid-'60s," p. 812.
54. Ibid., and Ungerleider, "The Army, the Soldier and the Psychiatrist," pp. 875-76.
55. A *psychiatric casualty* is defined as a soldier missing twenty-four hours or more of duty for psychiatric reasons.

Psychiatric Casualty Rates

WAR	*Rate per 1,000 Troops per year*
World War II	
Highest	101 (First U.S. Army, Europe)
Lowest	28 (Ninth U.S. Army, Europe)
Korea	
July 1950-December 1952	37
Vietnam	
Late 1965-Early 1970	13

According to Colbach, this combat psychiatric casualty rate is similar to the Army-wide rate, including garrison duty in the United States. The psychiatric evaluation rate has similarly dropped:

Evacuation Rate for Psychiatric Reasons

WAR	*Percent of All Evacuees*
World War II	23.0 percent
Korea	6.0 percent
Vietnam	3.4 percent

These figures are drawn from Colbach, "Morale and Mental Health," p. 11.

The low psychiatric casualty and evacuation rates continued until mid-1971, when the Army began a wide-scale urine-testing program to identify hard drug users. These addicted soldiers were usually evacuated from Vietnam for stateside involuntary detoxification. These cases were considered psychiatric casualties and as a result the psychiatric casualty and evacuation rates jumped ten or twenty times to rates comparable to those in World War II. This drug-screening program was begun after American participation in the Vietnam War had declined markedly as the "Vietnamization" policy shifted the burden of the fighting to the Army of the Republic of Vietnam. See Franklin Del Jones and Arnold W. Johnson, Jr., "Medical and Psychiatric Treatment Policy and Practice in Vietnam," *Journal of Social Issues* 31 (Fall 1975): 49-65. Jones and Johnson suggest that there was no effective policy for treating drug users in combat.

56. See Samuel A. Stouffer et al., *The American Soldier: Combat and Its Aftermath* (New York: John Wiley & Sons, 1949), pp. 96, 130-31, 135-39, 142-43, 148, 349-50, 382-83.

57. Roger W. Little, "Buddy Relations and Combat Performance," in *The New Military: Changing Patterns of Organization*, ed. Morris Janowitz (New York: W. W. Norton & Company, 1964), pp. 195-224.

58. Charles C. Moskos, Jr., *The American Enlisted Man: The Rank and File in Today's Military* (New York: Russell Sage Foundation, 1970), pp. 134-56.

59. Bourne, "Military Psychiatry and the Viet Nam Experience," p. 487.

60. Glass, "Advances in Military Psychiatry," p. 159.

61. Bourne, "Military Psychiatry and the Viet Nam Experience," pp. 123-29.

62. See Tiffany and Allerton, "Army Psychiatry in the Mid-'60s," p. 813, and Peterson, "Discussion," pp. 819-20.

6

Military Courts and the Law

Of all the systems of social control in the military, its justice system[1] has been the most extensively criticized. After every major war there has been considerable agitation for reform of military justice.[2] In the later 1960s, most well-known works on military social control focused mainly on military justice. Some examples are *Military Justice Is to Justice as Military Music Is to Music* by Robert Sherrill, *GI Rights and Army Justice* by Robert Rivkin, and *The Unlawful Concert* by Fred Gardner. Injustice in the military has also been the subject of several articles in popular magazines, such as *The New Republic and The Nation*. Civilian law journals—*American Bar Association Journal, Maine Law Review, Cleveland Marshall Law Review*, and others—have published articles concerning justice in the military and offering possibilities for reform. The close of the Vietnam War also saw some official committee reports on military justice. One study written by a civilian-military committee, the *Report of the Task Force on the Administration of Military Justice in the Armed Forces* (four volumes) by Nathaniel R. Jones and C. E. Hutchin, Jr., in November 1972 investigated racial discrimination in the administration of military justice.[3] Another official study was an in-house critique by an all-military committee headed by General S. H. Matheson; entitled *Report to General William C. Westmoreland, Chief of Staff, U.S. Army*; it was written in June 1971 by the Committee for Evaluation of the Effectiveness of the Administration of Military Justice. This study looked at the role of military justice in maintaining discipline (and morale) at the small-unit level and focused on the problems junior officers encountered.[4]

Others concerned with military justice included soldiers, veterans, lawyers, and reporters, and some of their criticisms resulted in congressional actions to modify the military justice system. For example, these pressures have helped to produce the passage of the Uniform Code of Military Justice (UCMJ) in 1950,[5] and the Military Justice Act of 1968. (The code is called *uniform* because it applies to all branches of the armed forces. Most of the following comments apply also to the other services even though the majority of sources here pertain to the Army.)

Although other sectors of military social control have had some civilian professional help, the Army usually remained free to decide the extent of application of modernization and new techniques. But with regard to the military justice system, the Army has not had a free hand in determining the development of this sector. Rather, the military justice system has changed as a result of civilian pressures and decisions. The state of the military justice system at any moment is the outcome of countervailing pressures between civilian (and ex-military) critics and military resistance (with some civilian support). The military justice system has become steadily "civilianized," particularly over the past twenty years.[6] (*Civilianization* refers to the increasing modification of the military justice system to resemble civilian, particularly federal, justice systems.) Soldiers' due-process rights have been increased as a direct result of congressional action and, indirectly, as a result of Supreme Court rulings. The outcome is an odd system with some elements that are fully as fair as civilian justice can be at present but with other elements that are blatantly unjust.

The Army's reaction to criticism of its military justice system is partly related to the contradictions within that system. One of the system's functions is to assist the commander in controlling his troops. Originally, military justice was a simple extension of the commander's power. *Drum-head justice* is a slang term that refers to the way a line officer handed out punishment at the front.[7] A drum was used as the judge's bench since there were no tables at the front, and the commander (who was also the judge) swiftly dealt out punishment to offenders in this decentralized system of "justice." The military justice system operated in a manner consistent with the other social control sectors, although possibly in a more routinized and specified way. Its assumptions and goals were consonant with the rest of the Army: to make for "good discipline and order" so the Army could function efficiently. Problems such as commanders' influencing outcomes of trials were not seen as particularly odd: commanders always influence outcomes—from major decisions on the battlefield all the way down to making decisions of who gets transferred.

From the Army's point of view, the justice system was never intended, nor is it intended today, to protect the individual from excesses of government. On the contrary, it exists to protect the organization from individuals. General Eisenhower once said, "I know that groups of lawyers in examining the legal procedures in the Army have believed that it would be very wise to observe . . . that great distinction that is made in our Governmental organization of power. . . . But I should like to call your attention to one fact about the Army. . . . It was never set up to insure justice."[8] Former Attorney General Ramsey Clark (in discussing the use of troops in urban riots) said, "Generals resent civilian presence and legal guidance. Their business is war. War knows few rules and forgets them when need arises. Attorneys from Justice concerned about civil liberties, excessive force and the rights of civilian populations and prisoners find it hard to influence military commanders."[9]

Former Justice William O. Douglas, speaking for the majority in the United States Supreme Court decision on *O'Callahan v. Parker* (1969), said:

> A court-martial is tried, not by a jury of the defendant's peers which must decide unanimously, but by a panel of officers empowered to act by a two-thirds vote. The presiding

> officer at a court-martial is not a judge whose objectivity and independence are protected by tenure and undiminishable salary and nurtured by the judicial tradition, but by a military law officer. Substantially different rules of evidence and procedure apply in military trials. Apart from these differences, the suggestion of the possibility of influence on the actions of the court-martial by the officer who convenes it, selects its members and the counsel on both sides, and who usually has direct command authority over its members is a pervasive one in military law, despite strenuous efforts to eliminate the danger.
>
> A court-martial is not yet an independent instrument of justice but remains to a significant degree a specialized part of the overall mechanism by which military discipline is preserved. . . .
>
> While the Court of Military Appeals takes cognizance of some constitutional rights of the accused who are court-martialed, courts-martial as an institution are singularly inept in dealing with the nice subtleties of constitutional law. . . . A civilian trial, in other words, is held in an atmosphere conducive to the protection of individual rights, while the military trial is marked by the age-old manifest destiny of retributive justice.[10]

Defenders of the military justice system always point to the uniqueness of military society in their attempt to justify the state of the system of military justice at the time they are writing. Military justice as a separate system is justified in the *International Encyclopedia of Social Science* by three basic reasons: (1) the need for swift and summary machinery for the maintenance of discipline; (2) the fact that the adjudication of military crimes may require military expertise by the court; and (3) the fact that the armed forces may be stationed abroad, outside the jurisdiction of their country's civil courts.[11] So military society is depicted as different from civilian society because its objective is to win battles; a lack of discipline would greatly impede this objective.[12] A justification of the military justice system on the basis of an argument that it maintains order and efficiency hardly placates critics. Citizens' rights are always at odds with societal efficiency. If efficiency were accepted as the highest value, there would be little place for the individual's rights.

Defenders of military justice recognize this argument and, paradoxically, attempt to justify their system by asserting that it is actually fairer than the civilian justice system. Supporters assert that the accused is more likely to be treated justly in military than in civilian courts.[13] Delmar Karlen, after bitterly criticizing the disorder, delays, and the assembly-line appearance of civilian criminal courts, extolled the military justice system:

> The military scene presents some refreshing contrasts to the civilian scene. A soldier in a court-martial is provided with meaningful counsel, not pro forma representation. He is not kept in the dark, but advised well in advance of trail what witnesses will testify against him and the substance of their expected testimony. He is made aware of what is happening at every stage of the proceedings. His trial is an individualized affair, separately scheduled and distinct from every other trial. The goal is a deliberative, thoughtful, unhurried proceeding, not a frantic ritual. This is true even when a plea of guilty is received. That being so, we must ask ourselves again: Why try to convert military justice into a carbon copy of civilian criminal justice?[14]

These somewhat contradictory assertions—that the military justice system protects the individual's rights, yet as a justice system it requires special prerogatives to maintain military efficiency—seem to be a constant feature of these pro-military justice arguments.

The soldier in the Army today does in fact have considerable procedural due-process rights according to law. However, in contrast, he has minimal substantive due-process rights. Substantive due process requires that the law itself (that a person is charged under) be reasonable and not arbitrary or invidiously discriminatory. According to this substantive requirement, the law should not be so vague that a normal person cannot tell whether his conduct falls within the language of the law or overly broad so that it goes much further in suppressing individual rights than is necessary to effect the desired results. There are also informal pressures within the military justice system that may result in an accused soldier's not even receiving his procedural due-process rights.

The legal base for the military justice system lies in the fact that it is specified by a law (or set of laws) passed by Congress. The 1951 Uniform Code of Military Justice is the main base of courts-martial structure and procedure and of statutes of offenses for all the United States military services. The law was passed in 1950 by Congress, which is empowered by the United States Constitution to make laws for the governing of military forces. Thus, the ultimate legitimacy for the military justice system, and for military laws generally, does lie in the Constitution. (The Constitution is, incidentally, included in the *Manual for Courts-Martial.*[15]) It is illegal for the military to countermand the United States Constitution.

Interpretation of the Constitution, however, is another matter. Because the federal courts and the United States Supreme Court have no direct power over the military,[16] a soldier cannot carry an appeal on a ruling he has received in a military court to the Supreme Court. The only way he might get his case into the federal court structure, and thus have a chance of taking it to the Supreme Court, is by claiming that the military does not have jurisdiction over him and therefore cannot try him.[17] The claim that the military does not have jurisdiction over a given individual is usually made through a writ of habeas corpus. A writ of habeas corpus does not assert that the individual is innocent or guilty of a specific crime; it simply states that the military does not have jurisdiction over the individual or possibly over a certain area of his activities.[18] Conscientious objectors often used the writ of habeas corpus, basing their argument on the assertion that, due to their beliefs, they should not have been in the military in the first place. The Supreme Court decision on *O'Callahan* held that the military cannot try a soldier for a wholly civilian crime when the soldier was on leave and out of uniform.[19] This decision eliminates the possibility that a soldier might be tried in a civilian court as well as a military court for the same offense. Occasionally a soldier may get a writ of habeas corpus if his constitutional rights of due process have been violated.[20] This issue is a hazier area and subject to several conditions, such as his having exhausted all appeal possibilities in the military.[21]

There really is no possibility for collateral review of military decisions in federal courts. Writs of habeas corpus are not, strictly speaking, reviews. A decision of a military court is never overturned or reversed; it is merely deemed inapplicable. A soldier's lawyer may appeal a writ of habeas corpus through a federal appeals court, and thus the case might eventually reach the Supreme Court with the Army and the soldier as adversaries. In general, federal courts have been reluctant to interfere with military courts.

In addition to congressional acts and the Constitution of the United States, the military itself produces laws. Army regulations have the force of law, and so do some local (post or base) directives.

In terms of judicial structure, the military justice system is composed of two separate functions: trial and review. (The following discussion will refer to military justice after the establishment of the Uniform Code of Military Justice in 1951, including the relatively minor revisions of the Military Justice Act of 1968. In many ways the military justice system in the past twenty years is substantially different from that during World War II and before.) Military trials occur at four different levels, depending on the maximum severity of the sentence that can be adjudged, the rank of the convening authority (who is not supposed to be the "accuser"),[22] and the rights accorded the accused. These levels are called nonjudicial punishment (as spelled out by Article 15 of the UCMJ), summary courts-martial, special courts-martial, and general courts-martial. Reviews are carried out by a separate set of structures. Thus a special court-martial decision would never be appealed to the general court-martial.

In 1972, the distribution of Army military justice actions appeared as follows:[23]

	Number of Actions for Fiscal Year 1972	*Rate per 1,000 (January-June 1972)*
General court-martial	1,877	.91
Special court-martial	15,239	6.89
Summary court-martial	12,134	6.02
Nonjudicial punishment	217,245	113.5

Nonjudicial punishment as specified by Article 15 is not adjudged in the way one would normally think of as a trial. Rather, analogous to being cited for violation of the traffic code (getting a ticket), the accused soldier may decide not to contest his case and accept the provisions of Article 15 and receive punishment without his guilt having been established in court. A soldier's use of the term *Article 15* is similar to a civilian's use of the term *ticket*. A soldier might say, "I got three Article 15s this year," just as a civilian might say, "I got three tickets this year." There are provisions for a limited appeal of Article 15s. My interviewees asserted that the Army tells soldiers that it is to the accused's advantage to accept an Article 15 because the offense does not appear on his record when he leaves the military. It does, of course, stay on his military record in his "201 file." If he refuses to take an Article 15, the case is tried at a court-martial, and he knowingly risks a more severe punishment. It is also to the Army's advantage to have soldiers accept Article 15s because the judicial system would be too clogged with cases if most minor offenses ended in court.[24]

To provide some idea of the extensive use by commanders of Article 15s, legal clerks have commented (in interviews) that the usual rate of Article 15s in a permanent party company (comprising around 200 to 300 men) is approximately ten or twenty a month. According to the interviewees, occasionally there are companies with very touchy company commanders who might give out as many as eighty Article 15s a month. Too many Article 15s, however, might suggest that the commander cannot control his men with leadership techniques and is resorting to harsher forms of punishment.

The limits to punishment under Article 15 vary and depend on whether the accused is an officer (a rare case) or where the act is committed (for example, on a vessel). The rank of the commanding officer (always a commissioned officer) also determines the degree of punishment. An Article 15 could result in restrictions to post, reduction in grade, forfeiture of pay, and correctional custody. For example, thirty days is the maximum prison term if the Article 15 is given by a field grade officer (major or above); by a company grade officer (captain), correctional custody might be seven days.

Article 15s, of course, can be given out only for infractions of the UCMJ, but, as we will see, almost any resistance to military authority can be construed as an offense against the UCMJ. Furthermore, they are only used for minor offenses. The main value of Article 15s for commanders is as a form of punishment to maintain discipline.[25]

The Task Force on the Administration of Military Justice criticized the great extent of discretionary powers given to commanders in Article 15 actions. This group would like to see all the armed services require a hearing, permit legal counsel, and provide clearer advice on the right to appeal. According to the task force, the wide discretionary powers of the commanders result in a great deal of racial discrimination; blacks receive Article 15 punishments at a much greater rate than their presence in the Army would suggest.[26]

Article 15s have been changed recently to give soldiers the right to consult with a Judge Advocate General's Corps (JAGC, or sometimes JAG) officer concerning punishment. The sentence is now given in the presence of the accused, and the results are posted.[27] Providing more safeguards for enlisted men results in more work for officers, however. One of the main complaints that junior level officers express about the military justice system is that Article 15 procedures have become too complex and require too much paperwork.[28]

The Article 15 is an enormously useful technique of social control; it is almost entirely in the province of the commanding officer, and there is little chance that the soldier will use his limited appeal rights. Some reasons the task force heard for the fact that most soldiers do not appeal their Article 15 punishments were that it would be a useless gesture or, worse, that it would result in some form of retaliation from their commanders. If the punishment of an Article 15 happened to be confinement or restriction, there would be little incentive to appeal because the appeal procedure is so slow that the soldier would have served his time before the appeal was processed.[29] If a soldier were likely to appeal, he probably would have turned down the Article 15 in the first place and asked for an actual trial, that is, a court-martial.

Military trial courts are ad hoc courts. In other words, they are created only to try certain individuals on specific charges brought by the commander with the power to convene them, termed the *convening authority*.[30]

A summary court-martial, the lowest level of military courts, has been described as a kind of "kangaroo court" because one commissioned officer (chosen by the convening authority) serves as judge, jury, prosecutor, defense counsel, and court reporter.[31] Before the 1968 Military Justice Act was put into effect, a soldier who refused an Article 15 would be tried by a summary court-martial and upon conviction could appeal only to the convening authority—who accused him in the first place—and to the staff judge advocate.[32] There was no record of the trial other than the charge sheet. This "kangaroo court" aspect of summary courts-martial has been recognized by soldiers and has been criticized extensively. For example, with reference to the Navy and Marine corps, "U.S. District Court Judge David Williams said that summary proceedings in which a single military officer acts as judge, jury, prosecutor and defense attorney, was illegal because it violated the right of the accused to counsel."[33] The Army and the Air Force had already begun to allow lawyers to represent the accused—a change that came as a result of a Supreme Court decision.

Since 1969 a soldier has been allowed to refuse trial by a summary court-martial in favor of trial by general or special court-martial. However, this request is made at considerable risk, since the latter courts-martial are empowered to hand down far more severe sentences than the relatively limited possibilities accorded to a summary court-martial. Thus, it may be seen that part of the military judicial system is structured in such a way as to frighten an accused soldier into giving up some due-process rights.

In addition to the newly established rights to refuse a summary court-martial, the accused may now subpoena witnesses and evidence, cross examine, remain silent, "discover a good deal of the prosecution's case," make statements in mitigation or extenuation after being found guilty, and obtain civilian counsel for his own defense.[34] However, he still has no right of challenge, either for cause or peremptorily, no right to appointed military counsel, and no right to a verbatim transcript or even a summary of the trial. The only review in a summary court-martial is a mandatory one by the convening authority and his staff judge advocate.[35]

Maximum punishments of summary courts-martial are similar to those of field grade Article 15s—that is, confinement for a month, hard labor for forty-five days, restriction to specified limits for two months, and forfeiture of two-thirds of a month's pay, or a combination of these.[36] But unlike a field grade Article 15, a summary court-martial is a federal conviction that stigmatizes a soldier after he leaves the Army. The task force argued that if an act is serious enough to warrant a criminal conviction, the soldier should have the due-process rights of a special court-martial; if the act is not serious, the soldier should receive a field grade Article 15. In essence, the task force said that the widely used summary court-martial, with its inadequate procedural protections, should be abolished.[37]

A special court-martial is an intermediate military court that can try the same crimes as a general court-martial. In practice it is usually used for less serious offenses because of UCMJ limits on the maximum sentence it can impose: six months' confinement, three months' hard labor, forfeiture of pay for six months, and, under certain conditions, a bad-conduct discharge.[38] While a commanding officer of a company may convene a summary court-martial, only a commanding officer of a brigade, regiment, or detached battalion may convene a special court-martial.[39] This officer is not supposed to be the "accuser."[40]

The court consists of either three or more members or a military judge, if one has been detailed to the court and if the accused requests it.[41] Members of the court are appointed by the convening authority because the UCMJ does not require random selection of court members.

> [It] requires a convening authority to select as members of a court-martial those members of the armed forces who in his opinion are best qualified for that duty by reason of "age, education, training, experience, length of service and judicial temperament" (Article 25 (d) (2)). . . . As a practical matter, most courts are empaneled with commissioned

> officers only. Even in the relatively rare case in which the accused requests enlisted men, senior non-commissioned officers are most often selected.[42]

The Task Force on the Administration of Military Justice argued that to fulfill the trial-by-jury clause of the Sixth Amendment and the due-process clause of the Fifth Amendment, the convening authority should play no part in the selection process, which should be completely random. The military judge should examine each prospective member as to grounds for possible disqualification, and these members should be subject to voir dire and challenge by counsel for either side.[43] Everett commented that there have been proposals for random selection of court-martial boards and that the Army had experimented with the procedure in a project at one post.[44]

The three officers who may compose the court are ordinarily not lawyers, and the highest ranking of these, the president, makes rulings on the admissibility of evidence and on motions. Since these officers have practically no legal training, and because they are hand-picked by the convening authority, accused soldiers often request that a military judge alone try the case.

This perception of military judges as more lenient is shared by commanding officers who cite this as one of their major criticisms of using JAG officers in courts-martial.[45] While trial by military judge alone is certainly far more common than using court members, it is not at all clear that these judges are any more lenient, as Table 1 demonstrates.[46]

In response to the criticism that trials were not really trials by one's peers, military law now allows the court members to include enlisted men, up to one-third of the court (this also applies to general courts-martial), at the request of the accused. In practice, they are usually career NCOs, E-7s to E-9s, because they are also picked by the convening authority. The result is that accused enlisted men rarely ask that other enlisted men serve on the court because the NCOs tend to make even harsher judgments than officers.[47] This is one of several examples whereby the rights of the accused have been increased by statute and countermanded in practice.[48]

Table 1. Non-BCD Special Court-Martial Data from Selected Commands,[a] January 1, 1971-March 31, 1971

	Court Members	*Military Judge Alone*
Persons tried	13	1,690
Persons convicted	11 (85%)	1,633 (97%)
Confinement adjudged[b]	10 (91%)	1,280 (78%)
0-2 months[c]	2 (20%)	319 (25%)
2-4 months[c]	3 (30%)	582 (45%)
4-6 months[c]	5 (50%)	379 (30%)

[a]These data are based on records maintained in the offices of the Staff Judge Advocates, Fort Dix, XVIII Corps & Fort Bragg, Fort Knox, Fort Jackson, Fort Benning, Fort Lee, and Fort Sill.

[b]Percentages based on number convicted.

[c]Percentages based on number of cases in which confinement adjudged.

In a special court-martial, the accused has, in addition to the summary court-martial rights, the right to a written trial summary (but not verbatim, unless a bad-conduct discharge has been adjudged), the right to have appointed military counsel (of his own choice if the convening authority deems it "reasonably available"), and the right to make some challenges.[49] Article 27 of the UCMJ states that the accused shall be accorded the opportunity to be represented by an attorney unless "counsel having such qualifications cannot be obtained on account of physical conditions or military exigency." It is possible, then, assuming the trial counsel (prosecutor) is not a lawyer, that the defense counsel need not be a lawyer.[50] Unless a bad-conduct discharge is adjudged, the only review of a special court-martial is by the convening authority and by a judge advocate officer.[51]

The general court-martial is the highest trial court in the military, and there are no limits to the sentences it can impose, assuming that the sentence is sanctioned by the UCMJ for the given offense. Most offenses are punishable "as a court-martial may direct"; in one case a soldier received a ten-year sentence for quietly communicating to another soldier his anti-war feelings.[52] A general court-martial may adjudge a death sentence if the offense is deemed so punishable by the UCMJ. In the Army, a general court-martial is convened by a "commanding officer of a territorial department, an Army group, an Army corps, a division, a separate brigade" or by the President of the United States, the Secretary concerned, and other commanding officers when empowered by the President or the Secretary.[53] General courts-martial are typically convened by post commanders. Those authorized to convene a general court-martial are authorized to convene a lesser court-martial.

The general court-martial consists of a military judge and five or more members, or only a military judge if the accused requests it.[54] Military judges for general courts-martial also tend to be less lenient than court members (see Table 2).[55]

In a general court-martial the convening authority details the judge, court members, trial and defense counsel, and reporters. Article 32 requires that there be a pretrial investigation of general court-martial charges, but, unlike a civilian grand jury's function, these findings are not binding. The accused has, in addition to the special court-martial rights, the right to have an attorney appointed as counsel and a verbatim transcript.[56] Re-

Table 2. Army-Wide General Court-Martial Data
January 1, 1971-March 31, 1971

	Court Members	*Military Judge Alone*
Persons tried	93	589
Persons convicted	79 (85%)	561 (95%)
Punitive discharge adjudged[a]	54 (68%)	509 (91%)
Confinement adjudged[a]	65 (82%)	518 (92%)
1-12 months[b]	34 (52%)	371 (72%)
13-24 months[b]	17 (27%)	88 (17%)
25-60 months[b]	8 (12%)	44 (8%)
61-120 months[b]	0	6 (1%)
More than 120 months[b]	6 (9%)	9 (2%)

[a]Percentages based on number convicted.

[b]Percentages based on number of cases in which confinement adjudged.

views are more extensive at this stage; the Court of Military Review must review all general courts-martial in addition to the mandatory review by the convening authority and his staff judge advocate.

It is clear that the omnipresent role of the convening authority in choosing the court members and counsel centralizes power in commanding officers and cannot help but compromise justice. Some parts of the review process are also structured to support military authority.

The first level of review is that by the convening authority himself. The convening authority can return the case to the same court for a variety of reasons, including his disapproval of the sentence or finding. He may reduce the sentence, and often he does. One of the reasons that all levels of courts-martial tend to impose severe sentences is because it is understood that the convening authority may lower the sentence.[57] This shifts much of the power back to the commanding officer and gives him additional control over the men.[58]

Everett questions the principle of having the convening authority review court-martial findings because he has so little training in law. He would prefer the convening authority review to be limited to clemency determinations.[59] Another difficulty with reviews at this level is the problem of administrative delay. The average number of days elapsed from date of trial to action by a convening authority steadily increased through the 1960s. By fiscal year 1970, it took an average of 71.9 days for the convening authority to review cases in which the accused entered a not-guilty plea, and an average of 48.2 days to review guilty pleas.[60]

The next level of review is by the staff judge advocate (SJA). The SJA has a peculiar position in the military justice system. He is the commanding general's legal adviser and is supposed to act as a nonpartisan administrator of the system.[61] In practice, however, he is the prosecutor's man because he helps the convening authority prepare charges, helps secure witnesses for prosecution and makes deals with those witnesses, and even provides a trial memorandum describing possible defenses the defense counsel might make and he suggests responses the trial counsel could use to overcome these defenses.[62] The SJA is obligated to remain in constant communication with the military police, the Criminal Investigation Division, the Federal Bureau of Investigation, and other agencies. According to Rivkin, these conflicts of impartiality and services for prosecution result in a "lawless role" for the staff judge advocate.

The highest appellate body within the Army itself is the Court of Military Review. The 1968 Military Justice Act upgraded the level, formerly called Boards of Military Review. The Army Courts of Military Review are composed of four panels of three military judges each.[63] This court automatically reviews all courts-martial that result in sentences of death, dishonorable discharge, bad-conduct discharge, dismissal of commissioned officer, or confinement for one year or more.[64] This last sentence—imprisonment for a year or more—accounts for a large number of cases reviewed by this court.

A study published in 1970 showed that the sentences of 43 percent of the inmates at the United States Disciplinary Barracks (USDB) had not gone through this automatic review.[65] It is possible to serve six months at the USDB and finally find out that one is adjudged innocent.

The Court of Military Appeals, the highest level of appeals for the entire court-martial structure, is composed of three civilian attorneys and functions for the entire military in much the same way that the Supreme Court functions for the federal justice system. This court must review cases in which a general officer is involved, or when a death sentence is passed, or when the JAG orders a case reviewed; it may also review on the petition of the accused.[66]

The Court of Military Appeals was set up as a response to civilian critics, and it has often functioned as an informal linkage to Supreme Court decisions.[67] For example, the 1966 *Miranda* decision by the Supreme Court, which extends substantial rights to the accused when in custody during investigation by police, was reflected by the Court of Military Appeals in its consideration of the *Tempia* case (1967). As a result of *Tempia* (and others), the interrogating police must inform the soldier that he has the right to counsel, that he has the right to remain silent, that what he says may be used against him, and that he may request to have counsel with him during police interrogation.[68] The lawyer may not necessarily be allowed at a special court-martial.[69]

The Court of Military Appeals has expanded other procedural rights of the accused. As a result, he has the right to a speedy and public trial, to confront witnesses, to be protected against unreasonable search and seizure,[70] and other rights.[71]

It may be apparent that several possibilities for injustice are built into the system of military justice by statute. Command influence (the ability of a commander to determine the outcome of a trial) is actually structured into parts of the military justice system; it is an important issue facing both commanders and accused soldiers.[72] It is important to accused soldiers because it violates their constitutional rights to a fair trial, and it is important to commanders because it allows them to have the direct control over the judicial means of punishment, the most extreme form of social control. Commanders pick court members, trial counsel, often defense counsel, investigating officers, and sometimes the judge. The commanding officer is prohibited from censuring or coercing any member, and he is expected to exclude himself in cases of personal interest. Personal interest in practice refers to issues such as money matters, but it is not extended to interest in his official role, that is, as a commander.[73]

The possibility for overt command influence is probably remote in most cases. It is a risk for a commanding officer to be caught in the act. Besides, a commander is just simply not concerned enough with, say, an AWOL case (the most common offense) to risk influencing an outcome. However, in cases that would threaten his ability to command, such as dissent, disobedience, barracks theft, and homosexuality, the commander is likely to be more involved.[74]

Overt command influence does seem to occur in spite of the risks involved. In 1967 alone the Court of Military Appeals overturned ninety-three convictions from Fort Leonard Wood because an officer there—General Lipscomb—was demonstrated to have exercised command influence.[75] Luther West, a former JAG officer, discusses other instances of command influence.[76]

It is probably a rare occurrence that a commander would be impolitic enough actually to tell a court member how to vote. His ability to select the participants and "stack the jury" may make this unnecessary. The Court of Military Appeals once reversed a conviction because the convening authority selected two provost marshals, an inspector general and an executive officer of a Marine brig as court members.[77] There are more subtle ways of communicating one's desire to see a given outcome to receptive officers in his command.

Army officers can use techniques that are less blatant and less obviously illegal to deny soldiers the rights they are guaranteed by statute. One of the most important ways of doing this is by carefully managing military lawyers so they would be unlikely to go out of their way to assist soldiers who are disciplinary problems.

Robert Rivkin, a lawyer and an ex-serviceman, believes the military distrusts lawyers.[78] Is there any evidence to back up this kind of feeling? In a survey, experienced line officers (students at the Army War College) were asked to evaluate military lawyers' performance along several lines.[79] They were most critical toward the lawyers' "appearance and bearing," "attitude toward own status," "concern with discipline," and "common sense." They were most pleased with JAG officers' "legal education and training," "concern for the soldier-client," "speaking and writing," and "job performance." These officers were evenly split on the issue of JAG officers' cooperation. Thus, at least some military officers disapprove of military lawyers.

The Matheson committee also recognized the conflict between JAG officers and line officers and suggested that

> a judge advocate, upon being commissioned and reporting to active duty for the first time, should attend a course conducted by one of the service schools, designed to acquaint him with the problems faced by commanders. Likewise, the Judge Advocate General's School should invite commanders and senior noncommissioned officers to personally present their views to the students concerning the administration of military justice. All judge advocates, including mili-

> tary judges, must understand that the needs of the Army, as well as the rights of the accused, must be taken into account before any system of military justice can be considered effective.[80]

One of the possible explanations for the rift between lawyers and commanders might be that lawyers come into the Army as an already professionalized group. This professionalism could be durable and may be based on different values than the professionalism of military officers. For example, a military officer might be afraid that a lawyer would hold a strong value for individuals' rights, which would seem to be more likely to protect the individual than to serve the Army. Historically and currently, military justice has been an important adjunct to a commander's ability to control his men, and at certain times military officers have formed much of the judicial system. If an officer were not certain of his capacity to threaten a recalcitrant soldier with a court-martial, his power would be considerably reduced. Furthermore, commanders might think that military lawyers, who are not in a position of command, might be insensitive to the requirements of discipline. Other officers, convinced that lawyers slow up proceedings and interfere with efficiency generally, would prefer to rely on them as little as possible.[81]

The distaste for lawyers is manifest in practice in two ways: lawyers are excluded from proceedings as much as possible, or they are controlled by line officers, albeit indirectly. The exclusion of lawyers occurs by attempting to keep trials at the lower levels of the hierarchy, that is, at summary courts-martial or nonjudicial punishments. However, even in a higher court-martial the Army need not offer a lawyer as defense counsel if it does not use a lawyer as trial counsel (but if the accused knows enough of military law, he may specifically demand a lawyer).

Sherman cites a U.S. Court of Military Appeals annual report finding that nonlawyers as military counsel "are more likely to advise the accused to plead guilty and not to bargain for a lesser sentence. . . .[They] are less likely to make pre-trial motions such as for suppression of evidence and confessions, to make timely objections to questions and evidence, and to cross examine witnesses."[82]

A JAG lawyer told me that this exclusion of lawyers sometimes forces each "counsel" to come to the JAG office and ask for advice on how to conduct the trial. Their unfamiliarity with legal procedure results in their quickly forgetting much of what they were told or what they might have read in the *Manual for Courts-Martial.* They neglect to establish basic conditions for proving their case. (The importance of denying the accused trial transcripts should be clear in this connection.) The *Manual for Courts-Martial* provides a word-by-word script for these trials. Of course the counsels do not always know why various phrases are included, and, according to my interviewee, sometimes a strange scenario results when one of the court members or counsels forgets to stop and reads on to someone else's lines.[83] The Matheson committee also commented on this issue: "Too often the uninitiated laymen, including the accused, gains the mistaken impression, because of the 'script' that all the members are following, that the trial is no more than a play, the lines of which the actors are mouthing, with completely foreordained results."[84] The committee suggested that excess verbiage be eliminated from the court-martial proceedings as a solution for this problem.

This exclusion of lawyers probably occurs less now than it did in the past, because recent civilianization (through the Court of Military Appeals and Congress) has increased the rights of the accused and possibly because soldiers today have a somewhat better knowledge of their rights in the military.

If simple exclusion cannot be relied upon as a technique of limiting lawyers' assistance to resisting GIs, then the Army would be expected to resort to pressures on the lawyers themselves.

I should point out that when I speak of a lawyer actually being dominated by the Army, I am speaking of numerically rather few cases at any one post. In the JAG section (typically a separate building on a post) there are probably only one or two lawyers (out of ten or twenty) who would be inclined to cause the Army some problems. The rest of the lawyers, either by training or by selection, are not inclined to provide exceptional help to an enlisted man. Lawyers may hold some of the same attitudes toward their clients who are in trouble with the military as the psychiatrists do. Many of those whom this study views as resisters are either incoherent politically or cannot express themselves in a way that these professionals would see as political resistance. Because these resisters are working class or lower class, a lawyer may not understand the nature of their nonideological resistance to the military. Many of these enlisted resisters are black and more than 98 percent of military lawyers are white, which tends to create a further gap in understanding.[85] A lawyer is not likely to make special efforts to defend his client if he has no rapport with him and if he does not respect or understand the reasons for the client's resistance. The Task Force on the Administration of Military Justice recommended that judge advocates receive additional training in human relations and in communicating with minority persons.[86]

One way for a commander to control lawyers is through the Army's promotion structure.[87] Promotion decisions are made on the basis of "efficiency reports." Efficiency reports for lawyers, particularly heads of JAG sections, are written by line officers.[88] The efficiency report does not focus on the officer's performance as a lawyer but rates him on his conduct, his sociability, his performance as an Army officer, his reliability, his dependability, and similar characteristics. A former JAG lieutenant colonel wrote:

> The commander concerned may note in the counsel's next efficiency report that he is an excellent officer, but of limited imagination and lacking in drive. He may state in this report that the officer concerned tries very hard to produce acceptable results but generally falls below accepted standards. He may note that the officer concerned is a neat dresser, but lacks self-confidence, and generally talks too much at social gatherings. The criticisms that a commander may level at a military lawyer in a situation of this nature are, of course, false and are designed solely to punish the officer concerned for "stepping out of line. . . ." The officer concerned is "low rated" and may well fail to be promoted along with his contemporaries at his next promotion period.[89]

During the Vietnam War, many lawyers enlisted as legal officers to avoid being drafted as enlisted men; these noncareer Army lawyers were probably those who were most sympathetic with enlisted men's problems. Even during the all-volunteer phase of the Army, there may be some noncareer Army lawyers who enlist for the experience or as a result of some problem of job shortage. As noncareer officers, an efficiency report probably would not matter very much to them. But it would matter a great deal more to the head of the JAG section, say a major (noncareer JAG officers usually are captains; the rank of major is an indication that the professional is career Army.) This major would try his utmost to please the line officer (a colonel or a general) who would be writing *his* efficiency report. Thus the career Army lawyer would be expected to transmit the pressure from command to the JAG officer under him.

Some of my JAG interviewees spoke of these pressures, and the findings of one of the official studies showed some corroboration of what they reported: "Although by no means a universal complaint, some defense counsel have stated to the Task Force that they have been harassed by their commanders and even, in some cases by their staff judge advocates, when they have defended cases of particular interest to the command."[90]

My interviewees identified some of the tactics that they have seen used by a head of a JAG section. The military provides this major (as any other officer) with a variety of rules that he can choose to enforce or not enforce. The lawyers under him are professionals; they are used to setting their own hours, not being particularly attentive about uniforms, and so forth. This major would tighten up on the rules by threatening these officers for even small violations, for example, arriving a few minutes late or walking out of the office without a hat. Interviewees reported that these sanctions were applied in subtle ways. One reported that his major simply arrived fifteen minutes early every day, and thus everyone else thought that he was watching for disciplinary infractions such as tardiness (a form of AWOL). According to interviewees, the liberal lawyers were sometimes harassed by their superior officers' manipulation of leaves and rotation schedules. There are many similar minor areas of administrative discretion that can be used as rewards or punishments.[91]

This harassment could lead to an office with a tense atmosphere, which would not be conducive to supporting soldiers in conflict with the Army. Similar to infantry units, when there is low morale the hostility is frequently misdirected horizontally, rather than vertically, to its source.

A second way to handle lawyers who are overzealous in their support of resisting enlisted men is to transfer them to a different job. This strategy was also noted in the task force report: "Some defense counsel . . . felt that, because they had conducted successful defenses in a number of cases of special interest to the commander, they had been reassigned to less desirable duties within the office of the staff judge advocate."[92] Some of my interviewees observed that a lawyer the Army distrusts might be put on "claims," where he would not be likely to see anyone with authority problems or political problems with the military.[93]

Younger, less experienced lawyers are likely to start out on the defense side. Those who are particularly competent in defending soldiers' cases may be transferred to prosecution.[94] So, ironically, a lawyer who makes a special effort to assist GIs is likely to be transferred to prosecution where he will be enforcing military discipline (it is a rare soldier who would risk seeing a prosecuting counselor for advice on how to avoid being prosecuted).

When lawyers who are sympathetic to GIs are transferred from defense to prosecution, some attitudinal changes may follow this attachment to a new role. Inevitably they will have to justify accepting their job in prosecution in order to retain their self-respect.[95] These lawyers are not likely to refuse this transfer. In an interview, a liberal noncareer lawyer who was transferred to prosecution justified his role in prosecuting GIs with whom he often sympathized by saying that he was a lawyer and the Army was his client; and a lawyer has a responsibility to his client, whether he agrees or disagrees with that client.

Their attitudes toward enlisted men may also change as a result of their new role. Company commanders with disciplinary problems in their command will be in contact with prosecution lawyers, rather than defense lawyers, since these commanding officers are putting the soldiers up for courts-martial. The effect of company commanders' bias on the conduct of the accused cannot fail to have some effect on the lawyers' attitudes toward them.[96]

The process of assigning a lawyer to prosecution or claims may sometimes be insufficient to isolate him from enlisted men because a network of communication may have been built up between the lawyer and various enlisted men. Contacts may have been made on off-duty hours or through various kinds of messengers, such as legal clerks. The lawyer might additionally have begun to influence other lawyers to act on their beliefs by his example. According to one of my JAG interviewees' experience, the Army's response to this state of affairs might be to transfer the lawyer to another base. At a new base, preferably one with a sleepy atmosphere and isolated from the politicizing influences of large cities, the lawyer would have to start anew the process of building relationships of trust among enlisted men and support among other lawyers. By this time the lawyer may be either fed up and cynical or he may be about to get out of the Army (as was the case with my interviewee) and thus not likely to make any great commitment to enlisted men.

This kind of transfer might be illegal if it could be defined as punitive.[97] But because lawyers are transferred from time to time as a matter of policy, it would be difficult to make this charge stand up in court.

Judges have been similarly subject to subtle kinds ofinfluence. Alley argues that the mingling of JAG judges and commanders as neighbors and officers has an important effect on the way the judges decide cases.[98] There are also more direct methods of managing certain JAG judges. If a JAG lawyer who is acting as a judge is sympathetic to soldiers and generally hands down light sentences, he may find that he is not assigned to the judge's position subsequently. The Military Justice Act of 1968 attempted to remove some of this influence by creating a "floating" or "field" (or independent and rotating) judiciary.[99] This supply of judges is used in the more serious cases and would be expected to be more immune to command influence.[100] The

Task Force on the Administration of Military Justice recommended that this be extended and urged that military judges and judge advocate defense councils be placed in an independent command chain through the judge advocate general.[101]

Yet another way of controlling lawyers and preventing them from assisting GIs is to issue a regulation to that effect. The Air Force, for example, once ordered its JAG officers not to help potential conscientious objectors in making their applications.[102] The Army has asked defense JAG officers to discourage clients from making appeals so as not to waste the government's money.[103]

The military can also set up an "obstacle course" for the occasional sympathetic defense lawyer and, of course, civilian lawyers.[104] The defense must request witnesses through prosecution, who can refuse to subpoena them. The Army has refused to allow, for example, a psychologist to appear at a trial.[105] The Army has threatened civilian defense lawyers with telling the state bar to reprimand them.[106] The lack of the requirement for verbatim transcripts works to the disadvantage of the defense.

According to the task force report, "Many enlisted men indicated a lack of confidence in military defense counsel. They believed that defense counsel are not truly representing the interest of the accused, but rather serving the commander."[107] A reason suggested for this is that the defense counsel does not have the trappings of professionalism. "An accused simply cannot walk into the office of his defense counsel—an office which is poorly furnished, inadequately lighted, shared with others, which has an inadequate reference library, and which is located in close proximity to that of the trial counsel—and feel that he will receive the services of a true professional."[108]

Some of my interviewees have asserted that there is a tendency for lawyers assigned to defense to be somewhat apathetic, alienated, or inexperienced. A trial counsel commented in an interview that occasionally a comic situation arose in which he, the prosecution lawyer, did the defense's work and told the defense how to argue in court. He looked up the precedents for the particular defense motion and the specific construction of the article. Another odd situation often arose when this prosecuting trial counsel "bent over backwards" to argue for a light sentence for the accused while the stricter court, composed of line officers, "Bent over backwards" to convict him and to give him a harsh sentence.

Other than the rather obvious problem of unenthusiastic courtroom performance, this lack of sympathy with resisting enlisted men might be manifested in a lawyer's lack of support for a soldier who feels he has been mistreated. Because officers are also subject to the UCMJ, they may be brought to trial, for example for harassing enlisted men (a violation of Article 93), through the procedure set forth in Article 138 of the UCMJ. But this accusation requires either a certain amount of technical skill or a sympathetic Army lawyer.[109]

One area in which an accused soldier might need a lawyer's support is during interrogations. Rivkin wrote that the rights guaranteed to the accused may be countermanded by interrogations by military police. Although the law requires the investigating agent to read a statement to the accused describing rights protecting him from self-incrimination and the right to counsel, the investigator may mask this information by telling the soldier he may be counseled by *anyone* he desires, such as his first sergeant, company commander, chaplain, IG, and lawyer.[110] Rivkin described other standard police bluffs used by both civilian and military interrogators such as (illegal) promises of immunity.[111]

Another point at which the soldier might need a JAG officer's support is when he has gotten into some kind of difficulty with the Army, such as in applying for an administrative discharge, or in the initial phases of a court-martial. Administrative delay in processing paperwork is often perceived by soldiers as a form of harassment. It is illegal, according to Article 10 and Article 98 of the UCMJ, to delay bringing a case to trial. In some cases, both trial and defense lawyers delay bringing a case to trial for so many months that it is embarrassing to both sides; and the enlisted man, who had already served many months in pretrial confinement, is let off with a light sentence.

One very common case of illegal processing of accused soldiers occurs when they are put in pretrial confinement. Pretrial restraint (a term that refers to orders to remain within certain specified limits, as well as confinement in a prison) of an accused soldier should not be "any more rigorous than the circumstances require(d) to insure his presence."[112] Normally, pretrial confinement should be used only when the soldier is a danger to himself or to others or seems likely to go AWOL, but at many bases, soldiers are regularly put into pretrial confinement for a variety of offenses.[113] The Matheson committee found that the overwhelming majority of the persons in the stockade—about 85 percent—are in pretrial confinement.[114]

> Many commanders interviewed by the Committee believe they should be able to place a member of their command in pretrial confinement without first obtaining permission from higher headquarters and without the necessity of making the often strained conclusion that the confinement is required to insure the presence of the individual at any future trial. These commanders feel, rightly or wrongly, that they should be able to confine any person who is a "trouble-maker," even though his alleged offense is not a serious transgression and even though there is no question of his being available for trial. This feeling, though understandable in some cases, betrays a certain lack of appreciation for the underlying rationale for pretrial confinement. . . .Stated bluntly, a commander simply cannot lock up a soldier merely because he is considered a "trouble-maker."[115]

A soldier in pretrial confinement is likely to be outraged or depressed and may get himself into even more trouble as a result. He may feel that justice has not been served and that he is being pushed around in the Army. He may think it would be an easy matter for a defense counsel to get him out of the stockade, but the soldier may not even have a defense counsel assigned to him, much less a concerned one.

Once in a stockade, accused or convicted soldiers have little contact with soldiers outside the stockade and have no one to complain to except their lawyer if beatings take place in stockades. These prisoners may show some evidence of being beaten by guards, such as blackened eyes, arm in a cast, and so forth, which the defense counsel could see if he ever conferred with his client. The defense counsel could easily bring charges against stockage guards and stockade commanders, but this is a rare occurrence.

Probably the last point at which a military lawyer can help a disciplinary offender is in the appeal and review process. But as a military lawyer complained in an interview, even when he wrote reviews of court-martial cases that criticized the proceedings or the sentence, there was no support from other lawyers whose role it was to include the review with the trial records. According to this lawyer, sometimes they would not even staple it to the back of the record.

Many varieties of social control are illegal by the Army's own standards, but they persist partly because commanders receive little military justice training and drill sergeants' schools do not teach any.[116] Lawyers should be the superego of the military, acting to prevent the use of these illegal controls. A lawyer need not threaten a line officer or a stockade commander with a court-martial. Sometimes a lawyer could prevent a commanding officer's excesses simply by advising him that he is overstepping his bounds. A post or brigade commander will often ask the head of the JAG section, another career officer, for legal advice before he takes some action. As discussed above, a legal officer who wants to please his superior officer can do so by telling him he can do something that is illegal. An interviewee recounted an incredible instance where one JAG officer told a post commander that it was all right for him to send some men to a local high school to tear anti-Army posters off a bulletin board.

Although procedural due-process rights of the accused may be abrogated for structural and for more informal reasons, there has been a gradual increase in laws and regulations guaranteeing procedural due-process rights to the accused. One result is that current apologists do have a basis for stating that the system is fair; in fact, they commonly assert that it is very rare that an innocent person will be convicted at a court-martial.[117] This argument is transmitted to civilians, but more importantly it is transmitted to soldiers, especially in basic training. Soldiers are assured in lectures that their rights will be protected and that they have more rights than a civilian has.[118] These are attempts to inculcate in soldiers a sense that the military justice system is very legitimate and very fair.

The most important defect in this argument lies in the difference between procedural due-process rights and what are sometimes called substantive due-process rights, or issues of substantive law. The term *substantive due-process rights* refers to the actual offenses that are specified, that is, what acts are deemed illegal. Even if the military defendant actually does have all the procedural due-process rights that a civilian has, his degree of freedom would still be very different because of problems with substantive law.

One substantive issue is the vagueness of law. It is a constitutional right that citizens should be able to distinguish between illegal acts and legal acts. In civilian law, vague laws have been declared unconstitutional for this reason. Some military regulations and laws, however, are written vaguely so that officers can maintain discipline and order. In fact, there are one or two "general articles" among UCMJ offenses that actually provide this important indeterminancy or vagueness.

Article 134, usually called the general punitive article, reads as follows:

> Though not specifically mentioned in this chapter, all disorders and neglects to the prejudice of good order and discipline in the armed forces, all conduct of a nature to bring discredit upon the armed forces, and crimes and offenses not capital, of which persons subject to this chapter may be guilty, shall be taken cognizance of by a general, special, or summary court-martial, according to the nature and degree of the offense, and shall be punished at the discretion of that court.

Noted in the *Manual for Courts-Martial*, as offenses against this article are such varied acts as the use of marijuana, assault with attempt to commit sodomy, dishonorable failure to pay debts, unauthorized use of passes, and escape from prison. This article has been particularly useful in dissent cases and disciplinary problems. Its (and other punitive articles') application to political resistance has become more specified due to the widening occurrence of resistance within the Army.[119]

Defenders of military justice assert that such articles as Article 134 are not unconstitutionally vague because their meaning is understood by all parties concerned.[120] Whether the meaning of such articles is clear is debatable, but their use is unquestionably clear to commanding officers. For example, legal clerks have told me that when a commanding officer finds that his charge is not going to stand up in court, his response may be, "Well, never mind, we'll just get him on some other charge then."

Some soldiers feel no one is innocent in the military, given the variety of offenses specified by the UCMJ. Of course, as already noted, those in authority who commit illegal acts in the course of controlling GIs are rarely brought to answer for them, unless a JAG lawyer is willing to push the paperwork.

Another "general article," Article 133, has been used to prosecute anti-war officers. It reads: "Any commissioned officer, cadet, or midshipman who is convicted of conduct unbecoming an officer and a gentleman shall be punished as a court-martial may direct."

As a result of Captain Howard Levy's statements in the presence of enlisted personnel and others concerning his strong opposition to the Vietnam War, the Army was able to court-martial him under Articles 133 and 134. The Court of Appeals for the Third Circuit found Articles 133 and 134 void for vagueness, but this appeal was reversed by the Supreme Court in *Parker* v. *Levy* (1974). Justice William Rehnquist's opinion emphasized that military law exists separate and apart from the law that governs the U.S. federal and judicial establishment and cannot be equated to a civilian criminal code. The failure of the challenge to Articles 133 and 134 may mean a significant reversal in the trend toward providing more due-process rights for soldiers. With conversion to the all-volunteer force, there is reason to suppose that there will be little progress made in the civilianization of the military justice system for several years to come.[121]

Young officers have also been convicted for their opposition to the Vietnam War under Article 88, which reads:

> Any commissioned officer who uses contemptuous words against the President, the Vice President, Congress, the Secretary of Defense, the Secretary of a military department, the Secretary of the Treasury, or the Governor or legislature of any State, Territory, Commonwealth, or possession in which he is on duty or present shall be punished as a court-martial may direct.[122]

An example of the use of Articles 133 and 88 to deny free-speech rights to officers who opposed the U.S. national policy was the case of Lieutenant Henry Howe. Howe was convicted and sentenced to two years of hard labor (later reduced to one year) for his part in a demonstration in which he carried a sign reading, "Let's have more than a choice between petty ignorant Fascists in 1968" on one side, and "End Johnson's Fascist Aggression in Vietnam" on the other.[123]

Other articles may be used against resisters who resist domination per se. Article 89 and Article 117 are particularly useful in controlling these resisters because they are vague enough and general enough to encompass the indirect kinds of resistance often expressed. Article 89 reads: "Any person subject to this chapter who behaves with disrespect toward his superior commissioned officer shall be punished as a court-martial may direct." Article 117 is similarly vague: "Any person subject to this chapter who uses provoking or reproachful words or gestures towards any other person subject to this chapter shall be punished as a court-martial may direct."

Most court-martial cases are for offenses that are not criminal offenses in civilian life. The majority are AWOL cases. Other offenses not considered crimes in civilian life are supports to military discipline and social control. Some of these are refusal to obey orders or regulations (Article 92 or Article 90), disrespect to a superior officer (Article 89), malingering (Article 115), insubordination to a noncommissioned officer (Article 91), and missing departure of a vessel (Article 87). That there are no civilian equivalents for these disciplinary offenses makes them particularly galling to soldiers.

In some cases, the Army itself provokes the infraction of disciplinary offenses. Prior to the recent volunteer Army changes, drill instructors in basic training have been reported as deliberately and explicitly attempting to drive recalcitrant soldiers AWOL. An AWOL case is taken off a commander's roll after a certain length of time and is no longer his problem; thus harsh officers can say they do not have any disciplinary problems. Legal clerk interviewees have asserted that soldiers often went AWOL for family or financial problems at home and may have even petitioned the Army for leave to go home to take care of their problems. When these requests for leave were refused, they went anyway.

It is through the broad specification of disciplinary offenses that the military can use its justice system to control GIs. To guarantee the soldier's right to counsel, right to fair trial by peers, and Fifth Amendment rights may be useful for maintaining legitimacy and commitment to the military organization. But in reality, and in connection with the fact that so many acts are illegal, the system can still easily overpower him.

The paternalism expressed by the protection of rights extolled in training lectures is in marked contrast with the experience of someone who does get into trouble.[124] Then the system can appear to be quite impersonal and frightening. The accused soldier may feel that the lawyer assigned to his defense has no interest in him and that his case is hopeless. In an actual court-martial there is little he is able to do. The accusers and the prosecution witnesses in disciplinary cases are likely to be experienced in these court-martial situations. The proceedings are usually brisk, and the case against him is not likely to fail (as Tables 1 and 2 show).

The process of achieving legitimacy for the military justice system has not been entirely effective. It was noted at the outset of this chapter that the military justice system has been the sector of military social control that has been most criticized by soldiers. The most obvious and perhaps the most important reason for criticizing this system rather than some other sector of social control is that military justice results in some of the more serious forms of repression, such as prison terms. Great numbers of soldiers remained in military prisons after each war was over. Court-martial convictions also leave a mark on an individual's life long after he has left military jurisdiction. A court-martial conviction is a federal conviction, and the offender has a federal record that follows him into civilian life. Similarly, a bad conduct discharge may follow a man for the rest of his life.

The military justice system, of course, is not the only sector of social control that can leave long-term marks on a soldier's life. An administrative discharge under less than honorable conditions, for example, might leave an equally debilitating effect on him as a veteran.[125] In such decisions, the soldier has no right to confront witnesses, no right to qualified counsel.[126] Some forms of administrative discharge are considered forms of punishment;[127] Dougherty and Lynch suggest methods of enhancing their punitive effects. Yet the system of administrative discharges retains a low profile and is not criticized very often.[128] So the existence of social control and repression alone is insufficient to explain the great deal of criticism that has been leveled at the military justice system.

Another explanation for the intense criticism of military justice by both GIs and concerned citizens is the presence of a civilian justice system with which to contrast the military equivalent. The United States Constitution, especially the Bill of Rights, is involved on a day-to-day basis in the civilian courts, and it provides a sense of the rights all Americans have. Whether corruption exists in civilian courts does not detract from the sense that, as Americans, there are certain rights that help in providing a self-identity. Injustices in the military justice system seem to be a result of the structure of courts and the statutes themselves, rather than simply of corrupt individuals. Thus it is thought that only revision of military justice laws would substantially change outcomes of military justice. Much of the agitation, therefore, is directed to congressional action to reform the military justice system. Chastising or removing certain individuals makes little sense once this kind of structural analysis has been made. So the presence of an alternative (that is, civilian) justice system that operates without those "structured-in" problems provides a model that legitimizes criticism.

This kind of critique does not emerge in such an articulate way with respect to other military sectors of control. GIs rarely perceive the controlling effects that attitude surveys, counseling sessions, rap sessions, character guidance classes, milieu therapy, and similar strategies have on their behavior and their attitude. In order to resist these forms of social control, soldiers would have to have a notion of their own rights against such forms of manipulation. As yet there is little basis on which to draw to delegitimize these modern, manipulative controls. The contrast between the many criticisms of the military justice system and the few criticisms of these other sectors shows that the most effective forms of social control and domination are based on acceptance and legitimacy, not on force.

NOTES

1. In this chapter, I will use the term *military justice system* to refer to the court structure, the military disciplinary and criminal laws, and the participants in that system. This usage of the term is similar to the Department of the Army usage; see its "Our Military Justice System," *Commander's Call* DA PAM 360-804 (3d Qtr Fy 1971). One could also consider the prison system to be part of the military justice system, but I will look at that subject in Chapter 7. The term *military law* is a broader category than the concerns of this book. Military law includes martial law, international law (see Joseph W. Bishop, Jr., "Military Law," *International Encyclopedia of Social Science* [New York: Macmillan, 1968], pp. 312-319), thousands of Army regulations (ARs), and many other elements extraneous to discipline (see James K. Gaynor, "The Military and the Law," *Cleveland State Law Review* 18 [1969]: 485-92). The term *military judicial system* is too restrictive a term because it does not include some actual laws and specifications of offenses, particularly criminal articles. *Military justice system* includes the articles of the Uniform Code of Military Justice (UCMJ), including offenses, specific court procedures and punishments, and rights of the accused.

2. See Edward F. Sherman, "The Civilianization of Military Law," *Maine Law Review* 22 (1970): 3-103.

3. This study also assessed some of the reasons behind the disparity of punishment rates between white and minority servicemen. The report was very critical of many aspects of the military justice system, generally arguing that the discretion given to commanders works to the disadvantage of enlisted men's individual rights and to the detriment of morale. It recommended some changes in the military justice system in the direction of the civilian justice system's protections of the accused.

4. Some of the junior officers' dissatisfactions with military justice focused on issues such as restrictions on search and seizure and Article 15 administration, the alleged leniency of military judges (JAG officers), and administrative delays in disciplinary cases. This report also looked at confinement policies and the limited legal training of junior officers. Like the earlier *Report to Honorable Wilber M. Brucker, Secretary of the Army* by the Committee on the Uniform Code of Military Justice, Good Order and Discipline in the Army, Department of the Army, January 18, 1960 (also called the *Powell Report*), this study sometimes recommended that the military justice system be made more efficient by removing some procedural safeguards.

5. See Robert E. Quinn, then chief justice of the Court of Military Appeals, "The Role of Criticism in the Development of Law," *Military Law Review* DA PAM 27-100-35, 35 (Winter 1967): 46-58. Alley noted that the military justice system is usually in a greater state of flux than the civilian justice system. Wayne E. Alley, "Determinants of Military Judicial Decisions," *Military Law Review* DA PAM 27-100-65, 65 (Summer 1974): 90.

6. Sherman, "Civilianization of Military Law," pp. 3-8. The task force commented that as a result of command influence over judicial proceedings, there are "vocal, well-placed critics who recommend total civilianization of the military justice system." Nathaniel Jones and C. E. Hutchin, Jr., *Report of the Task Force on the Administration of Military Justice in the Armed Forces*, 1:66 (hereafter *Task Force Report*). This report, incidentally, recommended only certain specific reforms.

7. Sherman, "Civilianization of Military Law," p. 4.

8. Quoted in Joseph N. Tenhet and Robert B. Clarke, "Attitude of US Army War College Students Toward the Administration of Military Justice," *Military Law Review* 27-100-59, 59 (Winter 1973): 32.

9. Ibid.

10. Ibid., p. 31.

11. Bishop, "Military Law," p. 312.

12. See Frederick Bernays Wiener, "Are the General Military Articles Unconstitutionally Vague?" *American Bar Association Journal* 54 (April 1968): 357-64; Department of the Army, "Our Military Justice System," pp. 7-8; and Gaynor, "The Military and the Law," pp. 485-92.

13. See Department of the Army, "Our Military Justice System," p. 8; Gaynor, "The Military and the Law," p. 492; Wiener, "Are the General Military Articles Unconstitutionally Vague?" p. 359; Edward J. Bellen, "The Revolution in Military Law," *American Bar Association Journal* 54 (December 1968): 1194; Army Digest Staff, "Subject: Military Justice, Memo to: Commanding Officer, B Company, 2d Battalion," *Army Digest* 24 (August 1969): 15; and Homer E. Moyer, Jr., "Procedural Rights of the Military Accused: Advantages Over a Civilian Defendant," *Military Law Review* DA PAM 27-100-51, 51 (Winter 1971): 1.

14. Delmar Karlen, "Civilianization of Military Justice: Good or Bad," *Military Law Review* DA PAM 27-100-60, 60 (Spring 1973): 118.

15. *Manual for Courts-Martial, United States*, rev. ed. (Washington, D.C.: U.S. Government Printing Office, 1969).

16. See Gaylord L. Finch, "Military Law and the Miranda Requirements," *Cleveland Marshall Law Review* 17 (September 1968): 547. For a general discussion of civilian reviews, see Thomas M. Strassburg, "Civilian Judicial Review of Military Criminal Justice," *Military Law Review* DA PAM 27-100-66, 66 (Fall 1974): 1-66.

17. See Edward F. Sherman, "Judicial Review of Military Determinations and the Exhaustion of Remedies Requirement," *Virginia Law Review* 55 (April 1969): 483-540; and Myron L. Birnbaum, "The Effect of Recent Supreme Court Decisions on Military Laws," *Fordham Law Review* 36 (December 1967): 153-74.

18. Richard J. Loeffler, "Military Justice and Due Process: Concerning the Rights of Representation and Judicial Review—An Analysis of *Kennedy v. Commandant* and *Application of Stapley*," *John Marshall Journal of Practice and Procedure* 2 (1969): 327-47.

19. Paul J. Rice, "Court-Martial Jurisdiction—The Service Connection Standard in Confusion," *Journal of Criminal Law, Criminology, and Police Science* 61 (1970): 339-51.

20. Loeffler, "Military Justice and Due Process," p. 333.

21. Sherman, "Judicial Review of Military Determinations," p. 500.

22. Birnbaum, "The Effect of Recent Supreme Court Decisions on Military Law," p. 155.

23. Drawn from *Task Force Report*, 1:11.

24. Hubert G. Miller, "The New Look in Article 15," *Army Information Digest* 18 (January 1963): 6.

25. See Thornton E. Ireland, "Article 15 Actions Are Command Actions," *Military Police Journal* 12 (June 1963): 15-16.

26. *Task Force Report*, 2: 37-44.

27. Department of the Army, "Our Military Justice System," p. 8.

28. Committee for Evaluation of the Effectiveness of the Administration of Military Justice, *Report to General William C. Westmoreland, Chief of Staff, U.S. Army*, pp. 9-10 (hereafter *Matheson Report*).

29. *Task Force Report*, 2: 39-40.

30. Robert S. Rivkin, *GI Rights and Army Justice: The Draftee's Guide to Military Life and Law* (New York: Grove Press, 1970).

31. Ibid., p. 227.

32. Ibid., p. 228.

33. *St. Louis Post-Dispatch*, April 15, 1973.

34. See Committee for Legal Research on the Draft, *Basic Resource Materials on Military Law*, 3d ed., (Cambridge: Harvard Law School, 1970), p. 10.

35. Ibid., p. 11 See also *Task Force Report*, 2: 75.

36. Article 20, Uniform Code of Military Justice (1950).

37. *Task Force Report*, 2: 46-47.

38. Article 19, UCMJ.

39. Article 23, UCMJ.

40. Birnbaum, "The Effect of Recent Supreme Court Decisions on Military Law," p. 155.

41. Committee for Legal Research on the Draft, *Basic Resource Materials*, p. 11.

42. *Task Force Report*, 2: 71.

43. Ibid., pp. 71-72.

44. Robinson O. Everett, "Military Justice in the Wake of *Parker v. Levy*," *Military Law Review* 27-100-67, 67 (Winter 1975): 13.

45. *Matheson Report*, pp. 23-24.

46. Drawn from ibid., p. 72. Table 1 excludes bad conduct discharges.

47. A study in 1966 showed that "officers consistently proposed less severe corrective action than NCOs." In addition, NCOs became more severe as they grew older and as their length of service increased. Interestingly, officers gave their highest effectiveness ratings to those NCOs who were most punitive and least like themselves; see Morris Showel, *Corrective Action Questionnaire: Development and Administration to Officers and NCOs*, Technical Report 66-5 (Alexandria, Virginia: Human Resources Research Office, The George Washington University, May 1966), p. iv. This is in contrast to studies in World War II that showed that officers had harsher attitudes toward soldiers.

48. Rivkin, *GI Rights and Army Justice*, pp. 249-51.

49. Committee for Legal Research on the Draft, *Basic Resource Materials*, p. 13.

50. Sherman, "Judicial Review of Military Determinations," p. 328.

51. Committee for Legal Research on the Draft, *Basic Resource Materials*, p. 13.

52. Robert Sherrill, in *Military Justice Is to Justice as Military Music Is to Music* (New York: Harper & Row, 1970), describes such an outcome on p. 41.

53. Article 22, UCMJ.

54. Committee for Legal Research on the Draft, *Basic Resource Materials*, p. 14.

55. Table 2 is drawn from *Matheson Report*, p. 78.

56. In order to make the judicial process more efficient, the Matheson committee suggested that the Army eliminate the requirement for a complete verbatim transcript of those general and bad-conduct special court-martial convictions that are based on guilty pleas. Ibid., p. 21.

57. Birnbaum, "The Effect of Recent Supreme Court Decisions on Military Law," p. 155.

58. *New York Times*, June 24, 1968.

59. Everett, "Military Justice in the Wake of *Parker v. Levy*," p. 13.

60. *Matheson Report*, p. 70.

61. Rivkin, *GI Rights and Army Justice*, p. 259.

62. Ibid., p. 260.

63. George F. Westerman, "Court of Military Review," *Army Digest* 24 (October 1969): 10. Civilians may serve on courts of military appeal. It even has been suggested that it might be desirable to authorize civilians to serve as mili-

tary trial judges. Everett, "Military Justice in the Wake of *Parker v. Levy*," p. 13.

64. In the vast majority of cases, the Court of Military Review takes no action. *Matheson Report*, p. 71.

65. Special Civilian Committee for the Study of the United States Army Confinement System, *Report of the Special Civilian Committee for the Study of the United States Army Confinement System*, Austin H. MacCormick, Chairman (Washington, D.C.: Department of the Army, 1970), p. 96.

66. Committee for Legal Research on the Draft, *Basic Resource Materials*, p. 18.

67. Birnbaum, "The Effect of Recent Supreme Court Decisions on Military Law," p. 154. The Matheson committee was not sympathetic with some of these recent changes in the interpretation of the Constitution: "It is recognized that the Court of Military Appeals in *United States v. Care*, 18 USCMA 535, 40 CMR 247 (1969) and *United States v. Donohew*, 18 USCMA 149, 39 CMR 149 (1969) held that the military judge must determine, and the record must so reflect, that the accused understands the meaning and effect of his plea of guilty (*Care*) and his rights to counsel (*Donohew*). These rules, especially the one announced in *Donohew*, are largely relics of an age of paternalistic concern for an accused who was not in every case represented by legally qualified counsel." *Matheson Report*, p. 22.

68. Birnbaum, "The Effect of Recent Supreme Court Decisions on Military Laws," p. 165; and George D. Schrader, "Miranda and the Military," *Georgia State Bar Journal* 5 (August 1968): 78. Some of these increased rights may be reversed as a result of the changing composition of the United States Supreme Court, which has recently tended to be much more sympathetic to military claims of its unique role. Everett, "Military Justice in the Wake of *Parker v. Levy*."

69. Sherman, "Judicial Review of Military Determinations," p. 866.

70. As a result, a major complaint of commanding officers is that they feel that their authority to order a search has been unduly restricted. The Matheson committee advised that the difference between an inspection and a search should be clarified. *Matheson Report*, pp. 11-13.

71. Sherman, "Civilianization of Military Law," p. 50.

72. On illegal command influence, see *Task Force Report*, 2: 66-70. The task force's discussion of command influence also included harassment of the defense counsel and influences over military judges.

73. Sherman, "Civilianization of Military Law," p. 91.

74. Ibid.

75. *New York Times*, June 24, 1968.

76. For a fuller discussion of command influence, see Luther Charles West, "The Command Domination of the Military Judicial Process" (Ph.D. diss., George Washington University, 1969).

77. Rivkin, *GI Rights and Army Justice*, p. 236.

78. Ibid., p. 243.

79. Tenhet and Clarke, "Attitude of US Army War College Students Toward the Administration of Military Justice," pp. 46-47.

80. *Matheson Report*, p. 33
81. Ireland, "Article 15 Actions Are Command Actions," pp. 15-16.
82. Sherman, "Judicial Review of Military Determinations," p. 869.
83. Ibid.
84. *Matheson Report*, p. 21.
85. In December 1971, according to the judge advocate general the Army had sixteen black judge advocates in the JAG Corps, which included 1,700 judge advocates. (Tenhet and Clarke, "Attitude of US Army War College Students Toward the Administration of Military Justice," p. 69.) Similarly, the task force reported that there were forty-five black and thirty Chicano and Puerto Rican judge advocates on active duty in the armed services. *Task Force Report*, 2: 60. Even in this case, this represents less than 2 percent of the total judge advocate strength. Ibid., 2: 60.
86. Ibid., p. 70.
87. Ibid., p. 67.
88. Rivkin, *GI Rights and Army Justice*, p. 262.
89. Ibid., p. 278, quoting Luther Charles West.
90. *Task Force Report*, 2: 67.
91. Rivkin, *GI Rights and Army Justice*, pp. 241-66.
92. *Task Force Report*, 2: 67.
93. *Claims* refers to those claims individuals make against the government for some financial loss they have incurred. For a brief discussion of this kind of military justice function, see Tenhet and Clarke, "Attitude of US Army War College Students Toward the Administration of Military Justice," p. 71.
94. See Rivkin, *GI Rights and Army Justice*, p. 264.
95. For a discussion of the role commitment plays in attitude changes, see Jack W. Brehm and Arthur R. Cohen, *Explorations in Cognitive Dissonance* (New York: John Wiley & Sons, 1962), pp. 286-96.
96. See Alley's discussion of commanders' informal influences on JAG judges for a similar view in "Determinants of Military Judicial Decisions," p. 99.
97. Being the only lawyer in a large graduating class to be transferred to Vietnam might be a clear case. See Sherrill, *Military Justice Is to Justice as Military Music Is to Music*, p. 89.
98. Alley, "Determinants of Military Judicial Decisions," p. 99.
99. James Mounts and Myron Sugarman, "The Military Justice Act of 1968," *American Bar Association Journal* 55 (May 1969): 470.
100. Alley comments on how judges of varying severity can cause significant differences in the overall disciplinary atmosphere of a unit. Alley, "Determinants of Military Judicial Decisions," p. 99.
101. *Task Force Report*, 2: 67.
102. "AF JAGs Warned Not to Help EM," *Camp News* 3 (March 15, 1972): 12.
103. Rivkin, *GI Rights and Army Justice*, p. 263.
104. Sherrill, *Military Justice Is to Justice as Military Music Is to Music*, pp. 84-90, 261-65.
105. Ibid., p. 88.

106. Ibid. The lawyer that Sherrill was referring to was using "unorthodox tactics," such as asking the commanding general of the post to testify.

107. *Task Force Report*, 2: 59-60.

108. Ibid.

109. See the recent Army Regulation 27-14 for the Army's attempt to rationalize the process. *Camp News* 3 (January 15, 1972): 11.

110. Rivkin, *GI Rights and Army Justice*, pp. 288-90.

111. Ibid., pp. 289-90.

112. Article 13, UCMJ.

113. See discussions in Richard R. Boller, "Pretrial Restraint in the Military," *Military Law Review* DA PAM 27-100-50, 50 (Fall 1970): 71-115; and Carroll J. Tichenor, "The Accused's Right to a Speedy Trial in Military Law," *Military Law Review* DA PAM 27-100-52, 52 (Spring 1971): 7-23.

114. *Matheson Report*, p. 38.

115. Ibid., pp. 34-35.

116. Ibid., pp. 28, 31.

117. See Karlen, "Civilianization of Military Justice: Good or Bad."

118. See Department of the Army, "Our Military Justice System," *Commander's Call* DA PAM 360-804 (3rd Qtr Fy 1971): 9-13.

119. According to the task force, Article 134 "historically provided, among other things, a vehicle whereby civilian-type offenses could be made punishable. That type of offense could not otherwise be tried by court-martial, except, for the most part and with respect to a limited number of offenses, during wartime, insurrection, or rebellion. This raison d'être—a vehicle for trying civilian offenses—for a general article no longer has significance, as the Uniform Code of Military Justice includes clearly defined civilian-type offenses in the punitive articles, without any limitation to times of war, rebellion or insurrection." *Task Force Report*, 2: 79-80. See also Ronald N. Boyce, "Freedom of Speech and the Military," *Utah Law Review* 240 (May 1968): 240-66.

120. See Wiener, "Are the General Military Articles Unconstitutionally Vague?" 357-64; and Gilbert G. Ackroyd, "The General Articles, Articles 133 and 134 of the Uniform Code of Military Justice," *St. John's Law Review* 35 (1961): 264-99.

121. Everett, "Military Justice in the Wake of *Parker v. Levy*."

122. See Sherman's eloquent response to the abrogation of free speech in an appeal. "Civilianization of Military Law," pp. 80-81.

123. Thomas C. Nord, "Constitutional Law—Freedom of Speech in the Military," *North Carolina Law Review* 46 (1968): 915-31.

124. See, for example, Department of the Army, "Our Military Justice System," pp. 9-13.

125. A JAG officer surveyed "employers, unions, colleges, and professional examiners" and found that there is a considerable degree of stigma concerning discharges other than honorable. See Bradley K. Jones, "The Gravity of Administration Discharges: A Legal and Empirical Evaluation," *Military Law Review* DA PAM 27-100-59, 59 (Winter 1973): 1-26. See also Robert K. Musil, "Amnesty and Bad Discharges," *Amnesty News*, Special Double Edition,

Americans for Amnesty, n.d., pp. 8-9. This article, in addition to discussing the shattering effects of a bad discharge, notes that many discharges hide the extent of anti-war activities and shift the burden of moral guilt on to the individual with labels like "homesickness" or "inability to adjust."

126. See Clifford A. Dougherty and Norman B. Lynch, "Loophole in Military Justice?" *Trial Magazine* (February-March 1968): 19-21. But, see statements of Major General Kenneth J. Hodson, the judge advocate general, U.S. Army, House of Representatives, Committee on Armed Services, Subcommittee No. 3, June 7, 1971 in House, *Hearings on H.R. 523*, 92d Cong., 1st sess., 1972, p. 5912.

127. See Richard J. Bednar, "Discharge and Dismissal as Punishment in the Armed Forces," *Military Law Review* DA PAM 27-100-51, 51 (Winter 1971): 71-115.

128. See Symposium on Military Justice, *Maine Law Review* 22 (1971); Dougherty and Lynch, "Loophole in Military Justice?" pp. 19-21; and Robinson O. Everett, "Military Administrative Discharge—The Pendulum Swings," *Duke Law Journal* 41 (1966).

7

Military Prisons and Rehabilitation

I have argued that psychiatrists perform social control functions for the military by minimizing the definition of soldiers as mentally ill. The reverse of this process occurs in correctional psychotherapy. Here psychiatric social control operates by attempting to confer a deviant label (as mentally ill) on the incarcerated soldier and inducing him to accept that new definition of himself. The Army can afford to try to transform the self-images of these soldiers because most of them have already been officially certified as deviant by the military justice system. In contrast, the Army could not afford this luxury for military psychiatry outside of prisons because the Army might be swamped with a much greater number of cases.

This methodical attempt to transform self-images refers only to the activities of prison therapists (including social workers and psychologists, as well as psychiatrists), who are not necessarily typical of the military prison system. In fact, there is little that can be said to be representative of this social control sector. Lags in modernization and contradictory styles of domination are more apparent in the military prison system than in any other sector of control in the Army.

There are three levels of prisons, which are related to the prisoner's length of sentence, the severity of the crime, and his potential for rehabilitation. The three levels are the post stockades, the Army's Correctional Training Facility (CTF), and the United States Disciplinary Barracks (USDB). Some military bases also have minimum security prisons, which are called Special Processing Detachments (SPD). These are run very much like ordinary barracks, and soldiers are not likely to be placed there for very long or for serious offenses. Rather, accused soldiers may be assigned to an SPD to wait for their courts-martial.

The stockades, located at each major base (now fewer than thirty), have been the most inhumane of the three types of prisons.

In an intermediate position in terms of severity and harshness is the armed forces' maximum security prison, the USDB. As we will see, the USDB makes only half-hearted attempts at reintegrating soldier-prisoners back into the Army. Its main emphasis seems to be directed at maintaining order within the prison by using techniques of social control that would not be subject to much criticism by civilians. The USDB at Fort Leavenworth is the only maximum security prison the Army (and the other services) has at the present time, and this relatively high visibility may help to account for its careful operation.

The most interesting prison for the purposes of this study is the CTF. Of the military prisons, it is the most co-optive, the most experimental, and the most oriented to rehabilitating soldiers and preserving military manpower. Unlike inmates in the USDB, soldiers who pass through the CTF are fully expected to return to active duty, and the CTF must reintegrate them into the rest of the Army. It does this (and maintains social control internally) by manipulating the convicted GI's self-image and his "definition of the situation." CTF principles may well be an anticipation of future trends in Army corrections.

The purpose of this chapter is to show how military prisons deal with their prisoners and to show how the behavioral sciences, including psychiatry, influence the modernization of prisons toward a greater reliance on manipulative forms of social control. After a brief review of some of the problems in the history of military prison modernization, I will discuss the various principles of operation behind these three rather different levels.

The unevenness in styles of control and the gaps between official statements of prison objectives and actual practices exist for several reasons. One reason is the lowly importance the Army has accorded to prisons.[1] Another explanation can be found in the history of military corrections in which it was continually shuttled from one branch of the Army to another.[2] The conflicting goals of various prison personnel provide for more confusion.[3] And yet another reason is the incompatibility between Army line officer goals and goals of the personnel at the prisons.[4] The Army, aware of all of these conflicts, has been making attempts to generate new ways of handling the problem of corrections and is trying to create convergences that may ultimately result in a more coherent military corrections system.

The U.S. Army did not always run its own prisons. Soldiers convicted of military crimes were put in state prisons until the early 1870s, when the Army was given a prison and a civilian-military committee was set up to govern it;[5] since 1875 this prison has been at Fort Leavenworth, Kansas. This was a late development vis-à-vis other branches of the Army. Huntington asserts that the last quarter of the nineteenth century was a time of great development in military professionalism.[6] However, the military prison staff could hardly have had a chance to develop its own professional standards and ideology, since it was in its infancy and going through processes of initial organization.

In 1913, jurisdiction over the military prison was given to the Judge Advocate General's Corps (JAGC). In 1915, the prison system was again reassigned to a different branch of the Army, the Adjutant General's branch (AG), which handles personnel records, casualty and prisoner-of-war records, strength accounting, office management, some personnel administration, most publications, and postal services. The final transfer came in 1954, when the military prison was given to the Provost Marshal General's Office.[7] The provost marshal general is the head of the military police. This last shift was a bit more gradual than the others. The provost marshal was given jurisdiction of post stockades and guardhouses gradually, beginning in 1946. Broadly, the two functions of the MP today are corrections and the usual police activities, such as traffic control, investigations, and arrests. It seems reasonable to suppose that these different branches of the Army are likely to view the proper way of administering the military prisons somewhat differently. In addition, the Leavenworth prison had been transferred twice to the U.S. Department of Justice and used for civil offenders. This occurred from 1895 to 1906 and again in 1929, this time following a major riot at the Justice Department's own overcrowded federal penitentiary. It was reestablished as the USDB near the end of 1940.[8] If the military prison system was late in becoming professionalized, any development in this direction was certainly impeded by this continual shifting of jurisdictions. Ranking officers in the USDB at Fort Leavenworth as late as 1970 complained that many of them were being transferred at one time, which tended to destroy the continuity of policies.[9]

Additional strains were put on the military prison system due to the rapidly shifting size of the military forces. During World War I and World War II, the military prisons multiplied fivefold and belatedly shrank after each war. When the Army had these large numbers of prisoners to deal with, it expanded the number of USDBs (from one to three in World War I, and from one to nine in World War II), and it instituted an intermediate level prison between the stockage and the USDB. These intermediate prisons, called *rehabilitation centers*, operated not only to relieve the load of the various USDBs but also functioned to keep the less serious offenders from being influenced by the more serious ones. The rehabilitation centers were closed or transferred to civilian agencies after World War II, but the Army has had to resort to this level again. In 1968, probably for the same two reasons, it opened a rehabilitation center at Fort Riley, Kansas, which was named a "Correctional Training Facility."

This kind of fluctuation in size of an organization may not be an insurmountable problem for line officers and training cadres, such as in the infantry. But the problem seems to become more acute when the number of guards rises and falls. Guards must be professionalized and must have a sense of responsibility and expertise. Without these qualities, a kind of anomic condition results in which each guard follows the dictates of his own whims. Recent experiments with college students in which they attempted a realistic form of role playing as prisoner and guard had to be terminated prematurely because some students in the guard role became brutal when they were not supervised.[10]

The official ideology of the military prison system, expressed by the provost marshal general in 1954, is centered around rehabilitation.[11] Military prisoners are a liability from the Army's point of view; they are a waste of manpower and training efforts, and they are costly to maintain. There is little return on an incarcerated soldier. Prisoner labor is used, but overall it is not a bargain since laboring prisoners must be watched, and every guard is another waste of Army manpower resources. The Army, like any other rationalistic bureaucracy, over the long run should be concerned not with revenge but with efficiency. But what does the word *rehabilitation* really mean? Or, perhaps the question should be, how seriously is this principle taken at different levels?

At the stockade level, rehabilitation of prisoners has not been much of a concern.[12] Soldiers are often in stockades for brief or varying periods, and a large proportion are held in pretrial confinement. While there are differences among stockades, some stockades have been brutally run, using some of the techniques of control that I described in the chapter on coercion.[13] In 1969, a pro-military, "blue ribbon," civilian inspection committee toured several stockades (but with advance warning to each post) and found several categories of problems.[14]

Probably the most immediate problem they found was the personnel. Guards were described as immature, untrained, inexperienced, nervous, and either too lenient or too harsh.[15] The stockade commanders were described in similar terms. Guards were sometimes assigned stockade duty as punishment, and they resented it. The special civilian committee found that some guards were drawn from infantry companies to serve thirty to ninety days as guards and received no training to speak of. They were frequently overworked and forced to work twelve-hour shifts for weeks on end, often without a break. Almost anyone would express some hostility under those conditions. Stockade duty even among MPs is seen as "bad duty."[16] Long hours and overwork seems odd in an organization that relies on large amounts of manpower to solve its problem of poorly motivated, inefficient workers, yet the Army seems not to want to waste many men in running stockades.[17] Stockade guards complained that stockade commanding officers do not bother to look out for their men or ease their work load.[18] A legal clerk, whose responsibility it was to interview stockade prisoners prior to their trials, gave me his impression of stockade conditions at a large midwestern Army post:

> I'd say a clear majority of the [inmates] who go out there get beaten up. . . . Once you come in, you're assigned to a barracks and you go to the barracks on the first night and that's invariably when the beating takes place: they throw him down the stairs, take him to the latrine and beat the shit out of him, beat him around, beat him in front of the other prisoners, they take him aside and beat him, [and if] the guy says anything at all they put him in the box ["administrative segregation"] and continue to beat him, [and leave] him in the box for a couple of days. I get the impression that it's very common for a guy to be put in a box for [his] first couple of days in jail, in pre-trial confinement. Then that subdues him . . . and they let him out of the box. By then they're pretty well beaten into the system.
>
> There was this case where this guy had been beaten up in pre-trial and he came to his trial with a cast on. They asked him if he had been beaten and he said no. They asked him how he got the cast on and he said he fell down the stairs. They said, "Well did anyone push you?" and he said, "No." You know that's a lie. He had told someone else that he had been beaten. But the reason he didn't say anything at his trial was because he knew he was going to be convicted and that he was going to go back to the stockade after he was convicted and they were really going to beat the shit out of him then. You can't get these guys who were beaten in pretrial to testify to anything because they know they're going to be convicted and that they're going to go back.
>
> [Two guards] were court-martialed recently for [beating

> inmates]; one was acquitted and the other was convicted and sentenced to a laughably light sentence (3 months or something like this). When they were brought in and read their rights and asked if they did it, they said, "shit, of course we did it." There was no doubt in their minds that they did it and that they were in their right in doing it. They said, "Sure, it's our god-damn job to beat those guys." I guess they thought they were going to be prosecuted for dereliction [of duty] for *not* doing it.

He contrasted these conditions with recent changes:

> [In 1971, a new commander was assigned to this stockade] and since then he has taken some very definite measures. He has increased the number of guards. It used to be that guards were temporary duty people. They just went into a permanent party company and said we need five guys to be guards for three months. And they were assigned right there and they were all pissed off because it was the worst duty. They couldn't get any leave. They took the jerk-offs and put them out there to work. They were very young and none of them had any formal training. Major —— changed that. There is now an MP company that does that. The age has been increased and these guys are given training classes. As a matter of fact they're given training classes as punishment a lot of time. If you're a guard and you come late to work one day, you have to go to training class for a week! . . . I think the brutality has decreased. . . . They now have a moderately elaborate stockade counseling system. They've got six enlisted men who have quasi-credentials to be social workers or guidance counselors and they have sessions to speak with prisoners.

The special civilian committee also found that the physical set-up contributed to bad stockade conditions. Some stockades were built as temporary World War II structures, never meant to be used today.[19] Others were constructed in such a way as to eliminate sunlight and fresh air from reaching many prisoners. The overabundance of security arrangements, such as many locks on intermediate doors and the separation of toilet facilities from the cells (requiring a guard to accompany each prisoner to the bathroom), make life for prisoners even more arduous.[20] Soldiers have asserted that some post commanders allow bad conditions in the stockade in order to prevent soldiers from malingering there.[21] The result is a high suicide rate, many mental breakdowns, and many riots.[22]

Stockades have been an unnecessary thorn in the Army's side. They result in bad public relations and lower Army legitimacy among GIs.

More serious offenders are sent to the USDB, which is not run in the brutal fashion that characterizes many stockades; yet there probably is little real rehabilitation going on there. In 1954, rehabilitation programs were at best rudimentary. The assumption seems to have been that the soldier-prisoner would so hate the experience of prison and of being away from his unit that he would want to reform himself, almost unaided, in prison. The soldier-prisoners were "given the opportunity to lift themselves by their own bootstraps back to duty."[23] Thus the burden for rehabilitation was placed on the soldier-prisoner.

In 1954, according to the provost marshal general of the Army, each new prisoner at the USDB was given an indoctrination session concerning the purpose of the prison and an orientation interview by the commandant or one of his representatives, where he would be assured that "he is part of an institution where the entire staff from the top officer down through the enlisted ranks has a warm interest in his personal problems and needs and his future welfare."[24] Later on he would be given what GIs call an "attitude check" to see how well he had responded to the "warm" concern. He was also interviewed by a social worker who elicited information on previous problems with school authorities, pastors, relatives, and employers, which was then worked up into a report of the psychiatry and neurology division.[25] This information, together with psychological tests, enabled the USDB classification board to make decisions as to the prisoner's custody, training, restoration to duty, or transfer to federal prison. Of course, the prisoner would not be restored to duty until he had spent a reasonable time in prison, so the classification board could make an accurate determination of his case. Thus, the main functions of psychiatrists and social workers were in screening and classifying.[26] Psychiatrists kept a close watch on each soldier-prisoner to determine when he had "improved" himself sufficiently to be released before his full term had been completed. A chaplain was involved in this setting, although only in an advisory capacity to the classification board. He was to ascertain the influence of religion in the prisoner's life.

Assuming a soldier wanted to return to duty or to civilian life, the classification board was an ominous judge. In order to see if he was worthy of favorable consideration, the board examined the soldier's attitude, adjustment to confinement, and "sincere attempt to better himself by taking advantage of the many opportunities to learn a trade or improve his education."[27] Rehabilitation in 1954, then, was officially a combination of some indoctrination, vocational training programs, and several "open doors" back to duty or out to civilian life.

From the recent prison experiences of Dr. Howard Levy, the basic principles of the USDB seem relatively unchanged.[28] The only difference is in a few minor modernizations. But, paradoxically, these modernizations, or liberalizations, have acted precisely to serve as techniques of control that replace older, brutal methods.[29]

The manifest function of the liberalizations is as techniques of rehabilitation, but their latent function is as techniques of domination. For example, parole was intended to ease the prisoner into civilian life gradually under the supervision of a parole officer. Yet in prison, the point at which the prisoner leaves for parole is under the nearly complete control of the prison warden, giving him great power over inmates. This has serious consequences; for example, if a political prisoner demonstrated his lack of "humility" by writing to his lawyer to complain about the extreme degree of censorship at the USDB, he would risk spending much more time behind walls.[30] Censorship of incoming correspondence and magazines and outgoing mail is presented as necessary to create a conducive environment for rehabilitation and to prevent outside agitation.[31] But according to Levy, it allows prison officials to continue their day-to-day oppression unimpeded. Similarly, Levy asserts that certain kinds of work, such as clerical or educational jobs, that are said to be mostly rehabilitative are used regularly as rewards for prisoner conformity and "humility." And much prison work, such as printing military decals for automobile bumpers, while useful for prison and military production, is useless for rehabilitation.

Military prisoners are sometimes transferred into the federal prison system, which includes facilities of varying levels of freedom and constraint—from maximum security, walled-in prisons to relatively open farm camps. The farm camps are justified as useful for rehabilitation as the prisoner gradually is reintegrated into civilian society and becomes accustomed to lessening formal controls. But assignment to these camps is also used as a technique of control; demonstrating humility in a maximum security prison may eventually bring a transfer to minimum security just as being uncooperative in minimum security might mean a transfer to maximum security. A prisoner who is called uncooperative may not necessarily be violent or thieving; he may be only criticizing prison policies or conditions. If a critic does appear to be gaining a following, the prison system can transfer him among several prisons, moving him slowly across the country from prison to prison. This transfer process can take weeks or even months.

Although the USDB and allied federal prisons differ from post stockades in some respects—guards do not routinely beat prisoners, and living conditions are not squalorous—they can easily substitute their own more neutral-appearing techniques.[32] As Levy said, "Anything given to an inmate beyond keeping him in 24-hour lock-up is a privilege contingent on his behavior."[33]

Thus it would appear that rehabilitation in the USDB in 1969 was still primarily a selective tool and had little lasting effect on soldiers' behavior. It selected those soldiers who were more easily manipulated or, perhaps more accurately, the ones who could most easily manipulate the prison by convincingly demonstrating their "humility" and their desire to be "rehabilitated." In either case, the USDB policies can be useful for the Army: the

USDB returns to service those soldier-prisoners the Army can use with minimal difficulty. Simultaneously, this prison can maintain a public-relations front of a modern, efficient, well-run prison, using "every modern principle of penology" so that "every possible effort will be made by industrial training, by education, morale and religion, by lectures and debates, by salutary contacts with families to create a sense of dignity and self-respect and of duty to the country and to fellow men."[34]

According to Berlien, correctional psychologists and psychiatrists during World War II had been unsatisfied with the limited role they played and wanted a greater role in planning and executing programs of rehabilitation.[35] They chafed at the classification and advisory function to which they were limited because they felt that sitting in judgment on a board precluded any therapy or counseling they might be able to provide because prisoners would distrust them. They wanted to prove their effectiveness and to demonstrate their support of military correctional objectives.

Psychology (and psychiatry) in the last few decades has taken the place of religion in maintaining mass discipline. Like religion, it operates by trying to convince the individual that it is trying to help him and has his interests at heart, all the while fairly self-consciously going about its role in creating and maintaining social order. Psychology not only provides techniques of control, such as various types of therapy and consultative assistance to those in authority, but it also parallels religion in providing an ideology. This ideology is one of "cooperation," "communication," "normalcy," and a distinct view of reality. In addition, psychology has a normative function, creating in individuals a sense of guilt, such as the anxiety that comes from feeling that one is not normal or socially acceptable. Instead of being sinful, today one is "sick." Like religion, psychology ministers to the guilt and anxiety that it was instrumental in creating.

In correctional settings, psychiatrists and psychologists use psychological definitions of the situation to reinterpret resistance so that it can be more easily managed and transformed. Mills has argued that the task of sociology is to interpret problems in an individual's life in the context of a social structure and public issues.[36] Correctional therapists "turn Mills on his head." For example, according to Holland and Luszki, "It can be assumed that each of the trainees [prisoners] has some kind of personal problem or maladjustment which was a factor in his getting in trouble."[37] Similarly, according to Abrahams and McCorkle, "rehabilitatees are considered for psychotherapeutic purposes to be socially ill."[38] Another correctional therapist said that the character and behavior disorder (a category that includes most soldiers who get in trouble with the Army) must "be made to see that there is something wrong with him and not with society."[39]

During World War II, psychiatrists and psychologists, like other professionals working for the military, had to manipulate and convince the more traditional authorities of their capabilities.[40] One strategy they occasionally used was to try to show the correctional staff that psychopaths could easily fool the latter but not the former.[41] A psychopath might look superficially normal, and an untrained observer would not be able to spot one. Some psychiatrists, for example, put up a scoreboard on these individuals' recidivism rates, comparing their predictions with those of the rest of the correctional staff.[42] Psychiatrists in the USDBs and rehabilitation centers in that era used connections in the Surgeon General's Office to make links with AG so they could get more involved.[43]

In World War II, occasionally a psychiatrist did have a chance to practice group therapy. One outstanding (although unusual for World War II) example of group therapy in prisons was at an Army rehabilitation center at Fort Knox, Kentucky.[44] This program generated new techniques that were later used more extensively.[45]

The psychiatrists at Fort Knox were careful to make sure the project would not backfire. They were dealing with two main problems at the prisoner level. One was in controlling small group attitudes and definitions of the situation in a manner consistent with the psychotherapists (and their several assistants).[46] A second problem was in dealing with the rebels who were potential organizers.[47] These individuals had displayed "gutsy," rather populist attitudes toward omnipotent bureaucratic authority and manipulative therapists. These rebels could have easily crystallized the resentful attitudes of many other prisoners.

The therapists handled the first problem by establishing a therapy program in three stages, a "preliminary," an "analytical," and a "synthetic" stage.[48] The preliminary stage, lasting nine weeks, consisted of lectures, discussions, and slide talks on such topics as the human personality, personality development, and methods of escape from reality. Thus psychology's definition of man and of resistance was well articulated, and a complete definition of the situation was well on its way.[49] As we shall see, resistance to regimentation was translated into antisocial attitudes; a withdrawn style was considered "uncooperative."

The analytical stage, lasting twelve weeks, used group discussions to analyze various group members' problems. AWOL, desertion, and the importance of authority were among topics discussed. The manner in which various group members responded to authority and the personality defects of various members came out in discussions. In fact, Abrahams and McCorkle utilized the "great 'gripe drive' of individuals under military control" as a tool for catharsis.[50] Additionally, the "rehabilitees" published an in-house paper, *Rehab Roundup*, and ran a broadcasting system that dealt with topics of "therapeutic value to the rehabilitees." These activities, under the control of the therapists, helped the latter get their perspective across without seeming to be saying much themselves.

The synthetic stage, consisting of the last five weeks of the program, was aimed at having each individual analyze the changes in himself and to rid himself of any residual hostilities or resentments.[51] Topics discussed included ways of adjusting to a new outfit and of adopting self-satisfying patterns of expression that are acceptable in a social situation. "Rehabilitees" who made a minimal commitment to this series of discussions inevitably found their attitudes changing. The force of his own uncoerced commitment would bring his attitudes "into line," and the power of the small group would confirm the job.

The second prisoner problem was the rebel. One strategy of dealing with him was to isolate him from the more passive prisoners and deal with him and other rebels as a special group.[52] In varying forms, this strategy of removing rebels from rehabilitation groups has remained in use at every level of corrections.[53]

Another strategy of dealing with the rebel was a result of the psychological definition of the situation: the rebel was particularly ill and in need of clinical help both from the psychotherapist and from his friends. If this ideology was not enough, the tendency of repressed people to turn on an isolate was encouraged.

The transformation of resistance and the conversion of the inmates in this therapy program can best be understood by reading an actual account of the interactions of the participants. The events in the following took place during the analytical stage of the program.

> The session started with a remark by A, an overtly aggressive rehabilitee, who yelled, "I don't like the way Sgt. — — treated K!" The group nodded approval and several remarked, "That's right." As the group quieted, I asked A what had happened and he replied, "He [the sergeant] is always doing things to us, especially to K." The group again emphasized approval and several started talking excitedly to the men close to their seats. I paused until the group stopped talking and asked A what the Sgt. had done to K. He said, "That g— —d— — Sgt. always punishes us and today he 'gigged' K for no reason." A continued talking rapidly, his face flushed. "That is the trouble around this place. I hate the whole bunch of the b— — who run this place. They won't give a guy a decent break."
>
> The group moved restlessly, and A continued, "Day and night you people tell us what to do and we never have a chance. I am sick of all this stuff and if I ever meet that Sgt. outside, I will break his neck." I asked A how he felt about other people in the Center and he said, "They are all the same, making us unhappy instead of giving us a break. I hate them all." The group became tense and looked expectantly at me as I asked A how he felt about me. He looked angry and defiant and said, "You are like the rest. I hate you too." A was making an obvious effort to keep himself

under control. His face was flushed and he gripped the chair in front of him. I asked A what he felt he would like to do to me now and with emotion he said, "I would like to take this chair and throw it at you because you always beat us down."

The group became tense and stiffened. Several of the rehabilitees in loud stage whispers gave support to A. C jumped up and said, "What the hell would you want to do that for. He never done anything to us." (C's remark was with warmth, indicating he accepted me as a group member, not a punishing agent.) After C's remark there was considerable confusion as the rehabilitees talked over his comment. Several yelled, "He (C) is hand-shaking," or, "You are right, C." A looked confused and turned angrily to the group and said, "He is no different than the Sgt., he just gives us a 'snow job.'" A rehabilitee near the front spoke up and said, "You are always bitching, A, about everybody and nobody could please you." The group laughed and A became more flushed as he turned and said, "Just because I don't let the b—— around here kid me, I stick up for my rights." Several group members yelled approval but a greater number "booed."

P, another rehabilitee, pointed at me, and said, "He understands us and tries to help us get out of here. He is on our side and most guys would have shut you up a long time ago. I don't like this place and there are a lot of people here I don't like but they're not all b——'s." A yelled at him, "You are just hand shaking to get out, that's all, you haven't got the guts to say what you think. You complain more than anyone else." P looked at A disgustedly and said, "If you think I haven't got as much guts as you, why don't you try finding out. Sure, I complain but that doesn't make me believe everybody is agin me. You make us all sick with your constant complaints."

A looked bewildered, and sensing the shift in the group's approval said, "That is the trouble around here, the prisoners don't stick together." P looked at him and the group and said, "I am no rat just because I don't agree with you, and you get the group in more trouble than anybody else." Several group members yelled, "That's right." By this time almost the entire group had rejected A and the members were anxious to criticize his behavior. One man yelled, "If he hadn't acted so damned smart maybe K would never have been 'gigged.'" The group looked angrily at A who guiltily replied, "You guys are all alike." I turned to A and asked him why he disliked me. Somewhat disturbed but with less emotion he said, "Because you are one of them. You don't give a damn about us." A rehabilitee's hand went up and I motioned to him to speak and with warmth he said, "That isn't true. He is our friend." The group accepted this remark and several commented to other rehabilitees about it. A looked guilty and dejected, but said nothing. I asked him if he could think of any reasons why he felt this way about me. He said, "No, I just know I don't like you. You never hurt me but you work from the front office." I asked A why he disliked the people in the front office and he replied, "They don't care about us, and never give us a break."

The group smiled as I asked A if he could tell us about other people he disliked. He said, "Sure, in this world it's every guy for himself and when you are down, the guys on top will give you a kick." I asked A if many people in life had given him kicks. He hesitated a minute and said, "No." I looked at A and asked him if he got kicked around in the army. He looked sullen and with rising emotion said, "Hell, everybody gets kicked around in the army. Of course, I got kicked around plenty. The Company Commander and 1st Sgt. never gave me a break." The group laughed and several members yelled, "Oh, oh, here it comes!"

A looked around at the group and laughed and I nodded to him to continue. A told of having more details than others, being refused passes, etc., and his subsequent AWOL. I asked him if he believed that some of his dislike for people in the front office might not come from the fact that they are like his Company Commander and 1st Sgt. A looked thoughtful and replied, "I guess so, they do the same things." I asked A if he could think of any reasons for his hatred of his Company Commander and 1st Sgt. besides their failure to give him a pass when he wanted to go home, and make him do K.P. He seemed puzzled by the question and asked, "What do you mean?" I explained to A that just as he disliked me because he identified me with his CO and 1st Sgt., perhaps he disliked them because he identified them with others.

A looked doubtful, perplexed, as he said, "This is a lot of b— — s— —." The group laughed and several members started to talk to one another. A's face became flushed and he excitedly said, "You are a 'con man,' we start to talk about one thing and you don't answer questions." Since the hour was closing I explained to A that we would talk about this tomorrow if he liked. . . .

The hour started with a remark by C, one of the men, that he believed that he was going to a disciplinary barracks Friday. I asked the rehabilitee how he felt about leaving and he replied, "I don't want to go to the disciplinary barracks and get a dishonorable discharge, but if that is where they want to send me, then I can take it." Several of the rehabilitees mumbled approval of this remark and one yelled, "Send me too. I am sick of this place." The group laughed and one of the men yelled, "He is frustrated!" (As a result of the didactic presentation of psychological concepts, the rehabilitees have acquired a vocabulary of psychological terms.)

I turned to the group and asked what they thought of the last two remarks. A rehabilitee said, "They are disgusted and have lost hope." I asked C if that was true and he said, "I guess so." I asked C if he could think of other times when he gave up hope easily. He looked thoughtful, laughed self-consciously and said, "Yes, a lot of times." I waited and he continued, "I wanted to get along in the Army but I quit after the 1st Sgt. picked on me." The men all laughed. I waited until the rehabilitees quieted down, and reminded them that C has a problem and we are to help him understand himself and find ways of getting along in the Army.

I asked C if he could think of other times he had stopped trying. He said, "Sure, I quit a lot of jobs and I quit school, even if I did want to graduate." I asked him if he could think of reasons why he stopped when he wanted to continue. He replied, "No, what the hell is the use? I can't make it anyway." I asked C if he could think of reasons why he can't make restoration. With pent up emotion he said, "I hate this place. They are always pushing you around making you do things you don't want to do." I asked C if people pushed him around more than others and he heatedly replied, "I like to do as I please without people sticking their noses in my business." "Why," I asked, and C disgustedly replied, "Because that is what I want."

The group remained tense and alert through the interaction between C and myself and in whispers expressed approval or disapproval. One of the rehabilitees said, "C wants his own way all the time and when he can't have it, he quits." Another yelled, "Quit brown nosing, C is right." As the rehabilitees quieted down, I asked the group if we could examine all that had been said and try to arrive at a conclusion.

I asked the group for possible reasons why people have trouble getting along and want to quit. I received a scattering of varied responses from—"Nobody can get along in the Army," to "Never learned to get along." I asked K what he meant by "never learned to get along." He replied, "C always had trouble adjusting to people." C looked a little confused and said, "I get along all right outside the Army." The rehabilitees laughed and C's face became red, and he looked angry. I reminded the men that we are helping C and his problem is also a problem that many of us have and how people can feel they get along but actually they aren't doing very well.

K said to C, "You didn't get along because you had trouble everywhere." C said, "Only with some people." I asked C what kind of people he had trouble with and he replied, "People who pick on me." I asked him what kind of people "picked on" him and he said, "A lot of b—— who don't like anybody." C became conscious of the smiles of

> the group and its enjoyment of his confusion. I helped C feel more at ease by asking to tell us about people he did get along with and liked. He told of a man who played ball with him who lived next door to his home and several friends of his adolescence.
>
> I asked C if the people he had most trouble with weren't people in authority. C looked guilty and said, "I guess so but that is because they pick on me." I asked him if the people who "picked on him" also "picked on" everybody else. He looked confused and annoyed and said angrily, "I don't know and don't care." I asked K, a more analytical rehabilitee, what he thought of this, and he said, "C has trouble getting along with people and won't admit it." I asked L, another rehabilitee, if he thought this was true and he replied, "Well, C can't be right and the world wrong." C yelled, "Sure, I am wrong a lot, we all have faults." I asked C if he believed that statement and he replied he did. I asked him what he thought was his biggest fault. He replied, "My temper, I blow my top too easy." I asked him if he could tell us about this, and as the session closed, he was reciting his impatience with people who attempted to restrain him, losing control when responsibilities mount and his general inability to conform.[54]

Since World War II, psychiatrists have been expanding their role in corrections. They have had a greater hand in designing corrections programs, and their participation as therapists rather than screening agents has increased somewhat. But this increased involvement has not come without costs to psychiatry. Psychiatrists have increasingly been compromising their techniques of therapy with military techniques of control.[55]

In particular, the practice of therapy becomes much more oriented to social control of the individual by the small group or team, which is characteristic of military organization in general. I have suggested that the offenders who must see therapists do not view themselves as ill. But according to one well-known therapist, confining soldiers in this "therapeutic community" contributes to these offenders' motivation for treatment. "Few retrainees not under detention would seek treatment for their maladaptive problems. This is because most feel little sense of guilt, are not highly anxious, and do not recognize that much of the problem resides within themselves."[56] This new role for therapists, that of forcefully attempting to transform soldiers' minds, results in a shift in the therapist's role. As Martin and Alvord wrote, "Since the goal of the group was to arouse in the patient the realization that something was wrong with him and that his problems are not necessarily caused by society, the therapist avoided functioning in the traditional passive manner."[57] They also noted that these individuals are "usually extremely resistant."[58]

Some of these young men may be able to lead fuller, more developed lives with the benefit of some kind of therapy. But the value of personal freedom, it seems to me, requires that these people should have the choice of whether they want to undergo such personality changes. The only real alternative they have to undergoing therapy is being sent to a harsher prison.

This convergence of psychiatry and military corrections should not be overrated. The convergence is greater between psychiatry and higher-ranking corrections staff, who function more as bureaucrats than as guards. There often remains a serious split between the corrections bureaucracy and the actual guard staff, particularly during transitional periods.[59] The convergence additionally exists only at some prisons, such as the USDB or the new CTF. Installation stockades are less likely to be influenced by modernization along psychiatric lines. But, as the following account demonstrates, convergences can even be created at the post stockade level.

Bushard, a psychiatrist, and Dahlgren, a stockade commander, reported in 1957 how they achieved a higher degree of cooperation between the Mental Hygiene Consulting Service (MHCS) and the post stockade at Fort Dix, New Jersey.[60] A serious riot at the Fort Dix stockade in 1954, in which nearly all control was lost over the prisoners, resulted in the Army's permitting an overall reorganization of the stockade operation.

Bushard and Dahlgren recognized that they were dealing with resisters who had not been quieted by the Army's "gentler" techniques, such as counseling and Article 15s. For example, they observed that co-optation through open communication is more difficult for the MHCS at the stockade (compared to nonstockade counseling) because the soldier-prisoner is likely to persist in feeling that he was right and that the Army was giving him a raw deal. Bushard and Dahlgren also noted that some prisoners were more likely to organize than others.

> The custodial personnel remain alert for evidence of the existence of "cliques" and other organized activities in the prisoner group. Suspected leaders are placed in an administrative, non-punitive segregation. Others so segregated are suspected or admitted homosexuals, alcoholics, drug addicts, noncommissioned officers, former stockade personnel, persons requiring extensive medical treatment, and others who, in the judgment of the confinement officer, represent a source for or a nidus of disruption, poor morale, or bad discipline.
>
> Disciplinary segregation and loss of accrued good conduct time are used when and if it becomes necessary, for any reason, to emphasize the punitive aspect of the confinement.[61]

With the remainder of the soldier-prisoners, the staff's concern was with changing attitudes, particularly the "misapprehension that delinquency is a pattern of behavior with social value."[62] Being aware that soldiers do not like being in prison, the MHCS staff manipulated the prisoner's desire to get out: "Rehabilitation is derived, then, partly from timing the offering of clemency at the moment when the more acceptable identification is in the ascendancy."[63]

In a way consistent with the rest of military practice, the psychiatrist and stockade commander designed a program "to promote group forces which tend to press individuals toward nondelinquent patterns of behavior. This is accomplished through providing the prisoner group with only that information on which they can predict what will occur if they conform with normal social attitudes and behavioral patterns."[64] However, Bushard and Dahlgren recognized that these techniques could lead to countertechniques on the part of the prisoners and thus the process must be carefully watched. "[The prisoners] must not be able to predict what frightening or threatening statements they can make to secure an early release, special attention, or disorganization of the administration."[65]

In this new program, the screening function was expanded, and several rehabilitation programs were established by the confinement officer. Prisoners were put to work in "menial, but not degrading" work.[66] Normal military discipline was maintained through the establishment of a rehabilitation company.[67] This company, a minimum security portion of the stockade, was located outside of the prison walls with prisoners in parolee status. The prisoner was attached during appropriate hours to a unit in its own phase of training, assuming the prisoner was a trainee (he was available for other work if he was not). After hours, he was required to return to the rehabilitation company. The system of parole and clemency was also expanded.[68] In addition to serving as the initiating agency in the new program, the MHCS also participated on a day-to-day basis in the stockade. This aspect of the program was described as follows:

> a. All prisoners are examined within 14 days after sentence is pronounced. Pretrial examinations are prompt if and when they are requested by the commander or the defense or trial counsels.
>
> b. Persons requiring psychotherapy receive it.
>
> c. Persons, especially first offenders, likely to benefit from transfer to the rehabilitation company are referred to the Classification Board at the appropriate time.
>
> d. Appearance before the Clemency Board is recommended at the appropriate time.
>
> e. Negative recommendations are made regarding both clemency and transfer to the rehabilitation comapny, if, for any reason, these appear inappropriate.
>
> f. Close liaison is maintained with the confinement officer in finding mutually agreed to solutions for such problems as tantrums, suicidal gestures, suspected psychosis, evidence of organized resistance, cliques, et cetera.
>
> g. When rehabilitative efforts have been attempted and

> significant evidence of their lack of success has been amassed, positive recommendations for separation from the service are made.[69]

The bulk of the work in the program was done by social workers. The most important function of the interview, which each prisoner went through when he arrived at the stockade, was to lay the groundwork for the rest of the program. The soldier-prisoner was "offered . . . an opportunity for coming to terms with the administration. The prisoner was shown that lack of social conformity had been of little value to him."[70]

One of the problems that emerged in using social workers in this kind of function was the morale of social workers, and "care was taken to make certain that the individuals doing this work did not become cynical" because the prisoner might begin to influence his therapist.[71]

The authors reported much improved rehabilitation rates and, importantly, better stockade control through this use of mutual cooperation between stockade and psychiatric personnel.

In July 1968, in response to the rising numbers of offenders, the Army reinstituted a rehabilitation program that worked well in World War II and was further developed in the 1950s. Certain offenders in World War II had been placed in minimum security retraining centers and, after going through a program there, were sent back into regular units. Today this program is carried out at a CTF at Fort Riley, Kansas.[72]

The CTF is an interesting amalgam of traditional military controls and those of modern behavioral science. Training is carried out in teams (like basic training companies), and each group of trainees is assigned to a specific team with which it stays until it has completed its ten-week cycle.[73] Among other things, these companies go through a process very similar to Army basic combat training—they are even trained with live ammunition and night fighting.[74] This standard, but closely supervised, military basic training keeps the trainees from developing a nonsoldiering self-image and is useful in helping to restore the offenders to duty (but this time with an acceptable attitude). Training cadres are themselves specially trained in corrections and leadership by CTF officers.

According to one anti-war organizer, other traditional military elements remain in use.[75] The CTF's slogan, "duty bound," seems to be inscribed everywhere—on the walls, buildings, even on the basketball court backboards.[76] Trainees must still salute officers but with a "spirited vocalization of the aforementioned slogan."[77] In the mess hall line, they are told "You WILL shout 'duty bound, sergeant' or you will find yourself at the end of the line."[78] This soldier asserted that if the charge of quarters finds anyone smoking in bed after lights out, the whole company has to get out of bed and stand outside in their underwear regardless of the temperature of a "fire drill."[79]

The CTF is located in an isolated part of Fort Riley. It is not difficult to escape the CTF (which is surrounded by barbed wire) because guard towers are few, and the guards are unarmed.[80] But once out of the CTF, according to this soldier's report of a company commander's comment, it can take five days to find one's way off post.[81] And once off post, civilian authorities will bring the escapee back.[82]

These aspects of traditional military discipline are combined with some rather more modern controls. The program starts out with a four-week motivation program, including lectures and discussions. Lecture topics might include moral and ethical matters from the chaplains; social adjustment, alcoholism and drug abuse, and personality growth and development from the social-work officers; and the disadvantages of a less then honorable discharge from the legal officers. Even though the trainees are closely supervised in this phase, they do not always "absorb the material given."[83] Reasons suggested for this problem are the trainees' own low educational and intellectual level.

The trainees are counseled by cadremen in their own units, and they are required to have four sessions with a member of the social work staff.[84] The social work staff also provides guidance to the cadremen who conduct the counseling program, and it advises the commander regarding disposition of trainees.[85]

The CTF is continuing to experiment with modifications of the techniques discussed. For example, the mandatory individual counseling program was modified to allow NCO social workers to conduct parts of the professional counseling. This was so successful that it was put to use in all the basic training companies before the end of 1972.[86] Individual and group counseling is reinforced by role-playing sessions and conferences.[87]

One battalion tested a technique that became known as "confrontation":

> The technique is employed with marginal trainees whose attitude constitutes a major obstacle to rehabilitation. In an informal atmosphere the trainee is confronted simultaneously by various members of the cadre and staff, normally including the unit commander, unit social worker, chaplain, members of the leadership team, and, when appropriate, members of the administrative or professional CTF staff elements. During these sessions the trainee's problems are discussed with a view toward causing him to accept responsibility for his problems and to select a course of action to resolve or reduce the intensity of his problems.[88]

Because of the great number of man-hours required, this technique continues to be employed on a selective basis.[89]

The CTF has also experimented with modifications in the basic training process. Officials attempted to use the "merit reward system" that was discussed in a previous chapter:

> Points were awarded for positive achievement, and deducted for negative behavior and disciplinary infractions. Rewards for scoring in the upper range included eligibility for late television viewing, exemption from Saturday morning inspections, and other similar privileges. . . . Trainees accepted the system readily. Cadremen in the participating leadership team, however, found that score keeping created an administrative overload when added to other required evaluation reports and routine administration. The system was therefore shelved with intentions to reimplement when feasible.[90]

It seems reasonable to suppose that this merit reward system will be more thoroughly implemented in the future.

One battalion experimented with a program it called "unit

adventure training," a vigorous training activity including tactical foot marches, rappelling, obstacle and confidence courses, and patrolling techniques.[91] "Energies were diverted to productive channels and disruptive behavior in the CTUs [Correctional Training Units] decreased perceptively."[92] In another experimental program, "units competed against one another in track and field events, unconventional relays, and military events. In the latter category, trainees participated in drill team competition, pup tent pitching contests, and hand grenade throwing for both accuracy and distance."[93]

The chaplain branch of the CTF appears to be quite active, offering a series of day-long retreats, formal instruction in "Life Issues Series" classes, and group counseling sessions that stress "freedom of expression on appropriate issues" and understanding the rights of others.[94] In 1972, the chaplains carried out 311 baptisms, 329 confirmations (Catholic), 306 first communions (Catholic), six weddings, and one funeral.[95] (The CTF usually has around 4,000 trainees in the facility at one time.) In a manner consistent with my earlier commentary about psychology supplanting religion, the chaplains brought two California psychologists to the facility to present a series of lectures and conferences on gestalt psychology and transactional analysis to selected CTF cadremen.[96]

Despite an overall program that appears to be quite pleasant[97] in contrast to those of other prisons, there are still "trainees who have been unresponsive to counseling by leadership team members."[98] In order to deal with this group, the CTF brought in a "Seventh Step Program." Seventh step counselors are civilian ex-convicts who stress the need for purpose in life and for trainees to "overcome future stress and temptation." The seven steps refer to a series of statements, such as "deciding we need to change" and realizing that there is some "power" that "we can use to overcome our weaknesses."[99]

Although it is probably the most successful prison project the Army has, the CTF also has a few problems.[100] While the stockades and the USDB send prisoners who "meet criteria for potential re-motivation and return to military duty,"[101] the CTF has not been able to screen its entrants.[102] The result is that some arrivals come to the facility and act as resistance organizers. The CTF's response is to quickly recommend them for an administrative discharge. The CTF has requisitioned for separate quarters for these individuals. "The discharge group interferes with the training program by their very presence and in many instances, are subversive in their contact with trainees."[103] If the CTF could screen its entrants and send some to the USDB, it would increase its capacity to control its soldier prisoners.

Another problem for this rehabilitation facility exists outside its "walls": secondary deviance.[104] Once a soldier who has been incarcerated has been restored to duty, some line commanders and other soldiers have a tendency to continue to view him as a potential offender. If he is not completely assimilated upon return to duty, his resistance sentiments will reappear. All the efforts at manipulating the prisoner's self-image and definition of the situation would be for naught. This has been a problem especially with soldiers who have no MOS or who are assigned to duty unrelated to their occupational specialty.[105] This process suggests that deviance is closely linked to the manner in which the soldier is treated by the Army and the nature of the group to which he is assigned.

What is the best explanation for deviance? I have suggested that some correctional psychiatrists and social workers argue that deviance resides in the sick individual. Yet, oddly, psychiatry does not come into the military setting with a notion of what the diseases are that it should be curing. Psychiatry's definition of the individual as ill is based on the Army's response to that person's behavior. Many of these responses occur when the young man refuses to "knuckle under" to some coercive action by the Army. (This refusal may occur for a wide range of reasons.) Usually these prisoners are in prison for repeated AWOLs, disrespect to an officer, or refusing an order. So the soldier is defined as a character and personality disorder after he has resisted the Army, not before.

The result of allowing the military to define psychiatrists' problems is that the therapists dutifully adapt their definitions of syndromes to match the criminal act.[106] Specifically, in terms of labeling the deviant, one finds circular, ex post facto clinical terms of personality and character disorders. A passive-aggressive personality is really someone who resists in a covert way. A disorder of the "immature" category is a soldier who impulsively reacts against domination.

There are other explanations for the character of deviance. Some sociologists have asserted that there is nothing inherently deviant about any act, either in terms of individual pathology or societal needs.[107] Deviance is something that is created "by making the rules whose infraction constitute deviance and by applying those rules to particular people and labeling them as outsiders."[108] Thus, persons in the social system take actions that define or confer on certain behavior the label of deviant. If the definition of deviance is located in the reaction rather than in the act or the actor, then there is little necessarily in common in terms of clinical characteristics among individuals who perform the same deviant behavior.

Looking at deviance as residing in the labelers might result in psychiatrists' examining their own preconceptions and affiliations. But this analysis is avoided as a consequence of focusing exclusively on the characteristics of the deviants themselves. As I have shown, the main finding seems to be that most deviants are working-class or former ghetto dwellers. There may be a lack of cross-class understanding operating to decrease the sensitivity that psychiatrists would otherwise have with their middle- or upper-class civilian clientele.[109]

Whatever the luxuries may be of labeling deviants, correctional psychiatrists and psychologists and social workers are practical people. In their practice, they seem to hold to a rather voluntaristic view of deviance and mental illness, perhaps in keeping with their variability of their labeling of offenders (that is, a person deviates or conforms partly as a result of his own choice). The selection function of the USDB is an implicit recognition of this role of intent in deviance. Therefore, social control can be achieved by managing the length and conditions of the stay in prison. This approach can be synthesized with the more deterministic view of the social nature of the self and the self-conception. As I have emphasized, the self-image can be manipulated. One continues on as a soldier or an offender mostly on the basis of pressures of the small group and other reference persons. So managing the definition of the situation[110] becomes very important for the rationalized co-optive style of corrections.

NOTES

1. See, for example, Bruce L. Bushard and Arnold W. Dahlgren, "A Technic for Military Delinquency Management: I," *U.S. Armed Forces Medical Journal* 8 (November 1957): 1619.

2. W. H. Maglin, "Rehabilitation the Keynote of the Army's Correctional Program," *Federal Probation* 19 (June 1955): 21-23.

3. Harvey Powelson and Reinhard Bendix, "Psychiatry in Prison," *Psychiatry* 14 (1951): 73-86.

4. See, for example, Jeremiah P. Holland and Walter A. Luszki, "A Balanced Rehabilitation Program for Military Offenders," *Military Review* 35 (1955): 52-54.

5. Maglin, "Rehabilitation the Keynote," pp. 23-24.

6. See Samuel P. Huntington, *The Soldier and the State: The Theory and Politics of Civil-Military Relations* (New York: Vintage Books, 1957), pp. 222-69.

7. Maglin, "Rehabilitation the Keynote," p. 22.

8. Special Civilian Committee for the Study of the United States Army Confinement System, *Report of the Special Civilian Committee for the Study of the United States Army Confinement System*, Austin H. MacCormick, Chairman (Washington, D.C.: Department of the Army, 1970), p. 73 (hereafter *MacCormick Report*).

9. See ibid.

10. Zimbardo, the psychologist who directed the project, said, "Another thing we've learned is that any prison, even a good prison, is terrible." *St. Louis Post-Dispatch,* August 22, 1971.

11. Maglin, "Rehabilitation the Keynote," pp. 21-28.

12. *MacCormick Report.*

13. Officially, the Army rarely acknowledges current bad stockade conditions. It does, however, in discussions of modernizations refer to how bad conditions *used* to be prior to being cleaned up. One of these recurring statements is that of the former Deputy Provost Marshal General Ramsey, who described Army stockades prior to his changes in 1957 as similar to county prisons with no rehabilitation programs and based only on principles of punishment, such as useless hard labor, and custody including maximum security type guarding. Raymond R. Ramsey, "The Army's New Correctional Program at Stockade Level," *Federal Probation* 23 (September 1959): 41-43.

14. *MacCormick Report*, p. 3-57.

15. Ibid. Rivkin cites a report of hogtied prisoners being dropped face down from various heights. See Robert S. Rivkin, *GI Rights and Army Justice: The Draftee's Guide to Military Life and Law* (New York: Grove Press, 1970), p. 272.

16. Richard L. Henshel, "Problems of Army Corrections: The Least Desired Duty . . . ," *Military Police Journal* 17 (July 1968): 9-11. Henshel surveyed military police officers in a training school and asked them to rank eight different military police activities. Corrections was by far the least desired duty, with 49 percent saying they would least wish to serve in that area. Some officers felt that too close an association with corrections would damage their future careers. Henshel cited a tendency to assign MPs to confinement work as a sort of punishment.

17. *MacCormick Report*.

18. Ibid.

19. For example, according to journalist Robert Sherrill, the Army stockade at the San Francisco Presidio held 120 soldiers in a space meant for eighty-eight. There was one toilet for every thirty-five prisoners because some of the toilets were unusable and backed up into the shower rooms, inundating them in two or three inches of foul water. The stockade was short of food and had very limited recreational possibilities. See Robert Sherrill, *Military Justice Is to Justice as Military Music Is to Music* (New York: Harper & Row, 1970), p. 6. See also Fred Gardner, *The Unlawful Concert: An Account of the Presidio Mutiny Case* (New York: The Viking Press, 1970), for a discussion of the Presidio stockade problems in the late 1960s.

20. The committee also criticized stockades for their lack of counselors, social workers, or psychiatrists; their lack of grievance machinery (and making it difficult for inmates to see a lawyer); the lack of participation by stockade personnel in professional meetings to learn about rehabilitation topics in civilian institutions; and the existence of anti-war GIs at every stockade fomenting discontent. See *MacCormick Report*.

21. Behavioral scientists who try to transform the style of stockades from a custodial orientation to a rehabilitation orientation sometimes encounter concern from line officers lest stockade conditions become so pleasant as to encourage soldiers to malinger there. But, according to Bushard and Dahlgren, "The social atmosphere of modern America and the pressures presently impinging upon the commander of a post in the U.S. Army are such that a stockade must be operated in a fashion that will avoid incidents leading to danger to life or limb." Bruce L. Bushard and Arnold W. Dahlgren, "A Technic for Military Delinquency Management: II. Methods and Results," *U.S. Armed Forces Medical Journal* 8 (December 1957): 1760.

22. One of the ways the Army tries to avoid the stockade riot problem is by putting potential organizers in solitary confinement ("disciplinary segregation" or "administrative segregation"). These small cells are intended to be miserable to live in. In addition, the diet is adjusted to contain little more than the officially required 2,100 calories per day. The Special Civilian Committee said that administrative segregation "should be brought up to Army regula-

tions (lighting, ventilation, size, exercise, food)" or abandoned. See *MacCormick Report,* p. 38.

23. Maglin, "Rehabilitation the Keynote," pp. 21-28.

24. Ibid., p. 24.

25. Ibid.

26. Ibid., pp. 24-26. See also Stanley L. Brodsky, "Some Observations of a Clinical Psychologist in a Military Penal Setting," *Corrective Psychiatry and the Journal of Social Therapy* 12 (November 1966): 467. One of the prisoners in the USDB, Howard Levy, saw this function as "identifying troublemakers." See Howard Levy and David Miller, *Going to Jail: The Political Prisoner* (New York, Grove Press, n.d.). Levy's interpretation of the role of these "helping professions" in prison is reflected in the writings of several social workers and psychiatrists. For example, a stockade social worker wrote that the intake interview (and later after-hours group meetings) by the social worker provides many purposes, including an occasion for the specialists to identify natural group leaders and, as such, to become aware of those confinees capable of instigating and/or leading a destructive group effort." George L. Raspa, "The Psychiatric Team . . . An Effective Tool in Correctional Programs," *Military Police Journal* 18 (August 1968): 8-10.

27. Maglin, "Rehabilitation the Keynote," p. 25.

28. Howard Levy was imprisoned from June 1967 to August 1969 by the Army for refusing to train Special Forces troops in medicine for foreign civic-action programs. *Going to Jail* is a result of his twenty-six months in military and federal prisons.

29. See, for example, Herman L. Goldberg and Frederick A. C. Hoefer, "The Army Parole System," *Journal of Criminal Law and Criminology* 40 (1949): 158-69, and Marion Rushton, "Military Clemency," *Federal Probation* 8 (1944): 9-13.

30. Levy and Miller, *Going to Jail,* p. 111.

31. Ibid., pp. 35-43.

32. According to Levy, beatings in these modern federal prisons do occasionally occur, such as during actual outbreaks of rebellion, or in cases of special prisoners. He commented that prison officials can bring criminal charges against inmates, greatly lengthening their stay in prison. They can more easily punish people by putting them in solitary confinement ("the hole"). Thus there are still techniques in use at the USDB that are not at all liberal and modern. See ibid., pp. 107-15.

33. Ibid., p. 107.

34. Maglin, "Rehabilitation the Keynote," p. 21.

35. Ivan C. Berlien, "Psychiatry in the Army," *Neuropsychiatry in World War II*, vol. 1 *Zone of Interior* (Washington, D.C.: Department of the Army, 1966), pp. 491-522. See especially Menninger's comments on pp. 502-503. The problems of a purely classificatory role were exacerbated by wide variation among different psychiatrists' diagnoses. For example, one psychiatrist might define 74 percent of the inmates as psychopaths, where a second psychiatrist might discover only 12 percent. Ibid., p. 496.

36. C. Wright Mills, *The Sociological Imagination* (New York: Grove Press, 1959).

37. Holland and Luszki, "A Balanced Rehabilitation Program," p. 53. Two Navy psychiatrists commented on the extensiveness of the military psychiatrists' task of transforming offenders. They wrote that, in order to achieve conformity, the individual offender's behavior patterns, attitudes, social techniques, and emotional expectations—his entire relationship to the world—may have to undergo considerable alteration. See John C. Kramer and John L. Young, "The Psychiatrist as Probation Officer," *U.S. Armed Forces Medical Journal*," 11 (April 1960): 454-55. A young man who went AWOL or talked back to his commanding officer certainly would not know what kind of bargain he had let himself in for.

38. Joseph Abrahams and Lloyd W. McCorkle, "Group Psychotherapy at an Army Rehabilitation Center," *Diseases of the Nervous System* 8 (February 1947): 51.

39. Clyde V. Martin, "Treatment of Character and Behavior Disorders in the Military," *Corrective Psychiatry and Journal of Social Therapy* 11 (1965): 166. Martin was a psychiatrist for the Air Force, which has developed rehabilitation centers along principles that are similar to those of Army rehabilitation centers and correctional training facilities.

40. For example, Holland and Luszki, "A Balanced Rehabilitation Program," p. 54, wrote that the commandant and his immediate superior must be aware of the permissive aspect of group therapy and that they should not misjudge these activities if they happen to observe groups enjoying a good joke or appearing to be "goldbricking" Air Force correctional innovators Hart and Hippchen wrote of transitional problems they encountered. They said the "correctional staff were initially resistant to the psychological services whom they felt were encroaching on their authority." Robert F. Hart and Leonard J. Hippchen, "Team Treatment of Air Force Offenders," *American Journal of Correction* (September-October 1966): 42. See also, Berlien, "Psychiatry in the Army," pp. 491-522.

41. Berlien, "Psychiatry in the Army," p. 497.

42. Ibid.

43. Ibid., p. 492.

44. See Jospeh Abrahams and Lloyd W. McCorkle, "Group Psychotherapy of Military Offenders," *American Journal of Sociology* 51 (March 1946): 455-63; and Joseph Abrahams and Lloyd W. McCorkle, "Group Psychotherapy at an Army Rehabilitation Center," *Diseases of the Nervous System* 8 (February 1947): 50-62.

45. Corrections psychologists and psychiatrists have described their work in a number of articles. See Stanley L. Brodsky and George V. Komaridis, "Military Prisonization," *Military Police Journal* 15 (July 1966): 8-9; L. H. Paul, "Morale Demoralizer," *Military Police Journal* 12 (April 1963): i-9; Jeremiah P. Holland and Walter A. Luszki, "Special Supervision for Military Offenders," *Journal of Criminal Law, Criminology, and Police Science* 49 (January-February 1959): 444-46; Ramsey, "The Army's New Correctional Program," pp. 41-

43; Raymond R. Ramsey, "Military Offenders and the Army Correctional Program," in *Crime in America*, ed. Herbert A. Bloch (New York: Philosophical Library, 1961), pp. 117-26; Robert E. Richardson, "Conserving Human Resources," *Army Information Digest* 18 (December 1963): 53-56; Adolf Haas and Edmund J. Kuras, "Some Antecedent Factors in Army Prisoners," *American Journal of Psychiatry* 115 (1958): 143-45; James J. Gibbs, "Handling the Military Offender," *Army Information Digest* 16 (February 1961): 52-58; Kramer and Young, "The Psychiatrist as Probation Officer," pp. 454-58; David B. Robbins, "Innovations in Military Corrections," *American Journal of Psychiatry* 123 (January 1967): 828-35; Eugene H. Czajkoski, "The New Wave of Therapy in Corrections," *American Journal of Correction* (January-February 1968): 17-18; Raspa, "The Psychiatric Team," pp. 8-10; Brodsky, "Some Observations of a Clinical Psychologist," pp. 466-71; Eugene Davidoff, "Disposition of the Unfit in an Army Service Forces Training Center," *Clinical Psychopathology* 8 (October 1964): 237-49; L. H. Paul, "Counselling the Youthful Offender," *Military Police Journal* 14 (October 1964): 20-21; Perry V. Wagley, "The Army Rehabilitates Military Offenders," *Federal Probation* 8 (January-March 1945): 7-11; William C. Menninger, "Psychiatry and the Military Offender," *Federal Probation* 9 (April-June 1945): 8-12; Leonard J. Hippchen, "The Air Force's 'Therapeutic Community' Concept," *American Journal of Correction* (September-October 1966): 40-45; John Morris Gray, "Straightening Out the Military Offender," *Army Digest* 24 (November 1969): 59-61; Stanley L. Brodsky and Paul W. Grosheim, "Custodial Personnel at the USDB: Observations on Their Roles and Activities," *Military Police Journal* 15 (November 1965): 10-11; Frank W. Hayes, "Community Mental Health and Resource Service at a Military Installation," *Military Medicine* (March 1968): 215-23; Fergus I. Monahan, "The Problem Soldier—Rehabilitation Through MHCS," *Infantry Journal* 52 (January-February 1962): 16-17; Holland and Luszki, "A Balanced Rehabilitation Program," pp. 52-54; Clyde V. Martin and Jack R. Alvord, "Long-Term Effects of Intensive Short-Term Treatment of the Character and Personality Disorder," *Corrective Psychiatry and Journal of Social Therapy* 12 (November 1966): 433-42; Joseph S. Skobba, "Military Psychiatry," *American Journal of Psychiatry* 117 (January 1960): 651-53; Martin, "Treatment of Character and Behavior Disorders," pp. 163-67; Sheldon B. Peizer, Edward B. Lewis, and Robert W. Scollon, "Correctional Rehabilitation as a Function of Interpersonal Relations," *Journal of Criminal Law, Criminology, and Police Science* 46 (1956): 632-40; John R. Cavanagh, "The Effect of Confinement on Psychiatric Patients," *U.S. Armed Forces Medical Journal* 11 (October 1951): 1479-82; Raymond R. Ramsey, "More Effective Manpower Through Improved Discipline," *Army Information Digest* 14 (March 1959): 22-25; Nathan Schlessinger and David Blau, "A Psychiatric Study of a Retraining Command," *U.S. Armed Forces Medical Journal* 8 (March 1957): 397-405; John R. Cavanagh and Samuel Gerstein, "Group Psychotherapy in a Naval Disciplinary Barracks," *Naval Medical Bulletin* 49 (July-August 1949): 645-54; John M. Murphy and J. Douglas Grant, "The Role of Psychiatry in Naval Retraining," *U.S. Armed Forces Medical Journal* 3 (April 1952): 631-34; Richard A. Chappell, "Naval

Offenders and Their Treatment," *Federal Probation* 9 (April-June 1945): 3-7; and Powelson and Bendix, "Psychiatry in Prison," pp. 73-86.

46. Abrahams and McCorkle, "Group Psychotherapy at an Army Rehabilitation Center," p. 52.

47. See Irving Louis Horowitz and Martin Liebowitz, "Social Deviance and Political Marginality: Toward a Redefinition of the Relation Between Sociology and Politics," *Social Problems* 15 (Winter 1968): 280-96, on the transformation of political resistance into mental abnormality terms. See also Abrahams and McCorkle, "Group Psychotherapy at an Army Rehabilitation Center."

48. Ibid., pp. 50-62.

49. Ibid.

50. Abrahams and McCorkle, "Group Psychotherapy of Military Offenders," p. 459.

51. Berlien, "Psychiatry in the Army," p. 507.

52. Abrahams and McCorkle, "Group Psychotherapy at an Army Rehabilitation Center," p. 59.

53. See, for example, Eugene Czajkoski, "The New Wave of Therapy in Corrections," pp. 17-18; James J. Gibbs, "Handling the Military Offender," p. 54.

54. Joseph Abrahams and Lloyd W. McCorkle, "Group Psychotherapy at an Army Rehabilitation Center," *Diseases of the Nervous System* 8 (February 2, 1947): 52-55. Quoted by permission of the publisher.

55. See the analysis suggested by Daniels, "The Captive Professional," pp. 255-65.

56. Hippchen, "The Air Force's 'Therapeutic Community' Concept," p. 15.

57. Martin and Alvord, "Long-Term Effects of Intensive Short-Term Treatment," p. 439. Martin and Alvord were so convinced of the legitimacy of their approach that they attempted to treat soldiers who were simply receiving administrative discharges from the Air Force on the basis of their being defined as character and behavior disorders. These disorders are not considered illnesses by the Air Force, although they often are so viewed by therapists. Although these soldiers could be discharged within a day of the determination of their status, normally it takes a couple of months for the paperwork to get through; these therapists can use that time to treat these young men because "we cannot continue to thrust this problem of the character and behavior disorder upon the overcrowded prisons and the understaffed welfare agencies." Ibid., pp. 437, 441.

58. Ibid., p. 438.

59. Powelson and Bendix, "Psychiatry in Prison," pp. 73-86. See also note 40 above.

60. Bushard and Dahlgren, "A Technic for Military Delinquency Management: I," pp. 1616-31, and "A Technic for Military Delinquency Management: II," pp. 1745-60. The mental hygiene staff is usually headed by a psychiatrist but often includes a psychologist and social workers. Thus the influence of modernization of corrections really comes from a variety of behavioral scientists.

61. Bushard and Dahlgren, "A Technic for Military Delinquency Management: I," p. 1623.

62. Ibid., p. 1626.

63. Ibid.
64. Ibid., p. 1629.
65. Ibid.
66. Ibid., p. 1622
67. Ibid.
68. Ibid., p. 1623.
69. Ibid.
70. Bushard and Dahlgren, "A Technic for Military Delinquency Management: II," p. 1750.
71. Ibid., p. 1751.
72. See Carl C. Turner, "New Army Correctional Training Facility Is Operational," *Military Police Journal* (August 1968): 5-7; and Larry Jackson, "How the Army Retains Deserters," *Parade Magazine* (March 18, 1973): 20-21. Most of the restoration functions of the USDB have been transferred to the CTF at Fort Riley. Many of the prisoners at Leavenworth (the "restorable" ones) were transferred to the CTF when it was opened. The "rehabilitative" function of the USDB today remains primarily one of reentry into civilian society.
73. Turner, "New Army Correctional Training Facility," pp. 5-7.
74. Jackson, "How the Army Retrains Deserters," pp. 20-21.
75. Greg Laxer, "Brass Brainwashing: Fort Riley 'Correctional Training,'" *The Bond* 4 (March 18, 1970): 6-7.
76. Ibid.
77. Ibid.
78. Ibid.
79. Ibid.
80. Ibid.
81. Ibid.
82. Ibid.
83. *MacCormick Report*, p. 65.
84. E. L. King, "The U.S. Army Correctional Training Facility: Annual Report, Fiscal Year 1972," U.S. Army Correctional Training Facility, Fort Riley, p. 33.
85. Ibid.
86. Ibid., pp. 27-28.
87. Ibid., p. 28.
88. Ibid., p. 27.
89. Ibid.
90. Ibid., p. 28.
91. Ibid., p. 29.
92. Ibid.
93. Ibid.
94. Ibid., p. 35.
95. Ibid., p. 36.
96. Ibid., p. 35.
97. Hamilton I. McCubbin et al., "Restoration of the Military Offender: A Follow-Up Study of CTF Graduates Returned to Duty," Final Report, U.S.

Army Correctional Training Facility, Fort Riley, Kansas, September 1971. In this follow-up interview study of graduates of the CTF, restorees and recidivists alike perceived the program as valuable. They liked the individual attention they received, the quality of military training, and its general lack of harassment (pp. 17-18).

98. King, "The U.S. Army Correctional Training Facility: Annual Report," p. 37.

99. Ibid.

100. In a thirty-month period, 9,784 soldiers had completed the CTF program and were reassigned. Of the 9,228 graduates whose status could be determined, 2,000 (21.7 percent) were serving in an honorable status within the Army, and 2,529 (27.4 percent) had been separated from the Army under honorable conditions. Together these figures represent a "restoration rate" of 49.1 percent of CTF graduates. Of the remainder, 4,280 (46.4 percent) had been separated under other than honorable conditions, twenty-one (0.2 percent) were currently in confinement, and 398 (4.3 percent) were listed as "dropped from rolls" (such as AWOL or desertion). Together these figures show a "recidivism rate" of 50.9 percent. See Lawrence J. Fox, Paul W. Nicholson, and Thomas W. Gooch, "Subsequent Performance of 9,228 Graduates of the Correctional Training Facility," Research and Evaluation Division, U.S. Army Retraining Brigade, Fort Riley, Kansas, November 1972, p. 3.

101. *MacCormick Report*, p. 62.

102. Only certain types of trainees are sent to the facility. They have been convicted for military offenses (mostly AWOL) rather than civilian offenses (such as assault or larceny). Unless restoration to duty is expected, no prisoners who are defined as having psychotic tendencies or severe character disorders are sent to the CTF.

103. *MacCormick Report*, p. 70. The currently contradictory set of approaches makes it possible to be punished more severely for a less serious offense than for a more serious one. A cunning resister could get himself out of the Army for a time and into a relatively comfortable prison situation by committing a crime serious enough to get beyond the stockade but seeming sufficiently capable of being rehabilitated to get sent to the CTF rather than the USDB. See Stanley L. Brodsky and Norman E. Eggleston, *The Military Prison: Theory, Research, and Practice* (Carbondale: Southern Illinois University Press, 1970), p. 27.

104. The term *secondary deviance* is from Edwin M. Lemert, *Human Deviance, Social Problems, and Social Control* (Englewood Cliffs: Prentice-Hall, 1967), pp. 40-64. *Secondary deviance* refers to the tendency of ex-convicts to commit a variety of deviant acts as a result of the expectations and labeling that they encounter after leaving prison.

105. McCubbin et al., "Restoration of the Military Offender," p. 25.

106. See, for example, the discussion of character and behavior disorders in Hippchen, "The Air Force's 'Therapeutic Community' Cqncept," p. 15; or Raspa, "The Psychiatric Team," p. 8; or Gibbs, "Handling the Military Offender," pp. 56-57. "Immaturity" is a common "disorder" within these categories.

107. See Jack P. Gibbs, "Conceptions of Deviant Behavior: The Old and the New," *Pacific Sociological Review* (Spring 1966): 9-14.

108. Ibid., quoting Howard Becker. See also quotations of John Kitsuse and Kai T. Erikson in ibid., p. 11.

109. For example, Czajkoski believes that therapists cannot do insight therapy with inmates, partly because the inmates are too inarticulate. He prefers "reality therapy," which emphasizes "better ways of behaving, not insight." It does not permit the patient to "excuse present behavior on the basis of unconscious motivations." This kind of "therapy" has the advantage of allowing the use of nonprofessionals as therapists and can be accomplished on "vast numbers of inarticulate, unintellectual and culturally deprived offenders." See Czajkoski, "The New Wave," pp. 17-18. The classic criticism of lower-class attitudes and personalities—the inability to delay gratification, and the lack of impulse control—is reflected in the writings of correctional therapists. See, for example, Bushard and Dahlgren, "A Technic for Military Delinquency Management: I," p. 1628.

110. This refers to the prevention of the development of "prisonization" (a prisoner counterculture). See Brodsky and Komaridis, "Military Prisonization," pp. 8-9.

Index

About the Author

Lawrence B. Radine is assistant professor of sociology at the University of Michigan at Dearborn and taught previously at Saint Louis University. His research interests are social organization and social control.